CLEARANCE DIVER

TONY EY

Copyright © 2014
All rights reserved.
ISBN-13: 978-1494348854
ISBN-10: 1494348853

Dedicated to the loving memory of Antoinette, my beautiful wife of 31 years who sadly departed this world long before her time - and to my two beautiful children, Jason and Kimberley, who day after day continue to make me so very proud to be their father.

FOREWORD

It is a great privilege and pleasure to be asked to write a foreword to Tony Ey's memoir *'Clearance Diver'*. This work gives the reader an inside look at the world of the Clearance Diver and a clear insight into the day to day life of Clearance Divers in Vietnam.

I had the great honour to serve in the Clearance Diving Branch of the RAN from 1955 to 1986 and have been and remain a staunch supporter of the Branch and the RAN Clearance Divers Association.

This book also provides great testament to the role the Clearance Diver has played in the Australian Defence Force, from humble beginnings as underwater workers, their role has become multi-faceted and incorporates much more than diving. Indeed, diving, to quote a high-ranking Clearance Diver, *"is just the way we get to work"*.

Tony's description of his career in *'the Branch'* will bring a smile of recognition to the faces of many of his contemporaries.

I have served with Tony on a number of occasions, consider him a close friend and am quietly honoured to be the basis of one of his characters in his first book, *'Can Do Easy'*.

I recommend his memoir to you as a definitive description of special forces personnel and especially the RAN Clearance Diver.

Edward (*Jake*) Linton
Commander BEM RAN Rtd.
Mine warfare and Clearance Diving Officer
Patron of the Clearance Divers Association.
Graduate of the 1st RAN Clearance Diving Course in 1955.

AUTHORS NOTE

This chronicle is in the main, a 20-year snapshot of my time spent as a Clearance Diver in the Royal Australian Navy from 1965 to 1985.

All of the events, dates, locations, names and characters described herein, to the best of my recollection, are true and accurate.

Looking back on my military life, I believe I had one of the best jobs in the world. I served with some damn fine people during my 20 years as a Clearance Diver, experienced many things which most people only read about, dream about, or see in the movies. It's been a good life all in all and I have very few regrets.

I am still *'living the dream'*.

Tony Ey
July 2014.

Other books by author:
'Can Do Easy –
Australian Navy Clearance Divers
in the Vietnam War'.
2013.

PREFACE

There were several reasons as to why I was stirred to put *'pen to paper'* and document the following events which occurred during my 20-year career spent as a Navy Clearance Diver.

Initially, I had decided to record the names, places and events associated with my service with *Clearance Diving Team 3* in South Vietnam during the early '70's before they completely faded from my memory. I was motivated to tackle this task solely for personal reasons, with no thought of anybody ever reading the final result.

As I began to tap away at my laptop, I became aware of a growing sense of relief, like a weight was being lifted from my shoulders. For a lot of years, many memories of Vietnam had remained tucked away somewhere within the dark recesses of my subconscious.

In hindsight, I have come to the realisation that my aversion to confronting those old memories and emotions *(perhaps more a case of 'let sleeping dogs lie')* most probably affected my ability over the years to relate in what may be considered a *'normal'* manner towards my family, friends and workmates.

Even though I found it a little unsettling to recall and think through some of those memories, the process began to stir recollections of the mates, the camaraderie, the characters I had met and the enjoyable moments - and there were many.

Apart from the very formal and somewhat tedious *'Report of Proceedings'* written by the eight Team OICs, I was also conscious that there was no published written record from a participant's perspective of the CDT3 Vietnam experience.

It began to dawn on me that the good to come from this delve into the past would far outweigh the bad.

When I had finished documenting my recollections of Vietnam; and feeling so much the better for it, it then occurred to me that there has been very little written about what Navy Clearance Divers (CDs) are and what they do. So, I just continued banging away at the keyboard and began to document my memories of CD training.

Then one day, like 'a *bolt from the blue*', I realised that I was enjoying the hell out of this dig into my past. Memories are probably not especially important to the younger generation, but to us older folk, they become priceless as the clock ticks on.

I knew that I had led a relatively interesting and unusual life in a relatively unknown branch of the service and that I probably had enough stories left to fill up a few more chapters. So I just kept tapping away at the keys of my trusty laptop.

I was encouraged in my endeavours by a publisher who often reminded me that first hand *'living'* memory is the most important record of *'how it really was'* and if I didn't document my memories as *'I saw it'*, many of the events which had transpired during my two decades in the Military would be forgotten and lost forever.

It also crossed my mind that maybe one day my kids or grandkids may be interested to read a little as to why the *'old man'* turned out the way he did; so I persevered.

School for most of us is quite boring, so my chronicle begins with a very brief glimpse at my life before joining the Navy and the influences which inspired me to choose a Military career.

If I have offended any by my writing, I make no apology - as a very famous Australian bushranger once said just before the hangman placed a noose around his neck:

'Such is life'.

Having borne arms in the service of my country, I believe I probably have as much right as anyone to express some of my one-eyed views and opinions.

And so I begin......

CONTENTS

1	THE BEGINNING	Pg 12
2	RECRUIT SCHOOL - 1965	Pg 22
3	HMAS RUSHCUTTER - 1965	Pg 27
4	HMAS MELBOURNE - 1966	Pg 36
5	CD TRAINING – 1966/67	Pg 51
6	HMAS YARRA – 1967/69	Pg 77
7	CDT2 – 1969/70	Pg 100
8	CDT3 VIETNAM – 1970/71	Pg 111
9	CDT2 - 1971	Pg 175
10	CDT1 -1972	Pg 177
11	ADVANCED COURSE -1973	Pg 192
12	CDT1 – 1974/75	Pg 194
13	DEMOLITION INSTUCTOR - 1976	Pg 203
14	USA – 1977/80	Pg 208
15	CDT1 -1980/83	Pg 235
16	HMAS MORETON – 1983/85	Pg 248
17	USA - 1985	Pg 254
18	DUPONT - 1986	Pg 258
19	RETIREMENT	Pg 275
20	POSTSCRIPTS	Pg 278
	ABOUT THE AUTHOR	Pg 290
	ADDENDUM	Pg 292
	GLOSSARY of TERMS	Pg 297

CLEARANCE DIVER

1
THE BEGINNING

As the Boeing 737 descended through the thin afternoon overcast, the hazy landscape looming into view below the aircraft gradually transformed itself into endless green rice paddies stretching to the visible horizon. My heart was racing and the adrenaline was surging through my veins.

Like an old ghost from the past, vivid memories were flashing through my mind of the last time I had arrived in this timeless land some 22 years earlier when on approach to Saigon's *Tan Son Nhat* airport.

The aircraft began a gentle bank to line up for its final approach into Hanoi's *Noi Bai* International airport and I could clearly see the single row of Russian MIG 21s of the Vietnamese Air Force parked menacingly alongside the approaching runway.

It was January 1993, and I was about to set foot into what had been the heartland of an old and dreaded enemy. A lot of water had *'passed under the bridge'* of time leading up to this - my return to Vietnam. Over 20 years had slipped by since I had last arrived in this country dressed in military uniform, but memories of the past and many old prejudices were still very much with me.

I still find it somewhat ironic when I reflect back on the thoughts which were germinating in my young mind way back in 1954, the very same year that Ho Chi Minh's *Viet Minh* 'liberation' forces soundly defeated Vietnam's French colonial masters at the battle of Dien Bien Phu and drove them from Indochina.

Little did I know back then that my future path was to become closely entwined with Vietnam and we were to become firm acquaintances during two separate and very distinct occasions in my distant future - firstly in 1970 and 1971 as an Australian serviceman serving in the Vietnam War, then much later in 1993, when I was to return as part of the flooding tide of foreigners anxious to capitalise on the potential business opportunities which were evolving in Vietnam as the country emerged from the drab and oppressive shadow of Soviet Communist influence and moved towards the relatively free-wheeling market economy of *'Doi Moi'* (Economic Renovation).

It was during 1954, while General Vo Nguyen Giap (who I was to eventually meet some 40 years later) was routing France's finest at Dien Bien Phu, that I, as an impressionable young six-year-old, had made up my mind to spend my life in the Navy, cruising the deep mysterious waters of the world's oceans and visiting the exotic ports of South East Asia aboard a sleek grey warship. This determination to join the Royal Australian Navy became firmly entrenched in my young mind at that time and I never wavered from my burning desire to become a Navy man.

I can still recall quite vividly at that time Navy advertisements in our local Adelaide newspaper with photos of warships at sea and groups of young uniformed sailors obviously enjoying the sights of Singapore and Hong Kong. I think every boy in the early stages of his life imagines himself in some sort of uniform, but to me the Navy's was particularly special.

Not for me the ordinary and comparatively boring Policeman's or Fireman's lot. Being paid to play grown-up war games and visit exotic foreign ports which most people only read or dream about - that was the life for me.

My father had spent the majority of World War II flying with the Royal Australian Air Force dropping bombs on the Axis forces throughout North Africa, the Mediterranean and the Middle East. Both pride and interest in my father's experiences resulted in my growing up with very romantic images of war machines, particularly aircraft and large warships.

I was probably about eight or nine years of age when I finally persuaded my Mother to take me to visit the Navy's recruiting centre in Adelaide. As we walked into the front office, a big bearded Petty Officer with a weather-beaten face grinned down at me and said, *"A little young to be joining the Navy aren't we son?"* My Mother quietly explained that her offspring had set his heart on joining the Navy, and any information or brochures, and particularly photos of warships, would help keep me quiet for at least a few days.

I sat in awe of this old *'sea dog'* as he patiently gave me some insight into life in the 'Senior Service' and explained the necessary qualifications required to enter the Navy. I doubt that he had ever had such an attentive audience, before or since. The bad news was that I had a few years to wait. The options available were Officer Entry at 14, Junior Recruit at 15½ or 17 for General Entry.

From that day forward every warship which visited my home town of Adelaide saw my eager young face in the long queue, waiting to climb the gangway. I would wander around the ship trying to imagine what it would be like to be a sailor and part of the ship's company, daydreaming as to how it would feel to be underway at sea heading for the next port of call or taking part in fleet exercises.

When the larger ships were in, such as the Aircraft Carriers, I would harass my father to occasionally take me down to the Outer Harbour to watch the ship's departure. Standing on the wharf listening to the hum from the ship's machinery and ventilation fans made me think of these steel monsters as living and breathing beings.

Once, when the aircraft carrier HMAS Melbourne was preparing to leave Adelaide's Outer Harbour, I watched in fascination and awe as a team of her ship's divers worked under the stern of this elegant grey lady; the Flagship of the Australian Fleet.

I would watch in envy as the sailors scuttled about preparing their ship for sea, and when the lines were finally slipped and the huge propellers started to churn the water, moving the mighty vessel gracefully away from the wharf, my heart would be pumping like the boiling wake she left behind.

Little did I know back then, that not only was the Melbourne to be my first sea posting in the RAN, but I was destined to spend twenty years of my life as a Navy Clearance Diver.

As most boys look forward to the age when they can obtain a driver's licence, I counted the months and years leading up to the day that I could apply to join the Royal Australian Navy.

There was absolutely no doubt in my mind that my future would be in the Navy. I shut my mind to all other potential careers, and unfortunately this mind-set clouded my attitude somewhat toward my school-work. I blissfully thought that most of the normal subjects were not particularly relevant to my chosen career as a Navy man.

Even though the recruiting Petty Officer had emphasised that a good all-round education with relatively high marks was required to enter officer training, I was doing well enough at school that I believed nothing could stop me from being accepted when the time came.

When I finally turned 14 and the big day arrived, there were a number of examinations followed by a long interview with the Selection Board. I was about to receive the first major disappointment of my life.

The long awaited letter arrived a few weeks later telling me that I hadn't been accepted - I thought they must have made a mistake. Perhaps they had confused my name or address with someone else. The letter explained that even though I had obtained straight A's in all the academic exams, the Board was not satisfied with the standard of my written school report. This suggested to them that I had not fully applied myself to my schoolwork. For the Navy's selection board, attitude towards school-work was all important, and mine was not up to the standard expected for officer entry.

This first major lesson in my young life was an extremely bitter one. I was advised to return to school, work a little harder and apply again for a later intake.

I am unsure if this prompted my parent's actions or not, however they decided that I should change schools. For a budding young Navy man, it was an unusual choice. I began my second year of high school at Urrbrae - South Australia's only Agricultural High School.

My attitude to school did improve however, for the obvious reason that acceptance into the Navy demanded it, and because both my parents came from rural backgrounds I felt very much at home with my new school.

Throughout my childhood I had spent many memorable and thoroughly enjoyable school holidays on my Grandparents' farm, driving tractors, cutting and baling Lucerne hay, milking cows, learning to shoot rifles, trapping and shooting rabbits, getting into mischief and generally doing all the things that little boys love to do.

During the three years that followed I settled down at school and had a thoroughly good time. I pitched for the baseball team, took up boxing and made some very good friends from amongst the numerous country lads attending Urrbrae. The only problem I encountered at my new school was with the resident school bully who thought my surname was quite funny and something to joke about amongst his wimpy group of followers. I ignored him for quite a while until one day he caught me in the wrong mood. By this stage I was well advanced in my boxing training and sparring with 'Golden Gloves' contenders. About thirty seconds on the school oval at lunchtime quickly put the issue to rest. Amazing how a bleeding nose and a missing tooth can change a bully's attitude....

During the school holidays Urrbrae arranged for students to spend time on various sponsor farms around the State gaining practical experience and consolidating the subjects we had studied throughout the year. I had a particularly enjoyable work experience at the end of my first year on a wheat and sheep property at Mount Hope, north west of Port Lincoln on Eyre Peninsula in South Australia. At a little over fifteen years of age, I was entrusted with a Land-Rover, spent my days looking after sheep, harvesting wheat aboard a huge Combine and even accompanied the farmer's daughter to the local Saturday night dances - not a bad life for a young city lad.

My older brother Mike had by this stage decided that life in the big city was pretty damn boring and perhaps he could do a lot worse than follow his younger brother's leanings.

I remember how envious I was as we farewelled Mike at the Adelaide railway station and I watched his train pull away, bound for Melbourne and the Navy's Recruit Training Centre at HMAS Cerberus in Westernport Bay, Victoria.

Every cloud however has a silver lining and for me it was in the shape of the 500cc BMW motorcycle that Mike had left behind.

During my final year at Urrbrae, I turned many jealous heads as I rode to and fro in my school uniform, sitting astride that gleaming German masterpiece of engineering with its black baked enamel paint and white pin-striping. I always took particular pains to ride quite slowly past the Girls High school just down the road. It did wonders for my ego.

Perhaps it was the school or perhaps it was the lure of the land, but at that stage I decided I would wait and apply for General Service entry to the Navy after I turned 17.

Urrbrae was an unusual school in that it assisted graduating students who weren't country lads in finding suitable employment on rural properties throughout South Australia. During my final year I was offered a position on a sheep property as a trainee station manager.

The property was named for its actual location on the River Murray where that wonderful old river takes a sharp southerly turn on its meandering westerly advance from its source in the Great Dividing Range. 'Nor' West Bend' was located 10 miles from the river town of Morgan (originally called 'North West Bend') and my new home bordered 5 miles of the northern bank of this graceful and majestic old river. In South Australia's pioneer days, Morgan was a bustling river town and the second biggest port in South Australia, regularly seeing long queues of heavily laden paddle steamers and barges stretching downstream from the wharf awaiting their turn to unload stores and pick up the huge wool bales which were brought down from the big stations spread throughout the far North.

My new boss was an elderly bachelor who normally worked the property on his own, apart from the busy times such as shearing and crutching.

The magnificent old homestead sat high on the riverbank with sweeping views of the flowing muddy Murray below. The house was built in the typical South Australian style of the early settlers; Limestone walls about 2 feet thick with 14 foot high ceilings. In its heyday when wool was 'King', Nor' West Bend would most certainly have been home to the local aristocracy.

At one time Nor' West Bend covered over 2,000 square miles - stretching all the way from Overland to Burra. But there were plenty of tough times. During the drought of the mid 1860s, 16,000 sheep died of starvation or were killed by wild dogs.

The largest building on the property was the huge wool store which could store up to 17,000 bales of wool. Mr. Brockmeyer told me that it had later been converted into a ballroom with an upper level where a small band played on Saturday evenings leaving the entire ground floor free for dancing. With its magnificent polished wooden floor, my boss had erected a net across the middle and turned it into a badminton court so I soon became pretty handy with a racquet.

We had a lovely old country lady who was our live-in housekeeper and she was an outstanding cook. She cooked and cleaned and fussed over the two of us as if we were her own family.

Most evenings after dinner were spent relaxing in the huge drawing room listening to Mr. Brockmeyer's collection of records consisting mainly of music played on the Wurlitzer Organ, an instrument which he loved with a passion.

Not exactly exciting stuff for a 17-year-old, however it did me no harm. The daily work routine kept me busy enough so that I could excuse myself reasonably early each evening on the pretext of being very tired. This slow pace at night was more than compensated for on weekends and on the odd afternoon when it was particularly hot and we had finished our work for the day.

For a seemingly quiet old non-smoking tee-total bachelor, Mr. Brockmeyer had an unusual passion. He loved to water-ski, and at every opportunity we would take to the river. His ski boat was a classic clinker-built wooden hull finished with a clear lacquer. It was a spectacular looking boat and certainly the best I ever saw on the river. The power-plant was a monstrous Chevy V8 which propelled it down the river like a rocket.

I quickly learnt to water-ski and in no time at all I was tearing up and down the river on a single ski. We spent many an enjoyable afternoon taking turn about, driving the boat and skiing.

With my new albeit modest income of 5 pounds, 2 shillings and sixpence a week (about $10.50), I decided I needed a set of wheels so that I had the freedom to come and go to Adelaide every second or third weekend, as I still had my mates and missed company my own age, particularly the female variety.

With a small loan from my father, I invested 220 pounds on a BSA 650cc *'Golden Flash'* motorcycle. It was an ex Police bike with low mileage and it had been perfectly maintained. A 650cc twin cylinder British bike was about as good as you could get and it became my pride and joy. This was prior to the Japanese invasion of motorcycles and compulsory safety helmets. The only Japanese bike in Australia at that time was a 50cc Honda Cub.

Those were the days when a motorcycle sounded like a motorcycle and you could still enjoy the wind in your hair. The disadvantage of course, was that as the South Australian winter approached, my trips back and forth to Adelaide became less and less pleasant. I still wonder how I survived those long wet trips on dark roads with hands so numb from the cold that I could barely maintain my grip on the handlebars.

Occasionally, if it was a particularly wet and cold Sunday afternoon, my mother would take pity on me as I was about to set off to return to the property and offer me the use of her little black Morris Minor. Typical of my mother, her son's comfort was more important than her considerable inconvenience of being left without a vehicle for two weeks. Unless the weather was particularly bleak, I always declined her offer.

My responsibilities around the property varied from crutching and shearing sheep, trapping and shooting rabbits, cutting the house lawns, fencing, towing a huge water cart to water the trees that lined the last half mile of the track down to the homestead, to picking oranges from the house orchard and delivering them to the local fruit juice factory across the river in Waikerie. I quickly became a jack of all trades.

One of my favourite memories of Nor' West Bend was sitting in the shade of massive River Red Gums on the banks of the river around noon. While the 'Billy' boiled with not a soul for miles around, I would sit back and watch the brown muddy water drifting lazily downstream just as it had done for the past tens of thousands of years. I can still recall quite vividly the feeling of absolute peace and tranquillity. I doubt that there could be found on this entire planet a more serene or relaxing place to be.

Other very fond recollections of Nor' West Bend include the lambing season during which my first and last task for the day was to drive around the 300 acre lambing paddock to check on the condition of the mothers and their newborn lambs. Watching a baby lamb struggling to stand for the first time in its short life was a sight and a joy of which I never tired.

On the larger river flats located downstream from the homestead there were a number of small lakes and billabongs that abounded with every example of South Australia's numerous native water-birds. Often on my return to the homestead in the early evenings, I would park the Land-Rover near these billabongs to ponder and take in the wonders of Nature's sights and sounds. This brief chapter of my life instilled in me a lifelong respect for 'Mother Nature' and a love of the Australian Bush.

The property had a large Aboriginal burial ground located a few kilometres downstream from the house. Very few people knew about it as my boss was very concerned that it could attract the wrong type of people if word got out, and he was a particularly private person. Only the Adelaide Museum was aware of the site so they occasionally sent their people to do whatever museums do with ancient burial sites. It consisted of a naturally occurring sand hill covering perhaps an acre of the riverbank and it did not take much effort to uncover large quantities of Aboriginal remains. Mr Brockmeyer was quite protective towards the site and discouraged even me from going there too often.

This was a thoroughly enjoyable chapter of my life and I occasionally reflect on what my future might have been had I stayed on the property. Mr. Brockmeyer's only living relative was an older spinster sister living in Adelaide and he made it quite clear to me that my future was assured if I wished to stay on at Nor' West Bend. The call of the sea however was too strong.

Many years later I was deeply saddened to discover that after the death of my old boss, Mr. Albert Brockmeyer, who had lived on the property for 70 years, the house was left empty and very quickly started to lose the roof and the ceilings. Doors were gone, half the house was still intact but the other half was pretty much missing. Such a terrible waste....

After I had spent eight months in the bush and three months after my seventeenth birthday, I again visited the Navy recruiting office.

With some regret at leaving the peaceful life on the land, I took the first of those major steps in life that ultimately determines the direction of one's destiny.

After several days in Adelaide and a round of farewells to my family, friends and girlfriend, I officially entered the Royal Australian Navy on the 28th of August 1965.

This was to be the biggest decision of my life as there was now no turning back. I had signed up for the minimum enlistment of 9 years so I now belonged to the Navy. I boarded the cattle truck that in those days passed for a passenger train for the overnight trip to Melbourne. I must admit that it wouldn't have really mattered if it were a cattle train, for I was off on the adventure of my young life. The Navy's recruiting team were there to ensure that we all actually boarded the train, as we were now officially Navy property. None of my fellow recruits, me included, slept much that night.

It was to be our last night as *'civvies'* for a very long time. In my case, 20 years.

2
RECRUIT SCHOOL 1965

Our arrival at HMAS Cerberus was a very exciting moment for me. I had been dreaming about this for most of my life.

The sight of uniformed sailors marching to and fro and the extremely military appearance of the base, with everything neatly positioned in its exact and appointed place (down to the white painted rocks surrounding the garden beds) confirmed that this was no dream.

Also called *'Flinders Naval Depot'*, Cerberus was the Recruit Training establishment for General Entry adult recruits (17-26 years of age). It was also the training school for numerous branches of the Navy, including Gunnery, Cookery and the Physical Training Instructors (PTI's). Unfortunately for us, we were to experience the worst aspects of all three branches.

Gunnery NCO's were the self-appointed disciplinarians and drill instructors of the RAN, and they were let loose on the new recruits from day one. I had thought that the Army was the only Service which had sadistic instructors who enjoyed bellowing their every command. How wrong I was.

The PTI's were responsible for our physical training and they obviously took great delight in running the recruits into the ground.

There is no need to explain the obvious down side of eating in the same establishment where the Navy's cooks were trained. In those days we intentionally called them cooks rather than chefs, although I must admit they made the best 'piss strainers' (*devilled kidneys*) and 'train smash' (*tomato and onion au gratin*) that I have ever tasted.

The 12 weeks which followed at Recruit school were far from a pleasant experience, however I accepted it as the price of entry into my chosen career.

Every minute of the day, and most evenings as well, were organised down to the last second. This was probably part of the shock therapy necessary to transform a group of young, slack and undisciplined civilian kids into responsible, professional sailors. There was no time to think about home or to feel sorry for yourself. We were pushed and shoved from one class to another with squad drill taking up any time between.

We had to double everywhere, call everyone 'Sir', and generally speak only when spoken to. The slightest sign of insolence or umbrage towards an instructor resulted in extra squad drill being inflicted during a time that would normally be spent washing clothes, studying or preparing for one of the endless Kit Musters.

The extra squad drill, or more accurately, punishment, was normally conducted by a PTI, and usually consisted of doubling around the parade ground with a SMLE (*Short Magazine Lee Enfield*) .303 rifle held high above your head. It weighed 3.9kg/8lb 10oz. This proved to be a very effective method of short circuiting any potential aggression.

The one thing I probably hated most of all was the Kit Muster. Every item of your kit had to be folded and laid out in a very exact manner for inspection. Failure to achieve perfection resulted in an additional kit muster being awarded. Very few recruits passed at their first attempt.

In hindsight the reason for this much hated harassment was obvious. Once aboard a warship the cramped conditions and limited locker space demanded that you were very neat and able to fit your entire kit issue into a very small space indeed.

The thing I could never understand was why we had to carry so much superfluous gear with us. The Navy insisted that at all times you had to have with you, every single item of kit you had been issued with. The old saying went *'if the Pusser issued it to you, you must need it'*. I soon discovered that we could have ditched at least half of the kit and gotten by very nicely. A variation to this expression was *'if the Navy wanted you to have a wife, they would have issued you with one'*.

Recruit school achieved its objectives in a very efficient manner. I could see the daily transformation of my fellow recruits from boys into well-disciplined young men. I presumed that the same changes were happening to me although I did manage to get into one punch up with a fellow recruit early on.

If the intensity of recruit training proved too much, recruits were given the opportunity after the first six weeks to change their minds and request a discharge. After this period however, there was no turning back. I cannot recall any of my intake taking this option.

After six weeks in the Navy we were all given a weekend leave pass and allowed to visit Melbourne. Most of us stayed at the *'White Ensign Club'*, a Navy sponsored haven for sailors. Accommodation and food were cheap - an important consideration when our salary was only 17 pounds ($34) per fortnight.

We were required to wear uniform on leave and warned by the Naval Patrol in extreme terms that if we brought any discredit upon the Navy, we would be dealt with in a very severe manner. As our uniforms made it obvious to all that we were recruits, we took the weekend very carefully. Melbourne was accustomed to seeing large numbers of sailors on leave, so to our disappointment, we were mostly ignored by the general public.

Real seagoing sailors were also on leave in Melbourne from the numerous warships alongside at Williamstown Naval dockyard and we tended to keep a low profile as they treated *'raw bones'* like us with contempt. However most of us managed to find some female company and have a good time. This was our first time in public as sailors in uniform and we were standing tall.

During the remaining six weeks of recruit training, the constant parade drill began to give way to the more serious aspects of Naval life. This was when I became seriously interested. I wanted to be a sailor, not a soldier. It was during this period that our instructors started to take note of which branch of the Navy each recruit would be most suited to. We were given basic lectures on the various branches and my initial thoughts leant towards an electrical career. I had not forgotten my father's wise advice to choose a branch which provided me with a qualification that was useful when I eventually left the Navy.

One of my three other room-mates, *'Snow'* Fogo, had joined the Navy with the sole intention of becoming a Clearance Diver. He was an excellent swimmer and I vaguely remember that he had already represented his home state of Western Australia in water polo.

Acceptance into Diver training required a physical aptitude test, and I think for the sake of a partner in crime, Snow pestered me for the week or so prior to the physical to try out with him. To keep him quiet I agreed.

I had no particular inclination to be a Diver at that time, other than a natural curiosity about what was renowned as the most difficult Branch in the Navy to enter.

As a lad, I had done my share of snorkelling and spear fishing however I laid no claim to being anything other than very ordinary, albeit comfortable, in the water. I had an older cousin who held some Australian spear fishing titles and was a professional Abalone diver but that obviously had no bearing on my abilities.

The actual diving aptitude test was conducted by a very British, very *'old school'* ex Royal Navy Lieutenant Commander who had once in his distant past qualified as a *'shallow water'* Diving Officer. I will never forget him. His name was *'Plum'* ...... and in hindsight he was quite unfit to be testing potential Navy divers. I think it was pure good luck that he had never caused a serious diving accident. His reputation preceded him and I think his particularly obnoxious manner deterred many potential divers from taking the test.

The diving aptitude test consisted of donning surface supplied breathing apparatus and descending into the cold and murky waters of Westernport Bay with *Plum*. Just being underwater with diving gear was enough of a shock however we weren't allowed the luxury of taking in our new environment.

No sooner had we reached the bottom than our facemask was torn off. We were expected to calmly continue breathing while refitting our facemask and clearing it of water. Once that was completed, Plum ripped out our mouthpiece and this then had to be replaced and cleared. Most of the would be *'frogmen'* decided at that point that a warm and comfortable job on the surface was more to their liking. Only three of the budding divers had passed to Plum's satisfaction. Two being Snow and me.

Our entire Intake was given three career choices with every effort supposedly being made to allow each recruit's first preference. Thinking *'what the hell'*, I opted for Clearance Diver as my first choice.

In 20 years, I never lost the stupid inclination to volunteer for everything. As only three of us had passed the test, we were all assured of being accepted for the first phase of diving training. I didn't think this would be such a bad thing as the Navy diving school was situated on Sydney Harbour and I had never been to Sydney. The last thing I wanted to do was to spend six months doing branch training at Cerberus. I had seen all I wanted to see of Flinders Naval Depot and I had joined the Navy to travel and sooner was much better than later.

With a tremendous amount of relief, we finally arrived at the time of our *'passing out'* parade. Recruit school had been an unpleasant although necessary evil on the way to becoming a *'Matelot'*. It had been akin to what I imagined prison to be like and best forgotten.

And so we all headed off on our second major train trip.

We were all very pleased with ourselves as we were no longer recruits. We had made it to the dizzy heights of *'Ordinary Seaman'*, with even a pay rise thrown in.

3
HMAS RUSHCUTTER 1965

On arrival in Sydney, we three would be divers *'drafted'* into HMAS Watson, a spectacular piece of real estate situated on the South Head of one of the most beautiful harbours in the world.

My fellow recruits went straight to their first sea posting, which turned out to be the Navy's Flagship HMAS Melbourne. In those days, with the exception of prospective divers, Ordinary Seamen, commonly called *'Ords'*, or *'OD's'*, spent up to 12 months at sea before starting their branch training. During this time, they learnt how to be seamen and were introduced to their chosen career at the sharp end, as well as learning how to wash dishes, scrub decks, chip paint and clean toilets.

We however were to be given the opportunity to take the first steps towards becoming a Clearance Diver.

The Navy's diving school, HMAS Rushcutter, was located in Rushcutters Bay, next to the Sydney Yacht Squadron from where the famous Sydney to Hobart yacht race starts every year. It was a magnificent location and from the moment I set foot in Rushcutter, I knew that being a diver was going to be totally different from anything else the Navy had to offer. For a start, nobody seemed to care about uniforms, which was in complete contrast to the attitude drummed into us at recruit school.

Divers under training ran around the depot in swimming trunks while the instructors went about in shorts and barefoot.

Instead of addressing diving officers as *''Sir'*, qualified divers all called their officers *'Boss'*. I immediately thought that this was the Navy for me as I was not cut out for the highly regimented *'left, right, left, right'* garbage that I had been subjected to in recruit school.

The RAN Clearance Diving Branch was only about 10 years old at that time and had been broadly based on the structure and training methods of the British Navy's CD branch and the Bomb and Mine Disposal teams of World War II. Many of our senior instructors were in fact amongst the first to have qualified as Clearance Divers in the Royal Australian Navy.

The first step in our training was to qualify as regular shallow water divers or *'Ship's Divers'*. This entailed becoming qualified to dive on air to a depth of 66 feet (20 metres) using surface supplied (SSBA) and self-contained (SCUBA) breathing apparatus.

We were joined on our course by regular volunteers from various branches of the Navy, including officers, who would return to their ships, providing they qualified, as members of their respective ship's diving teams. These teams were primarily responsible for carrying out hull searches as part of their Ship's defense against possible swimmer attack when visiting foreign ports.

At the completion of 3 weeks of intensive training, the survivors were classified as shallow water divers and thereafter entitled to wear a 'gold wire' diver's helmet sewn onto the right cuff of their dress uniform as opposed to their main rate badge which was worn on the right upper arm. These ships divers were then forever referred to by CD's as *'cuff rate divers'*.

From memory, about 18 sailors started my course and 8 or 9 qualified. Reasons for failure varied from fear of the water - particularly at night, to folding under the constant physical regime.

Our day began with joint physical training on the parade ground conducted by one of the more *'hard-ass'* Clearance Diving instructors. The morning sessions included all classes whether they were cuff rates or the more advanced CD courses, and most instructors joined in.

We were lucky that our dress for PT was only overalls. The less fortunate CD classes were usually attired in Dry suits. These were heavy sealed rubber suits which left only the face and hands exposed - a miniature sauna bath. I was to become well acquainted with these relics from WWII in the years to come.

On completion of our parade ground work-out, we would take to the streets in our overalls, with a pair of swim fins tucked under our arms for a barefoot run through several of the surrounding suburbs. These less than pleasant morning jogs finished in one of the many bays in Sydney Harbour from which we would then swim several miles back to Rushcutter, escorted by a diving workboat.

We were required to swim on our backs keeping our arms at our sides or crossed over our chest. This form of swimming strengthened our legs considerably and was essential for us to reach the level of fitness and endurance that was required of Navy divers.

On arrival back at the school, we could look forward to *'duck diving'* for a handful of mud at the end of the wharf – you just kept at it until you either got mud or quit. Next followed *'unders and overs'* Depending on the state of the tide, these could be relatively easy or next to impossible.

Still wearing overalls, everyone was required to climb over the highest cross member under the wharf and then duck dive under the lowest for the full length of the wharf, and to achieve this, we all had our first lesson on the importance of teamwork. To complete this obstacle course, we had to work as a team with the first one being hoisted up to the cross beam, and then he in turn hauling the rest up and over. At the end of this obstacle course, it was time to start the day's diving instruction, regularly interrupted by more PT.

Each class had a Petty Officer Clearance Diver in charge and he was assisted by a recently qualified Able Seaman CD, known by all as the *'2nd dickey'*. These fellows were extremely proud of their newly acquired status and were determined to make sure that we did not suffer any less than they had done during their training. The slightest imagined infringement by a trainee incurred the wrath of the 2nd dickey.

This usually involved spending most of one's precious spare time doing push ups, running around the parade ground or jumping into the water to free dive for a handful of mud.

Once the instructors had removed the students who were not considered suitable - many left the course voluntarily and some were advised that they were not up to the standard required - the basic diving skills were hammered home.

The training began to concentrate on proficiency in such things as basic seabed searches, ship's bottom searches and general ability to work underwater.

All skills were practised during the day and then repeated at night. The night diving definitely separated the men from the boys. This was the stage when most voluntarily withdrew from the course. Imaginations can run wild at night and some feel they are constantly surrounded by monsters of the deep.

Night diving took place twice a week on Tuesdays and Thursdays. Prior to the night dives, it was common at Rushcutter during the 60's to carry out what were called *'initiative runs'* (all divers were expected to have considerably more initiative and intelligence than the average sailor). To put us to the test, we were loaded into the back of an enclosed truck and driven to some unknown destination, arriving after dark. We were dressed in our wet suits or overalls with a pair of fins, with no identification and no money. As most of us were unfamiliar with Sydney, we did not have a clue where we were. We were split into pairs and given a task to carry out prior to returning to Rushcutter in time for our night dive.

Most of the population would have found it a little perplexing to be accosted in the outer suburbs of Sydney after dark by two young men dressed in wetsuits, with some absurd request.

Some of the stories as to how we accomplished our tasks and made it back to the diving school are probably best left untold due to the long memory of the law, however, one memorable night two students were given the task of obtaining the signatures of the two star strippers at the most popular strip club in Kings Cross.

Not only did they obtain their signatures, they were invited to stay and watch part of the show from the best seats in the house, in their wetsuits and with drinks *'on the house'*. Unfortunately, they had to decline this generous offer for obvious and more pressing reasons, so as an alternative the owner presented them with free lifetime entry to the club.

One incident sticks in my mind and always brings a smile to my face - my class was using the reasonably large vessel MSL 707 as our diving boat and because of her size, she required a stoker in the engine room to man the engine controls. One morning our friendly stoker asked if he could join in with the class for the swim back to Rushcutter. Our 2nd dickey, Noel (*Stewy*) Stewart said no worries, he would look after the engine room. As we arrived back at Rushcutter and the 707 idled towards the wharves, our instructor, Bluey Johnson, who was driving 707, rang down to the engine room to go half astern as she came in. Stewy being unfamiliar with the controls, put it half ahead. As the boat surged forward, Blue rang down full astern and Stewy obligingly went to full throttle as she raced towards the Yacht squadron next door. Blue had nowhere to go.... It was quite spectacular from our sea level view to watch the 707 plough full ahead into the wharves of the posh yacht squadron. Luckily she missed some very expensive yachts and only demolished one of their wharves.

At the end of three harrowing weeks, the newly qualified and very proud ship's divers returned to their ships with a gold diver's helmet sown on the cuff of their dress uniforms.

The remaining few *'would be Clearance Divers'* stayed behind for a further week of suffering to determine if we were suitable for selection to undergo the *'real'* diving course. Snow Fogo and I both made it through to this stage along with a couple of other potentials from our course.

It was not uncommon for sailors already qualified in other seaman categories to attempt to *'change their rate'* after obtaining a ship's diver qualification. After a taste of Rushcutter many envied the CD's unique lifestyle. In some cases, these were sailors who had reached Leading Seaman rank and been in the Navy for perhaps five or six years.

My older brother, Mike, who had originally qualified as a Radar Plotter, did just this after I had qualified as a Clearance Diver.

During the fourth week we continued with the normal morning PT sessions, however the days were spent undergoing extensive medical, psychological and suitability tests.

The most important of these tests was the ability to withstand breathing pure oxygen.

Oxygen has some surprising characteristics and not everyone can tolerate this life supporting element in its purest form. We were introduced to the CD's Oxygen Breathing Apparatus, then known as a UBA (Universal Breathing Apparatus), a British set which was refined during World War 2 by the famous Royal Navy frogman, Buster Crabb.

The UBA was basically a copy of an oxygen re-breather set which was found on the body of an Italian frogman; recovered during the infamous underwater chariot raids during WW2 on British warships in Gibraltar. Italian frogmen aboard their human torpedoes, or *'pigs'* as they were known, were later responsible for the sinking of HM's Battleships *'Queen Elizabeth'* and *'Valiant'* in Alexandria Harbour.

The set consisted of a rubberised harness and breathing bag with a *'pendulum'* type breathing system. The pendulum system was later replaced with a circulatory system on more modern re-breather sets for safety reasons. A full facemask was worn with a single flexible hose connected to a canister situated in the breathing bag. This canister contained a white granulated carbon dioxide absorbent (known as Protosorb) sufficient at that time for 90 minutes of use. This was later reduced to 60 minutes to provide a greater margin of safety for the diver. Two small cylinders, pressurised to 3,000 psi, provided pure oxygen through a reducing valve at a constant flow rate of 1.5 litres per minute, and a single cylinder of pure oxygen supplied an emergency backup.

Essentially, the set produced a sufficient flow of oxygen for a fit diver to perform at a predetermined level *(swimming underwater for an hour)* and the harmful carbon dioxide (CO_2) exhaled by the diver was removed by the *'Protosorb'* absorbent in the canister as it passed through to the breathing bag. If needed, the diver could use a by-pass valve to top up the bag with fresh oxygen as required. This meant that a constant volume of gas was being maintained in the breathing loop - the body was consuming the oxygen provided by the set and the CO_2 given off by the body was being chemically removed. The upshot of all this was that the set emitted no tell-tale bubbles and hence its reason for being - the perfect diving rig for ship attack.

Unfortunately, there were a number of downsides to this outstanding piece of equipment.

Firstly, even though human life cannot survive without oxygen, if 100% pure oxygen is breathed in an atmosphere in excess of two atmospheres absolute (29.4psi or 33 feet of seawater), it is toxic to humans and will kill quite quickly, particularly when breathing underwater.

Secondly, the pendulum breathing system (essentially the breathing medium moving backwards and forwards through the single hose) meant that there was a dead space in the hose and if a diver did not breathe deeply enough, he would be re-breathing a large percentage of his already exhaled CO_2, resulting in a *'CO_2 build-up'* and subsequent blackout.

Thirdly, should the CO_2 absorbent become overly damp (some of the older sets leaked a little), its life would be considerably shortened and if the canister was packed incorrectly, *'channelling'* could occur whereby the exhaled gas followed the resulting channels and the efficiency of the *'proto'* was considerably reduced.

If the Proto became wet, the resultant mixture frothed up through the breathing tube into your mouth and this brew then removed the lining from your throat.

For these reasons, it was absolutely imperative that all students experienced both oxygen poisoning and a carbon dioxide build-up. Both effects were hard to pick when working underwater so it was extremely important that the symptoms were experienced during the early stages of training.

Having elaborated on all its faults, it was the most comfortable piece of diving equipment I was to use in my 20 years of Navy diving. It was like a temperamental woman. If you were aware of its dangers and treated it with care and respect, it was a delight. I loved it. Unfortunately, the UBA was responsible for more deaths in the Branch than any other diving set.

As ship attack swimming was a key role for CDs, failure to pass the O_2 tolerance test meant instant removal from the program and there were always several who could not tolerate oxygen.

On completion of my CD acceptance course, I was advised that I would join the remainder of my intake for my first sea posting. They had all joined the aircraft carrier HMAS Melbourne a month or two earlier while she lay alongside in Garden Island dockyard in Sydney. When I completed my course however, she was exercising off Jervis Bay, over 100 miles to the south of Sydney.

In typical Navy fashion, I and Jeff (*Cowby*) Garrett, who had qualified with me, were ordered to proceed by train to the Naval College at Jervis Bay and await the Melbourne should she enter the bay and to board at the first opportunity.

As it turned out, her program was changed and the next thing we were told was to report to the college parade ground with all our kit. To my delight, a Wessex helicopter was waiting to transport us to our new ship. This was extremely exciting and exactly what I thought was befitting a Navy frogman.

The ship was steaming quite a long way off the coast so we had the opportunity to sit back and enjoy our first flight in a helicopter. Fortunately, it was a beautiful day and I'll never forget the sight of Melbourne underway as we approached her from her port quarter.

After drafting in and stowing my kit in my mess-deck, I was assigned to my *'part of ship'*. My first job aboard the Melbourne was chipping paint and rust on one of the boat decks; those openings under the flight deck where the ship's boats are stowed.

However, on this my first day at sea, with a superb view of the gentle blue ocean swell slipping by at 20 knots, with flying operations being conducted on the flight deck above my head, nothing could dampen my excitement or enthusiasm.

I was in the Navy, at sea aboard the Flagship - and a qualified Ordinary Seaman Clearance Diver to boot. Couldn't get any better than that....

4

HMAS MELBOURNE - 1966

The following few months were spent preparing Melbourne for her next deployment to the Far East, planned for early '66.

Most of our sea-time leading up to our departure was conducted off the coast of Jervis Bay, exercising with the Fleet Air Arm. The airborne or *'Birdie'* branch of the Navy was based at HMAS Albatross, near Nowra in NSW, when it wasn't aboard our floating *'bird farm'*.

Life aboard the Melbourne was reasonable for ordinary seamen, although being the flagship, discipline was rigidly enforced by the Naval Patrolmen, who were known as *'crushers'*. These sadistic bastards were despised by regular sailors and were a breed of their own. Being such a large ship, it was relatively easy to stay out of their way and keep your nose clean.

As a qualified member of the ship's diving team, and being an Ord CD, I spent a lot of time in the diving store maintaining equipment under the watchful eye of Bruce Paulson, the ship's AB Clearance Diver. This suited me as it was a vast improvement on chipping paint all day.

My clearest memory of this period was putting to sea early one February morning in 1966 after an overnight anchorage in Jervis Bay. The weather was deteriorating rapidly and the ship was heading directly into a rising easterly swell which had the Melbourne pitching quite heavily. I was thoroughly enjoying the experience as we fell in on the Quarterdeck at 0800 that memorable morning.

Not only was it my first exposure to bad weather in a big ship, it was pay day, and we received our first pay in Australia's brand-new decimal currency – dollars instead of pounds.

During this *'work up'* period, the Birdies were constantly conducting *'touch and go's'* in their Sea Venoms and Fairey Gannets. It was still quite comfortable aboard as the ship did not have its full complement of crew.

Once we loaded the aircraft, aircrew and support sailors aboard in preparation for our Far East cruise, conditions became a little more crowded. The other downside of having them onboard was that they considered the ship and all aboard her were there purely for their benefit; and they were probably right. There was a lot of animosity between the Birdies and the ship's crew. This dislike of each other was I think historical. The crew held the Birdies in contempt as they were not considered to be real sailors and the Airmen obviously thought they were a cut above regular sailors.

Finally, on the 24th March 1966, we sailed from Sydney on the first of my many trips *'up top'*. In those days, Australia was a member of SEATO *(South East Asian Treaty Organisation)* and it was common for ships to spend between 6 to 7 months exercising in Asian waters with other member Navies. SEATO then included Australia, France, New Zealand, Pakistan, the Philippines, Thailand, the United Kingdom and the United States. Australia normally sent the Melbourne to show the *'flag'* with two or three Destroyer escorts/Frigates and the ex-Royal Navy fleet replenishment tanker, HMAS Supply *(previously the Tide Austral)*. The SEATO treaty was intended to create alliances that could contain communist powers in the region.

It was normal practice in all Navies to conduct a *'crossing the line ceremony'* for all first timers as the ship passed over the equator, and Melbourne was no exception. A senior sailor usually acted as *King Neptune* and the uninitiated are accepted into his realm. The youngest sailor on board becomes Captain for the day, or at least wears his uniform. This ceremony varies from ship to ship, but without exception it provides a laugh for all and fond memories for the newly initiated. Today it would be considered *'politically incorrect'* by the socialist wimps of our current society.

The Melbourne was also carrying the newly formed Clearance Diving Team One on our journey north. They were to leave the ship in Singapore, our first Asian port of call. The team was scheduled to participate in exercises with the Royal Navy's Far East Fleet Clearance Diving Team, including a dive on the HMS Repulse, a British Battleship sunk by the Japanese during WW2. As it turned out the team unexpectedly deployed at short notice to Vietnam for several days and as a consequence, began what was to be the four and half years of CD involvement in the war in Vietnam.

Singapore's Sembawang Naval base was home to the Royal Navy's Far East Fleet. It was a huge dockyard with sufficient infrastructure to carry out major refits in its dry-docks, and was at that time, home to thousands of British sailors and Royal Marines.

One of the several *'entering harbour'* procedures of the Navy was for all rates not on watch to fall in on the upper deck. This entailed standing shoulder to shoulder around the perimeter of the flight deck in our white *'dress for entering harbour'*. It was a very exciting feeling to be entering our first port of call in the mystical *Far East*, as it was then called. With the advent of the Jumbo jet, it is no longer considered to be *'Far'* as it is now commonly referred to as just South East Asia.

To be standing high on the flight deck of an aircraft carrier, with a bird's eye view of the Sembawang dockyard as the ship glided slowly towards its berth and the unique smells of Singapore wafting on the breeze, was quite an exhilarating experience for a 17-year-old. The wild stories told by the *'old salts'* during our last few days at sea had stirred some very active young imaginations and we were all chafing at the bit to get ashore. It was a tradition of sorts for one or two of the older Able Seamen to take a few of the young OD's under their wing and look after them on their first *run ashore*.

In retrospect, I think it was a case of the blind leading the blind. They invariably took the young seamen to the most decadent bars that they knew, where the Mama Sans took great delight in trying to entice these young *cherry boys* into accompanying one of their more experienced bar-girls for a *short time*. I believe that some bars actually paid off these old hands in the form of a few free beers to bring in the young sailors. My mates and I were no exception to this tradition and several of us finished up in some sleazy little bar in downtown Singapore on our first day ashore. Finally, we felt like real sailors – dressed in white fronts and white bell bottom trousers sitting in a real Asian bar in the mystical Far East drinking Anchor beer with our mates....

As the Naval dockyard was a considerable distance from the city of Singapore, it was normal practice to start with a few beers in the bars of Sembawang and Nee Soon, both located just outside the dockyard gates. As the sun went down we would jump into cabs for the hair-raising ride into town. The majority of taxis in those days were old Mercedes Benz's and the drivers were all lunatics. With a little prompting, normally in the form of a partly intoxicated sailor saying *'faster John, faster'* (sailors called all Singapore taxi drivers John), the drivers would endeavour to show us that they had missed their calling and should have been Grand Prix racers at Monte Carlo rather than driving taxis. I recall some very exciting cab rides. Fortunately, we were rarely completely sober during these trips.

In those days Singapore was a shopper's paradise with one Australian dollar buying three Singapore dollars. After the first couple of wild nights ashore to clear the cobwebs from two or three weeks at sea, most sailors went shopping for their wives, girlfriends and families.

Anything purchased to take home was referred to as a *'rabbit'* and every previously empty space on the ship began to fill rapidly with these rabbits. Almost everything was reasonably priced and even on our low salaries we could afford to buy the best selection of the available electrical and sound equipment. The buyer however had to beware as was proven on one occasion when a mate of mine couldn't wait to show me the flashy diver's watch he had bought at a bargain price. The tag said it was guaranteed to a depth of 600 feet so I suggested we take it to the nearest hand-basin to put it to the test. He stared in disbelief as we watched the water slowly drip in under the glass.

Once the obligations to family and friends were fulfilled, it was back to the many delights of Singapore. In those days Singapore was still very much old Asia, albeit with a distinct British colonial feel. The shops and street stalls were as they had been for centuries with life scurrying along in every narrow laneway and back street. Bamboo poles loaded down with washed clothes jutted from every window and cast shadows over the streets below. The sights and smells were quite intoxicating and it was an extremely exciting place to be. I particularly loved the food which was cooked before our eyes in the street stalls. The blend of Chinese, Indian and Malay spices produced flavours that were unique to Singapore and the curries, satays, laksas, fried rice and egg *'banjos'* were a connoisseur's delight.

The Raffles Hotel was at that stage one of the most imposing buildings in town whereas today Singapore almost resembles New York in terms of skyscrapers. Places like *'Change Alley'* and *'Bugis Street'* were amongst the major attractions for both sailors and tourists. From midnight, the only place to be was Bugis Street (pronounced Boogie), or *'the Bugin Straza'* as it was often called by sailors.

At night this infamous street became an open-air mall with every imaginable type of food and drink available and of course its most famous attraction, *'Beanie Boys'* or *'Kai-tais'*. These ladyboys of almost every Asian nationality would parade up and down the length and breadth of Bugis street in their finest feminine attire from midnight until dawn, with sailors' wolf whistling and urging them on. Real females also frequented Bugis street however they usually looked quite drab alongside the *'Beanies'*. Tourists from all corners of the globe visited Bugis street as well although I'm not sure if they came to gape at the Beanie Boys or watch the sailor's behaviour. Both were a major spectacle of their own. Sailors were known far and wide for their tendency to spontaneously perform the *'dance of the flaming assholes'* when *'under the weather'* – usually done on the roof of the toilet block in full view of all the tourists and much to the delight of the *Beanie boys*.......

We often dropped into the Royal Navy's NAAFI club for a cold beer. The NAAFI was a civilian run outfit which managed bars and clubs exclusively for the use of the Navy. It was located quite close to the Raffles Hotel downtown and had cheap cold beer with a spectacular view of Singapore harbour. Australian sailors used the term NAAFI to describe anyone who had 'No Ambition And F**k all Interest'.

On arrival in Singapore the ship took on board a number of Chinese workers. They were laundry-men, tailors and shoe makers and they were to stay with us until we departed the Far East on our way home. In my opinion it seemed quite strange for a warship to be carrying around a group of Asian civilians, however it was a long accepted tradition which the RAN had inherited from the Royal Navy's Far East Fleet. The young sailors whose part of ship was the laundry thought it was an absolute blessing. The Melbourne was an old ship designed and built by the British for the North Atlantic and she was not suited to the hot and humid climes of the Far East. With the exception of the engine room, the laundry was probably the hottest place on the ship. These Chinese *'dhobymen'* worked like Trojans in conditions that were relatively comfortable to them.

I later discovered that these men spent most of their lives at sea aboard warships, quite often transferring between ships at sea as one ship left the Far East station and another arrived. The shoe maker was called *'wac-a-tac'* and was given a small compartment from where he turned-out tailor-made shoes.

The Melbourne continued its deployment throughout the Far East with ports of call at Hong Kong, Manila and Penang. In between these visits we played war games at sea with the Brits, Yanks and Kiwis.

Life at sea aboard an aircraft carrier can be quite boring as it is a little like being the Queen Bee. We steamed along in the centre of the fleet being mothered and protected by the real warships which were racing around the edges of the convoy searching for and keeping submarines away.

Things livened up however when flying operations were underway. The fleet turned into the wind and increased speed to

20 plus knots (37+ kms/hr). With the wind howling over the flight deck at perhaps 30 or 40 knots and the ship ploughing into a reasonable sized swell, life became much more interesting. The ship would feel alive as it gently pitched into a head sea with its hive of aircraft busily launching and recovering.

On two occasions, we had aircraft crash, or miss the arrestor wires altogether on touchdown and plunge off the flight deck into the ocean. I recall a *'Sea Venom'* (all weather night fighter) touching down and it seemed that the pilot thought he had hooked one of the seven arrestor wires so he pulled his engines to idle – unfortunately he had missed all the wires. The aircraft sailed off the forward end of the flight deck and began to roll inverted as the two crew members ejected. Sadly, the pilot left his ejection a fraction late and slammed into the water at a great rate of knots, sinking immediately while still strapped in his seat. Memorial services at sea for lost pilots was not such an unusual occurrence on Carrier deployments. On the same cruise, a *'Fairy Gannet'* (a mid-wing monoplane with a tricycle undercarriage and a crew of three, and a double turboprop engine driving two contra-rotating propellers) did the opposite to the Sea Venom. He had hooked a wire but applied full power to his engines. This caused the heavy aircraft to lift slightly before slewing to the left and sliding over the ship's side. There it was hanging by the wire and the arrestor hook with the crew still inside. Once the Melbourne had come to a stop, the seaboat was launched and the crew jumped into the water to be picked up. Very shortly after, the arrestor hook snapped and the aircraft slipped to a watery grave.

As an Ord CD, I often had the task of Swimmer of the Watch *(ready to go over the side in an emergency)*. At sea, 24 hours around the clock, there is a *'watch on deck'* comprised of seamen rates who rotate through hourly stints as lookouts, helmsman, lifebuoy sentry and standby to launch the ship's seaboat in the event of an emergency.

Watch on Deck was done in addition to normal daytime duties and was a four-hour watch with the exception of the afternoon *'dog watches'* which were two hours each.

The watches were as follows: -

	'Middle'	0000 - 0400
	'Morning'	0400 - 0800
	'Forenoon'	0800 - 1200
	'Afternoon'	1200 - 1600
	'First Dog'	1600 - 1800
	'Last Dog'	1800 - 2000
	'First'	2000 – 0000

Even though the watch officially began and ended on the hour, it was an unwritten law of the Navy that you relieved the watch ten minutes before the hour and woe betide anyone who wasn't there on time. There was no greater sin at sea than to be late for your watch.

The most unpopular watch was the Middle as it effectively put a four-hour hole in your night's sleep. At least the Morning watchmen did not have to *'turn to'* to work until 0900.

Most seamen resented the fact that apart from the engine-room stokers, many other rates did not keep any night watches at sea. While in harbour, seamen kept a full one-day duty in every four whilst stores rates and electrical sailors sometimes kept one in five or six. This obviously meant more time ashore for them and may explain why seamen rates normally played harder and got into more trouble during their less frequent time ashore. Most mornings there were several seamen *'defaulters'* at the Captain's table with caps in hand.

The old British Naval tradition of a rum issue at sea had long been replaced in the RAN by a beer issue although the Brits and Kiwis still retained their rum issue. It was pure Jamaican made especially for the Navy and it was the best rum I have ever tasted.

With the exception of the first night at sea and during exercises, an evening issue of one 26oz (750ml) can of beer was made to all the crew with the exception of officers and those having the First watch. After the HMAS Voyager disaster *(where the Melbourne sliced her in half)*, officers were not permitted to drink at sea. It was not unusual for off duty sailors to negotiate extra cans from their non-drinking mates although I recall several sailors who were quite heavy drinkers ashore but wouldn't touch a drop of alcohol at sea.

Life at sea aboard an Aircraft Carrier continued to fascinate me. Apart from *'Watch on Deck'* no two days were the same. The ship was constantly on the move at a speed of about 16 knots and spread over 24 hours a day, we covered a lot of ocean. When steaming in a northerly or southerly direction the weather changes could be quite spectacular from one day to the next. It was the rough weather however that was exciting. Every minute of the day and night you were constantly reminded that you were at sea. The ship felt alive as it was constantly rolling or pitching and it was surprising how much a relatively large ship like the Melbourne did move about in a big sea. To wander out onto the boat decks or gun sponsons and watch the big dark swells rolling down the ship's side and the constant sea-spray being flung aside by the ship's bow as it pounded through the oncoming waves always brought to my mind such classics as *'H.M.S. Ulysses'* and *'Victory at Sea'*.

In very heavy weather the exposed weather decks, including the fo'c'sle and flight deck, were out of bounds as the risk of being swept overboard was quite real. The only sailor permitted to be outside was the lifebuoy sentry and he was stationed in the relative security of the quarter-deck, right at the very stern or rear end of the ship. His task was to keep a lookout for anyone who may accidentally fall or be swept overboard. He was the last line of defence for any poor soul who went over the side out in the middle of that very big and very lonely ocean.

In between SEATO exercises our visits to the exotic ports of Asia continued.

Our several days alongside in Hong Kong was a roaring success. As the Flagship of the RAN, we drew a berth alongside at HMS Tamar, the Royal Naval base located on prime real estate on Hong Kong island, midway between the bar district of Wanchai and the business district of Victoria. We had no sooner tied up when 20 or 30 women came alongside in sampans and began washing the ship's side. The old girl in charge came aboard and in no time at all drums of *'ship's side grey'* paint were being passed over the side and down to her ladies. This was the famous matriarch of *'Jenny's side party'* and over the years she had probably painted every warship of the British, Australian and New Zealand Navies. Very few old sailors haven't heard of Jenny. Her mother, the original Jenny, began painting British warships refitting in Hong Kong back in 1925. We all thought she was wonderful as it allowed us to get on with having a good time ashore rather than cleaning and painting the rust streaked ship's side.

Hong Kong in the mid 60's was truly a great town. The hordes of tourists in their Jumbo jets hadn't yet descended on the place and our Australian Dollar bought HK$6. Beer was cheap and the girls very friendly. Every bar was full of sailors in a variety of uniforms – Australian, British, Kiwis and Americans, all in various stages of intoxication. Every bar had a *'Mama San'* who supervised the proceedings and, in those days, and I believe they genuinely liked Australian sailors. Many a young sailor was taken under the wing of a Mama San who made sure he was looked after. They did think that Yankee sailors were very gullible and happily took full advantage of their free spending ways at every opportunity.

Within a few days of a ship's arrival in Hong Kong, it was traditional that every Messdeck on the ship had a Mess Party. This was all planned out well ahead of time by the old salts who had their favourite bars in Wanchai or to a lesser extent then, Kowloon. Since leaving Australia, every crew member had contributed from every pay day towards their respective Mess party fund and by the time we arrived, each mess had collected a considerable amount of money. A bar would be booked for the night and entry was restricted to members of that particular mess. The beer and female company were non-stop.

To every sailor of that era, if you hadn't been to Hong Kong, you hadn't been anywhere.

During the day, work routines went on as normal, albeit with hangovers and some unusual tales from the night before. Most of the young sailors returned with bright new tattoos to show off. I accompanied several mates to tattoo artists however I was never tempted. I was content to sit back, drink free beer and watch them as they became marked for life.

While in Hong Kong, all of the Ords were given the opportunity to obtain their Marksman badges or *'Crossed Rifles'*. We were taken to the British Army's rifle range on Stonecutter's Island and put through our paces.

As a lad I had been a pretty fair rifle shot, and bagged more than my share of rabbits. My Father and Grandfather were both State trophy holders and on my Mother's side, some of her uncles had coached and represented Australia against the Brits.

We were using the old Lee Enfield SMLE .303, an outstanding bolt action rifle which had been used by the British and Australian forces throughout both WW I & II. I was a little hung over on the day and assumed that I wouldn't have much of a chance. However, about halfway through the shoot, one of the gunnery instructors told me that I was well on target to qualify for the gold wire badge so I decided that maybe I should get a little more serious. As it turned out, I breezed it in and was one of only about three to qualify on the day. The only problem was that the Crossed Rifle's badge was to be worn on the right cuff of our dress uniform and I already had my Shallow Water Diver's helmet proudly sown there. Apparently the Navy had never taken into account that sailors might qualify for both cuff rates, as they only allowed one badge to be worn on the cuff under the dress regulations. If I remember correctly, we were paid a small annuity for the qualification.

After more fleet exercises in the South China Sea, we visited Manila, the capital of the Philippines, while the city was still under President Marcos's decree of Martial Law. The city was a little like the US Wild West - totally lawless.

The anti-submarine Frigate, HMAS Yarra, was one of Melbourne's escorts and it so happened that my brother Mike, an Able Seaman Radar Plotter at the time, was part of her crew. We often met each other ashore in our various ports of call and in combination with his mates, I and my mates were often led astray by these experienced old salts who were mostly on their second or third deployment *'up top'*. I don't remember many of the details but I spent my 18th birthday in Manila with Mike and we celebrated it in style. I had a ball.

While we were ashore, we kept in groups of at least six or seven and we always walked down the middle of the street after dark. I remember going to one infamous bar called *'Bill's Place'* which was tucked away down some little side alley. There was a large sign hanging at the front door - *'Please leave your guns at the bar'*. It became one of our favourite drinking holes as it was always overflowing with friendly girls and sailors.

During broad daylight in downtown Manila one of my mates witnessed a thief steal a watch from a tourist's wrist and before the thief had run 20 metres, a policeman had drawn his pistol and shot him dead.

Aside from the dangers of the city, we loved it and all had a great time. It was a thoroughly good run. So good in fact that some sailors didn't want to leave. Because of her size, the Melbourne had to anchor a few kilometres out in Manila Bay, with liberty boats regularly running backwards and forwards.

On our final night in port I was on the last liberty boat back to the ship and as we neared the Melbourne, one Leading Seaman who was *'several sheets to the wind'* decided that Manila was so good that he had no intention of leaving. With a wild "Yee-haa", he jumped over the side and began swimming back towards the city lights. We all cheered him on as the boat's coxswain nonchalantly turned the boat around and the crew dragged the waterlogged sailor back onboard. The Leading Seaman coxswain had obviously witnessed similar proceedings before and took it all in his stride.

During our cruise, all Ords of the seaman category were required to qualify for their Helmsman Certificate. This meant from memory, spending a total of 10 hours on the helm of Melbourne. The wheelhouse was located below the bridge in a tiny compartment big enough for 3 people and the *'wheel'*. The only thing visible to the helmsman was the ships' compass repeater by which he steered while receiving orders from the bridge. The wheel was spoked and constructed of varnished timber and polished brass and it was huge. About 5 feet in diameter from memory.

Our deployment passed all too quickly and after a short visit to Penang in Malaya, we returned to Australia, our first port of call being the city of Perth. Our stopover there was brief and we were all looking forward to getting back to Sydney, which was home port for the majority of the crew.

We departed Fremantle Port in company with Yarra in deteriorating weather and by the time we cleared Cape Leeuwin to the south and turned east into the Great Australian Bight, we were experiencing the full brunt of a ferocious *'Roaring Forties'* storm. For the next 4 or 5 days we were hammered by the worst weather I was to experience in my 20 years in the RAN.

Apart from essential watch-keepers, work on both ships came to a complete halt. Nobody was allowed on the upper decks and everything that was movable was secured and battened down. It was awesome to see Mother Nature unleash her fury on these two insignificant blips on the surface of that vast ocean. Yarra began to take such a beating that the Admiral ordered both ships to reduce speed to about 7 knots.

I spent my *'watches'* as a lookout on the bridge and it occurred to me what a complete waste of time it was as no other vessel would have dared venture into such weather. Yarra had shut down and secured her LWO2 *(main radar antenna)* for fear of it being broken away.

From the Bridge I watched the immense swells bearing down, with the Melbourne's bow virtually disappearing into the troughs as the oncoming crest rose ominously above the flight deck. Many times I watched the bow of the ship being driven into a huge trough and the tip of the flight deck actually dig into a solid wall of water. The ship would shudder and struggle to lift its nose clear and the water would then roll along the flight deck like surf breaking on the beach. It was quite frightening as we all knew Melbourne was an old ship and the word had quickly spread that the bulkheads in 3 Bravo *(3 Bravo being the 3rd deck down and second watertight compartment back from the bow)* were beginning to buckle by up to 2 feet.

After the Voyager collision in 1964, Melbourne had had a new bow fitted and it appeared that the replacement was not as sound or as strong as the original. Damage Control parties reported that the ship's boats were being torn out of their cradles as the huge waves rolled down the ship's sides, slamming them against the overheads and destroying their cabins. Several small aircraft tractors and a forklift had broken their chain moorings and been badly damaged. Luckily, none of our aircraft had sustained any serious damage.

If a relatively large ship like an Aircraft Carrier was suffering so badly, we all wondered what life was like aboard the Yarra *(only 2,750 tons)*. Mike told me later that all except essential watch-keepers had been confined to their bunks. While he was lookout on the Bridge, Mike took several outstanding photographs of Yarra's fo'c'sle as it sliced down into oncoming waves with solid walls of water rising vertically past 1 deck level. He told me that there were times when the watch-keepers on the Bridge thought the ship may not recover from its downward plunge and keep going down as if it were a submarine.

As the weather finally began to abate, it was decided to conduct a RAS *(replenishment at sea)* with the Yarra as she was in need of fuel. When Yarra made her approach from astern, I was quite shocked to see the damage inflicted by the storm. Large strips of paint had been peeled off exposing bare hull and her small boat's boom had come adrift and smashed a hole in the ship's side. The wind had eased a little but the swells were still huge so we knew this would be a dangerous transfer.

The Melbourne had to maintain sufficient speed to guarantee steerage way so the Yarra made her run in with a few extra knots *'rung on'*. It was most spectacular to see her during the approach with her bow rising sharply out of the water and baring her keel as far back as the Sonar dome followed by her bow burying itself again in the next swell. As she arrived alongside and reduced speed to keep station on Melbourne, she was pitching very heavily and I could see the tips of her twin propellers under her stern thrashing clear of the water as the bow buried itself again into the oncoming swells. We knew the ship's coxswain would be working up quite a sweat as it was imperative in these close and dangerous conditions that he maintained perfect station.

The RAS was not to be, as no sooner had the Yarra settled down to a parallel course and speed when a monster wave corkscrewed her bow and swung her stern in towards Melbourne's side. I was standing in a gun sponson at the edge of the flight deck and in the blink of an eye I found myself looking directly down onto Yarra's quarter-deck. I braced for the inevitable crunch as the two ships came together however the reaction on the bridge of Yarra had been immediate and decisive. There was obviously a frantic correction and engine order in the wheel-house and a black stream of smoke poured out of her funnel as she accelerated away from us like a racehorse out of the starting gate. All thoughts of another attempt were squashed by the Admiral. I'm sure he didn't wish to answer to the Naval Board as to why he had a collision at sea, however minor.

The buzzes *(rumours)* were flying around the ship that Yarra would have to divert to Adelaide but fortunately the weather continued to abate, so both ships pushed on ahead to the warm homecoming awaiting us in Sydney.

We arrived back at Garden Island dockyard on the 1st July '66 and I was immediately posted to HMAS Rushcutter; to start down the long hard road that would eventually lead to me becoming a fully-fledged Navy Clearance Diver.

5
CD TRAINING -1966/67

From memory we started the course with about a dozen or so hopefuls. With the exception of John Branch who had been back classed and Snow Fogo, Cowby Garrett and myself, the remainder were ex junior recruits who had completed their sea time aboard the troop transport HMAS Sydney, Melbourne's sister ship.

Prior to starting any diving, we all had to pass the Seamanship and NBCD (*Nuclear Biological Chemical Defence*) courses for Able Seaman and so moved across to HMAS Penguin which at that time was home to the RAN's future submariners and housed the Naval hospital, Seamanship and NBCD schools.

Most of the class enjoyed this short respite as there were a number of WRANS (female sailors) stationed at Penguin. Little did I know at that time that I would be returning to Penguin much sooner than I could ever have imagined.

Finally, we were ready to start the serious side of being in the Navy. As Rushcutter had no accommodation other than for the nightly duty watch, everyone was billeted at HMAS Watson; the Torpedo Anti-Submarine (TAS) school located atop Sydney's South Head. Either Navy buses or trucks shuttled us backwards and forwards each day.

Everybody from Rushcutter hated Watson for a number of reasons. Watson was real Navy, much like Cerberus; full of bullshit and regulations. Whereas Rushcutter was within walking distance of King's Cross, Watson was at the end of the world and worst of all as far as we were concerned, it was compulsory to go to church on Sundays if you were onboard. For these and a number of other reasons, a large percentage of the qualified CD's shared flats up near the *'Cross'*, either with other divers, or with girlfriends.

The worst part about church on Sundays was that most of us had hit the town on the only night of the week that we had to spare, and the last thing we wanted to do was be up and dressed in full uniform by 0800 on Sunday morning; for whatever reason. The only alternative for us was to be out the gate on the first and only *'Liberty Boat'* at 0800 and this unfortunately also entailed being in full dress uniform. We all lined up at attention as the duty officer inspected every detail of our uniforms before allowing us ashore, knowing full well that we were only going ashore to avoid church and would be back at about 1100. The second liberty boat would not be until after the completion of church.

Hard to believe in this day and age that only a few short years ago it was a chargeable offence to not attend church on Sundays if you were on the base. The Navy had a long tradition of strong religious convictions and I strongly objected to it being pushed down my neck.

The local civilian population must have thought we were a weird bunch. Sunday morning and Watson's Bay full of sailors wandering around in dress uniform. The only consolation was that it was normal for a number of young ladies to be sun-baking topless on the beach on the weekends.

Our course began with basic air diving to refresh our skills in the water and lots of *'run jumps'*. We were pushed and harassed constantly with not a second to spare. The minute the second dickey, at that time Scotty Allan, thought you had nothing to do; as when divers were in the water and all spare hands had finished recharging and lugging about the 220 cubic feet air cylinders that we seemed to use by the dozens every day, he felt it his duty to keep us busy. This usually entailed laps of the parade ground, *'speed dressing and undressing'* in both wet and dry suits, any number of push-ups, jumping over the side to get a handful of mud, or any other sadistic exercise that came into his devious mind.

Speed dressing in dry suits was the worst of these evolutions. The dry suit was a one-piece heavy reinforced diving suit which only had openings in the neck and the wrists. The only way to put it on was through the narrow soft rubber neck opening and it was impossible to put it on without the assistance of a buddy. Once inside the suit, a neck ring had to be fitted followed by a soft rubber neck seal which then had to clamped down tight over the neck ring. We had 2 minutes in total from the word 'go' to being fully dressed, so in actual fact we were allowed 60 seconds per diver to be ready for the water. At the end of 2 minutes, it was into the water without fins whether you were fully dressed or not. I can remember on several occasions jumping into the water without the neck ring fitted which meant the suit would immediately start to fill with water. Then we had to get mud and returning to the surface without fins and with a suit full of water was a very difficult undertaking. This exercise was repeated over and over until the whole class was fully dressed inside the 2 minutes. It was exhausting...

Normally during the day, it was a relief to get into the water although even then you had no peace. Some sort of physical task was usually required and a stream of directional signals from the surface would have us on the move constantly. There were a number of reasons for this assault on our minds and bodies. Firstly, it was a necessary part of being a Clearance Diver to be super fit and able to respond immediately, and secondly, they wished to sort the *'stayers'* out from the *'non hackers'* as soon as possible. They did not wish to waste an excessive amount of time on individuals who may drop out later in the course as things became tougher both mentally and physically.

At the end of our first week, our joint Petty Officer instructors, Brian *'Badger'* Dall and Harry Bingham told us that a maximum of six of us would qualify. We had about 12 or 14 on the course at that time so everyone wondered who would go and who would stay.

It was Harry who gave Jeff Garrett his lifelong moniker of *Cowby*. One day after an oxygen compass swim, Harry said in front of the class – *'Garrett, you're wandering all over the shop like a bluddy cowboy from western Queensland'*. The class shortened it to Cowby and he's lived with it ever since.

Every Friday afternoon Badger would bring us one at a time into his cabin on our diving boat *'Tortoise'* to read us our *'horoscopes'*. I remember on about the second or third Friday, four of our course mates emerged from Badger's cabin with very long faces. They had just been told that they would make better Sonar operators than divers and were off course from that moment. There was no room for discussion or second chances, the instructor's word was final. Snow was one of them. I don't recall the exact reason for his removal but I remember he was devastated and he was forced to choose another Branch. His sole reason for joining the Navy was to become a Clearance Diver. The only consolation he had was that he retained his ships diver cuff rate.

As the numbers were whittled away, we that remained slowly gained in confidence that we might make it, me included.

Then disaster struck….

We had been night diving and finished quite late. So late that the duty driver had to make a special one-off trip to Watson for our class. The driver was new to Rushcutter and was an unfriendly and very surly *'A stroke'* (acting) Leading Stoker who didn't have much time for Ord CDs.

I always found it strange how certain branches of the Navy had it in for Divers. Perhaps it was jealousy or envy, perhaps they knew they could never hack the pace, I'm not sure, however this turkey was one of those.

According to the regulations, when we travelled backwards and forwards to Watson we were supposed to be in the working dress of the day; at that time of the year shorts, shirt and long socks and shoes. That was usually fine however at 11PM and after a full day in the water, we were not inclined to worry too much about it, as most drivers usually had the decency to drop us off right outside our accommodation block.

It was quite normal practice after night diving to travel back to Watson in bare feet. On this particular night our less than friendly driver decided that he would deposit us at the main gate where we would be under the eyes of the duty gangway staff as we left the bus. This meant shoes and socks on. Unfortunately, I was at the back of the bus and therefore last off after scrambling to get my shoes and socks on in the dark. As I had obviously kept him from his rack (bed) for an extra 30 seconds, he came apart at the seams and accused me of being out of the *'dress of the day'* and told me to report to the duty Petty Officer at Rushcutter the following morning.

At that phase of our course we were required to be fallen in as a class on the parade ground dressed in the dreaded dry suits in time for *'Colours'* by 0800, come hell or high water. As the bus arrived late at about 0750, I decided that the sensible thing to do was to scramble into my dry suit, fall in for Colours, tell Badger what had happened and then report to the Duty PO. My instructor was one hard ass – Badger had played 1st grade rugby league for the Balmain Tigers in his younger days, was built like a brick shithouse and he was a man who expected his instructions to be followed to the letter. As far as I was concerned, Badger's instructions came before those of a bus driver….

As I flew off the bus, our arrogant and angry driver reminded me to report to the Duty PO as directed. I told him I had no choice other than to assemble with my class and would report immediately after Colours. I did exactly that, however when I reported to Acting Petty Officer Billy Burrows no more than 12 minutes later, he informed me that the bus driver was charging me with *'disobeying a direct order'* and *'silent contempt'*. Both very serious charges.

Bill was a CD and explained that he thought it was a ridiculous charge, however he had no choice but to follow through with the formal charge. The seriousness of these charges meant that only the Captain could decide the outcome.

As I was told by everyone, this could not have happened at a worse time. The Captain of Rushcutter *(in fact a very pompous Commander and non-diver)* was hell bent on introducing formal Naval discipline to Rushcutter, which was perceived by many outsiders, him included, as the Aussie version of McHale's Navy.

What this officer and his ilk failed to understand was that Clearance Divers were the most disciplined sailors in the RAN - when it really counted. How could they be otherwise when they operated in such a hostile and dangerous environment where each man puts his life in the hands of his team-mates every time he enters the water or handles explosives. CD's were disciplined when it really counted and put little value in the pompous *'parade ground'* bullshit blindly adhered to and enforced by *'non-combatants'*.

However, I digress. I knew I was in trouble when the Captain found me guilty and my punishment would be announced in front of the whole ship's company. At the *'Clear Lower Deck'* I was almost in a state of shock. I was about to be sentenced in front of my peers and I was thinking, what had I done that deserved this, and worst of all, I thought my diving career had come to an abrupt end. How could I possibly be allowed to remain on course?

I stood at attention with cap in hand as the Captain, with all the formality of a hanging judge, announced that I was to be confined to *'cells'* for 5 days. A paddy wagon was waiting outside and I was handcuffed and locked in the back like the dangerous criminal that I was and immediately taken to the cells at HMAS Penguin. As I left, I could see from the looks on the faces of the ship's company that they were just as shocked as I was.

During my 5 days' detention, I was confined in solitary in a cold windowless cell which had no furniture other than a raised timber board which I soon realised was my bed. A smooth rectangular block of wood served as my pillow and I had one very thin blanket.

Every morning I was brought my daily allowance of food and this comprised exactly 18 dry Sao biscuits, and as much water as I wanted. To this day, 48 years later, I have never eaten another Sao biscuit. They left me with several 30-centimetre lengths of hawser rope and by *'lights out'* in the evening, I was required to have unpicked this rope down to every single strand. The only reading material in the cell was a Bible and that held about as much interest for me as the *'Women's Weekly'*.

Every evening during *'rounds'* I was visited by the duty Medical officer and I had to stand at attention while he, dressed in his best Mess uniform and stinking of port, asked me if I was fit and well. This was purely a formality and I doubt he even listened to my reply.

I had developed quite a bad ear infection by the second day and it took until the fourth day before anyone took any notice. Instead of having my ears checked on that first evening, the duty MO waited 2 days before allowing me to be taken the 200 metres to the hospital for a check-up. I think he was more interested in getting back to his glass of port and the warmth of the Wardroom.

Next morning, I was handcuffed and escorted by two Naval patrolmen to the out-patients section. It was soul destroying to be treated like a dangerous criminal. When I was taken in to see the Doctor, he proved to be a decent type and told the *'crushers'* that he was not going to examine anyone wearing handcuffs and they were to remove them immediately. It was with great reluctance that they obeyed. Perhaps they thought I would thump them and abscond *(the thought had crossed my mind. I would dearly have loved to belt the mongrels).*

After checking my ears, the Doctor severely reprimanded them for not bringing me for treatment sooner, as the infection was quite advanced.

During this nightmare experience, my biggest concern was that I would be kicked off my CD course, not because I couldn't handle it or was not suited, but because of some pathetic little power-crazy acting/LS. I had a lot of time to think during those 5 days and I discovered a valuable lesson about the Navy. Discipline is a very necessary part of the Military but unfortunately the system provides many incompetent characters with more authority than they are fit to handle.

When I was released and taken back to Rushcutter, I was ordered to report immediately to my Course officer, Lieutenant Alex Donald. As I entered his office, I braced myself for the worst. To my great surprise, he was quite friendly and attempted to cheer me up by telling me that he had obtained his officer's commission after having spent time in cells as a young sailor. He gave me quite a fatherly talk and then told me to *"get the hell out of my office"* and back to my class and prove to him that I had what it took to be a Clearance Diver.

My instructor acted as if I had never been away. My cell time was not mentioned; however it was obvious to all that he expected me to swim harder, run faster, do more push-ups and generally outperform everyone else in my class. I realised that I was being tested and had to shine.

After about 2 or 3 weeks of steady pressure which would have been called victimisation or bastardisation anywhere else, Badger called me in for the weekly horoscope session. He told me that I had probably noticed *(a bit of an understatement I thought)* that he and the second dickey had been giving me a hard time since my short *'absence'* however he felt that I had suffered it gladly and with a smile on my face, as any potential CD should. He said because of my positive and determined attitude I was once again just one of the class and not to let him down because he thought I was *'CD material'*. I left his cabin feeling about 8 feet tall with a fierce determination to do everything possible to justify the faith which was being placed in me. Another valuable lesson for me – Clearance Divers possessed a stronger level of loyalty than the rest of the Navy and they would close ranks around their own. My loyalty from that point on was first and foremost to the CD branch, not the Navy.

As with most things in life, we usually only remember the good things, and training to be a Clearance Diver was in hindsight, a very interesting, demanding, exciting and challenging experience. The only downside at the time was the intense mental and physical demands placed on us however we were all mature enough to realise that we were undergoing some very serious character building.

To become a CD, you had to be able to *'hack it'* and have a very positive *'can do easy'* attitude. On the one hand it was drummed into us how important it was to be part of a team, as your life would one day depend on your team-mates, yet on the other hand you had to have many of the characteristics of a loner.

On the surface you were always part of a team, whether it was on a diving boat or in a pub, but when you were on the bottom of the seabed, cold and miserable in zero visibility, trying to locate or deal with a piece of ordnance, you most definitely had to be your own man. However, it was always comforting to know that topside there were a bunch of your mates whose only interest in life at that particular moment was to keep you alive.

As we started to feel totally at home in the water, emphasis was shifted towards actually being able to perform useful work underwater. We learnt to use underwater oxy-hydrogen cutting equipment and we mastered the difficult art of underwater welding.

We were gradually introduced to more and more complex items of diving equipment. Once we were considered proficient in one, we moved on to the next. The one real constant however was building experience with the Oxygen Re-breather. This was the one potential killer that could sneak up on the unwary. Because it was our mainstream diving set, the UBA had applications other than attack swimming. By removing the small oxygen cylinders in the front and attaching larger twin cylinders of mixture gas to the rear of the harness, the set could then be used for deep diving and in that configuration became the CDBA, or Clearance Diving Breathing Apparatus.

We had three gas mixtures available to us; 60% oxygen/40% nitrogen, 40% oxygen/60% nitrogen, and 32½% oxygen/67½% nitrogen. Once again because of the *'partial pressure'* of oxygen in the mixture, each of these had a depth limitation. *60/40* had a maximum safe depth of 77 feet, *40/60* - 132 feet, and *32½/67½* - 170 feet.

Because of the different percentages of oxygen in each gas mixture, different flow rates had to be set on the reducing valve, and with the higher nitrogen content, the unused gas had to be exhausted through a relief valve in the breathing bag. This valve was designed to break up the exhaust gas into a steady stream of small bubbles. A necessity because this set was also used for the CD's primary role of mine disposal. Because the magnetic and acoustic signatures of the set were quite low, it was relatively safe for the diver when dealing with magnetic and acoustic mines. Occasionally the CDBA was worn for deep swimming and normally this was done within the depth limitations of 60/40, down to 77 feet.

Normally when diving with this set in the CDBA mode, we would wear boots instead of fins. These were heavy rubber boots with lead sole inserts and a quick release flexible brass rod. It was also normal to wear the dreaded *'dry suit'* with this set although it was an extremely rare and lucky diver who had a suit that was in fact dry. If you managed to get your hands on a dry *'dry suit'* you treated it like a baby.

The final stage of our diving training was to work-up for deep diving. As qualified CDs, we had to be proficient with all equipment and be able to perform effectively at all depths down to 180 feet. Weekly dives in the 10-man RCC kept us acclimatised to the effects of nitrogen under pressure.

Nitrogen is a strange gas. It is inert, yet it affects the human body in an unusual manner. *'Nitrogen Narcosis'* generally starts to take effect at a depth below 100 feet, depending on individual tolerance, and its effect is very similar to drinking too much alcohol. Non worked-up divers have been known to exhibit some very irrational and alarming behaviour when under the influence of the *'Narcs'*. Fortunately, any diver who dives to depth regularly becomes temporarily immune to the potentially dangerous effects. I suppose a little like a seasoned drinker does to the intoxicating effects of alcohol. One of the amusing side effects of nitrogen is the way that it alters the human voice. At 180 feet, every diver's voice is several octaves higher than normal, although Helium produces a more pronounced *'Donald Duck'* characteristic.

One of the not so pleasant side effects of nitrogen is Decompression Sickness; more commonly known to the layman as the *'Bends'*. Depending on the severity, this deadly condition if not treated quickly and properly advances from severe pain in the joints, through loss of muscle control and coordination, to ultimately unconsciousness and death. The only effective treatment is to get the diver back under pressure as quickly as possible and gradually, in accordance with a very strict set of tables, stage him back to normal atmospheric pressure.

The air we breathe contains 79% nitrogen and to my knowledge the only useful purpose of this inert gas is that it acts as a diluent in our planet's atmosphere. To the diver, this inert characteristic becomes a major problem.

Briefly, the gases taken into the lungs are passed into solution and carried to the body tissues by the blood. There is a natural equilibrium as oxygen is consumed and carbon dioxide is given off from the cells. As the human body is subjected to increases in ambient pressure, as in diving, these gases are compressed and absorbed in increasing quantities into the tissue. This *'on-gassing'* of the tissue will continue as pressure increases until equilibrium is reached. Nitrogen being inert cannot be used by the body in any way so that when the pressure is relieved, as in a diver ascending, the nitrogen must then have sufficient time to *'off-gas'* from the tissue and be carried by the blood back to the lungs where it is exhaled. Hence the necessity for decompression after long and/or deep dives. The requirement to decompress can begin from dives as shallow as 40 feet. Saturation divers in the offshore oil industry often undergo many days of decompression after a long dive.

The big problem for divers arises when the pressure is relieved too quickly, as in ascending too rapidly and failing to adhere to the decompression tables. The nitrogen still remaining in the tissue and the blood begins to expand and coalesce into tiny bubbles. In severe cases the blood actually appears to *'boil'*. These bubbles collect in various parts of the body and continue to expand and grow in size as more nitrogen is released from solution by the decreasing pressure. If these albeit tiny gas bubbles are not rapidly reduced in size by recompression to allow the necessary time for *'off-gassing'*, irreparable tissue damage, or worst case, death will result.

The interesting thing about decompression is that there was no formula. All the tables in use were arrived at by trial and error and many divers have died in the process of developing safe tables.

An instructor once told me that to be a good diver you had to be a 1st class seaman. I have always held that to be true. A diver who could not apply sound seamanship skills when working under the worst of conditions was of no value to his mates or the diving profession. As a consequence, our instructors went out of their way to ensure that we dived and worked in the worst places that they could find. The darker the hole, the stronger the current and the deeper the mud, the more they liked it. They told us often enough that we did not need to see what we were doing, as we had five eyes on each hand. By the second or third month we were wondering if there was such a thing as good visibility and perhaps it was against Navy regulations to dive in clear water anyway. Anything over about 3 feet was considered by us to be great *'vis'*.

It obviously all had its purpose as we realised that we needed to become perfectly comfortable with working under the worst possible conditions while still in the relatively safe and highly supervised environment of the Diving School.

Later, whenever diving in exceptionally good visibility, I always had a feeling of being half naked. Bad visibility feels a little like being cocooned in a protective blanket.

Our initial deep dives were done in the blackest and deepest hole in Sydney harbour. It was only 120 feet deep however in broad daylight it was as black as a *'goat's guts'*.

We gradually progressed to our deeper air dives outside Sydney Heads. Using the diving boat's depth sounder, we would find bottom as close as possible to 180-190 feet, lower a 56-pound concrete shot over the side to 180 feet and start diving while the boat drifted, as it was far too deep to get any small boats' anchor to hold.

I remember our first dive off the Heads on a lovely calm sunny day. Jim Henry was *'first dip'* and he took a sealed empty Protosorb tin with him to the bottom. When he surfaced, he held it up for all to see. It had completely imploded under the additional pressure of 80 pounds per square inch it had been subjected to when it accompanied him down the shot line to the bottom. Jim said he had actually reached the bottom, but when it came time for my dive, the boat had been drifting seaward. When I arrived at the shot, it was suspended perhaps 30 or 40 feet from the clean sandy bottom. I clearly remember the cold and eerie deep blue half-light. The warmer colours of the spectrum are completely filtered out at that depth and everything takes on a dark blue green shade. The visibility was quite good but I remember feeling that this was probably the loneliest place on the face of the earth. All sensations at that depth were intensified by a mild touch of the *Narcs* and I wanted to stay there for much longer than our 11 minutes *'bottom time'* allowed. Our first deep ocean dive was most definitely a very exhilarating experience.

For decompression purposes, all dives are timed from when leaving the surface until leaving the bottom, so a rather rapid descent is called for if you wish to spend any time at all on the bottom. A slow descent can result in no more than a bounce dive if you wish to avoid lengthy decompression. Ascents are more controlled and a rule of thumb for the diver is to follow his smaller bubbles towards the surface.

We conducted *'stops'* in the water from a *'lazy shot'*. This is another heavy shot which is lowered from the boat to a pre-determined depth, depending where the *stops* are to begin. When the diver arrives at the shot, he signals the surface, from where his decompression is totally controlled by the diving supervisor topside. At the set stoppage time intervals, the shot is raised to the next shallower depth, usually in 10-foot increments, with the diver only required to hang onto the shot as if it were his favourite girlfriend.

In between diving and constant physical exercise we also had our regular share of classroom work. Diving theory had to be mastered as did underwater medicine. Henry's Law, Boyle's Law, endurance and maximum safe depths formulae still bounce around in my head to this day.

The ability to be able to maintain every piece of equipment in the CD inventory had to be learnt in meticulous detail. The potential consequences of poor maintenance were painfully clear to us. We had all been issued with personal items of diving equipment and were individually responsible for their maintenance and safe operation. As our lives depended on it, we all took this obligation very seriously.

With the bulk of the diving phase almost over, it was time to become adept at some of the other areas of expertise expected of a Clearance Diver. These other areas focused on the use of high explosives and the disposal of explosive ordnance both above and below the surface.

CD's had inherited the role of Mine and Bomb Disposal from the famous and very courageous joint British/Australian bomb disposal teams formed during the German blitz of London in WWII. Strange as it may sound, all of the Australians involved in this highly dangerous work were Naval personnel.

The CD branch actually had its own Bomb & Mine Disposal section. These instructor CD's were not only responsible for training but also for ensuring that the branch kept up to date with state of the art technology.

To the credit of the RAN CD branch, a major step forward in mine identification *(named AUSMIS)* was made by a Chief Petty Officer CD 'Dixie' Foord and Mike Turner, a civilian scientist from the RAN Experimental Laboratories *(RANEL)*. Prior to this development, mine disposal was a particularly hazardous occupation.

Each major world power had developed its own technology in sea-mines and these included magnetic, acoustic, contact, combination, buoyant and ground mines, all with various types of actuating mechanisms. There were several hundred types of different mines and before a diver could attempt to deal with one, he firstly had to identify it. Documentation was available on most mass-produced sea mines however it was impossible for any diver to remember them all. That meant in sometimes zero visibility he had to take note of and recognise a large number of key identification characteristics that he could take back to the surface to help identify the mine. This often meant several dives and thumbing through volumes of publications to narrow down and confirm its possible identity and country of origin. This was not a healthy occupation for a diver to be returning on a regular basis to a live mine containing several hundred pounds of high explosives.

Dixie and Mike developed an ingenious system of cards, one card for every known mine. The diver would take down a checklist and a measuring tape to gather key data in a set sequence such as the mine's shape, was it a buoyant or a ground mine, was it spherical, hemispherical or semi-hemispherical? What was its diameter, its length, what type of horns did it have, how many horns in the upper hemisphere, how many in the lower etc. etc.

This information was brought to the surface where the ID could take place within a few minutes. Every card had holes punched around its perimeter and every hole corresponded to a particular characteristic. The trick was that where a mine had a certain feature, the hole was open to the side of the card. When a thin spike was placed through the corresponding hole of that feature, all the cards that possessed that feature would fall away from the rest. These were collected and spiked for the next feature.

Step by step, cards that did not fit the diver's checklist were returned to the box until only the mines that had all the observed features were left. This usually came down to one or two cards. Each card was numbered and corresponded with a mine in the detailed publications which were carried on the diving boat and the diver could then quickly identify the culprit. This meant that on the diver's second trip back to the mine, he knew the exact type of mine, its dangers, how it functioned and what the recommended RSP (Render Safe Procedure) was. Prior to about 1966 these procedures were known as RMS (Render Mine Safe) – British terminology. When I left the Navy in 1985, there was still no better system in the world for mine identification.

An underwater minefield was set up with real mines off Clark island in Sydney Harbour. These mines had the main explosive filling removed however when actuated by a careless or incorrect procedure, they fired a small charge close enough to the diver to let him know in no uncertain manner that he had made a fatal mistake. We spent many days and nights proving the simple brilliance of AUSMIS *(Australian Mine Identification System)*.

The dry part of the course began with training in surface explosive ordnance identification and disposal which was conducted at the Army's Engineering school near Liverpool in Sydney's Western suburbs.

For us, our training was taking on a buzz as the Army was training its people for Vietnam and actual experiences of recently returned veterans were being included in the training curriculum. On our last day at Liverpool we took part in a combined sweep for booby traps in a mock-up of a Vietnamese village which was a meticulous copy of the real thing - tunnels and weapons caches included. What was particularly interesting for us was that we were undergoing some of our training in parallel with the recently formed Clearance Diving Team 3. This six-man team was about to open a new chapter in Clearance Diving history. They were preparing to deploy to Vietnam in what was to be the beginning of several very exciting years for *'the Branch'*.

We lesser mortals continued along our not so glamorous path with hands on explosives training at Marangaroo, deep in the Blue Mountains west of Sydney. I particularly enjoyed this phase of training as I took to explosives like a duck to water. In later years I had a natural leaning towards the explosives and demolition side of the Branch.

Marangaroo was home to the Army's 223 Supply Company which consisted of a small detachment of regular soldiers and a few civilians. They were responsible for the storage and security of Military munitions which the Army stored in large explosive magazines spread around the numerous valleys and gullies of this rugged mountain landscape on the western side of the Blue Mountains.

I thought it a great place and I never tired of going back there. Being a small depot, it was very relaxed and provided we behaved ourselves, the Army pretty much left us alone. With the CO's house within earshot of the junior rates mess, we didn't have much choice as Officer's wives, in particular CO's wives, are well known for their intolerance of anyone of a lower rank than their husbands. The slightest sign of an infraction of any rule would bring the wrath of the *'real'* CO upon us, via her husband. This was even true for the Diving School. It was common knowledge that the wife of the CO of Rushcutter *(the very same gentleman who gave me the all expenses holiday in the Penguin cells)* would often sit in her upstairs bedroom window with binoculars ensuring that correct Naval behaviour was being observed by all. It was rumoured that perhaps the diver's skimpy swimmers may have had something to do with her enthusiasm. The fact remained that her husband knew about everything occurring within the diving school grounds.

Marangaroo had incredible shifts in temperatures. During the day we cooked and at night we froze. The two demolition ranges known as the *'inner'* and *'outer'* were deep in blind gullies and for the first few hours of the morning they always seemed to be thick with frost. By mid-morning as the sun rose above the near vertical cliffs, the still gullies turned into hot ovens. The inner range was used for small scale demolitions and basic instruction and from memory had a 250kg explosive weight limit. The outer, being miles from anywhere was where we conducted our *'big bangs'*.

We were taught to look on explosives purely as another tool and as I soon discovered, what a devastating tool it was. It was the ability of explosives to do useful and calculated work and the challenge of mastering that awesome power that intrigued me.

Along with most people I had always thought of explosives as being no more than an uncontrollable and incredibly destructive force. We began by learning the various initiation methods. The detonation of high explosives needs to be set in train by a sequence of steps and the first step is normally by either electric or non-electric means.

Electric initiation is where a current is generated sufficient to fire an electric detonator/s which in turn will fire a further circuit until ultimately the main charge or charges, detonate. An entire circuit can be electric and fired singly in, or in combinations of, series or parallel.

The non-electric system was the old *'safety'* or black powder time fuse. Both systems were designed to give the firing party sufficient time to withdraw a safe distance before all hell was unleashed. Both systems had their advantages and disadvantages. Electric's single biggest advantage was that it gave exact control over the time of firing, but it required more time to set up and check. Dynamo type generators and firing cable had to be lugged about, cable had to be run out and checked for resistance and continuity, as did the electric detonators. Safety fuse on the other hand was simple and lightweight, however once the fuse was lit, everything was out of your hands and short of some gutsy heroics, there's not too many options to stop the inevitable from happening.

In the field, non-electric initiation was used almost exclusively as electric initiation was a luxury for those who had lots of time. Detonating cord circuits were my favourite. In those days it was known by its manufacturer's brand name - *'Cordtex'*. It came on reels, looked very much like white heavy duty clothes line and contained 10 grams per metre of a high explosives known as PETN. This wonderfully versatile cord detonated at a velocity in excess of 21,000 feet per second and was *'cap'* (detonator) sensitive. It allowed us to connect up an unlimited number of shots and initiate the lot with a single *'cap and fuse'*.

While under training, we would work in pairs and when we had all completed our assigned projects, it was a simple matter of running a Cordtex *'ring-main'* for all to connect to, and then shooting with a cap and fuse.

We also had a lot of fun with Plastic explosives. This relatively new product became our main tool of trade and we *'never left home without it'*.

'PE4' was made up of 90% RDX and 10% plasticiser. A major advantage of PE4 was that it was very stable and insensitive to most physical shocks and could easily be moulded into any desired shape. It could be pressed into gaps, cracks, holes and voids in buildings, bridges, equipment or machinery. PE4 had a slightly greater velocity of detonation than the US manufactured C4 plastic explosive - 8,210 m/s or 26,900 ft./s.

American soldiers during the Vietnam War era would sometimes use small amounts of C4 as a fuel for heating rations. The downside was that burning C4 produced poisonous fumes.

It could be used in everything from opening bomb cases to expose the main charge, to cutting 17-inch (43cm) diameter ship's propeller shafts in half.

I began to realise that any *'mug'* could overkill with explosives. The art was in learning to use it as an artist uses his brush, and the only way to acquire the skill was attention to detail and lots of practice.

In later years after I left the Navy, I worked for a commercial explosives manufacturer alongside Mining Engineers who had a string of academic qualifications but I quickly discovered that my years of wide ranging military experience in the handling and application of explosives gave me a tremendous advantage over them.

On completing surface demolition training it was time to learn the real art. As Navy pilots say; *'Any mug can land an aircraft on a runway, it takes talent and real skill to land on a small pitching carrier deck in the black of night in the middle of the ocean'*. It was our turn to learn how to apply our demolition skills underwater in bad visibility and at night. I don't recall having any great difficulty with this phase of training which speaks highly of the talent of both our diving and demolition instructors. There was the occasional misfire but we quickly learnt from our mistakes.

We approached the end of the course with both excitement and dread. Soon we hoped we would be Clearance Divers however there was one hurdle remaining. It was known to all in the branch as *'Hate week'*. Our second dickey, who by that stage was Phil Tonks, had been relating horror stories to us for the previous six months about this final hurdle that had to be overcome prior to passing out as a CD. From what we had heard we could look forward to a solid week of putting everything we had learnt into practice, with heaps of bastardisation (character building) laid on. The major difference from the rest of the course was that it was to be done at a nonstop pace with everyone being pushed to their breaking point and beyond. This final saga was conducted at Port Stephens on the NSW central coast, normally an idyllic fishing village and popular tourist spot. The trip north proved interesting in our two diving boats. Neither vessel was built for the open ocean and both were more at home in the tranquil waters of Sydney Harbour. The weather was quite rough and the 40-foot workboat that I was aboard did not handle the conditions at all well.

When we were about halfway up the coast with our stoker hanging over the side being violently sea-sick, the engine decided it didn't like water in the fuel and abruptly died. The seas and wind were driving us shoreward at a reasonable clip so it was quite urgent that the problem be fixed quickly. After a very unpleasant 30 minutes or so wallowing beam on to the approaching waves, our jack of all trades boat coxswain for the trip, Petty Officer CD *'Smiley'* Asher BEM had it running again, so we pushed on into the fading light for a late night arrival at our mooring 10 metres off the Fisherman's Co-op wharf.

There was to be no rest for the wicked and we were up at the crack of dawn to begin the dreaded hate week.

The first thing we noticed about the place on that first morning was the number of fisherman's houses and shacks that were painted in predominantly Navy *'ship's side grey'*. We soon learnt that the steady flow of divers through the place had created a close bond between the fishermen and the Navy. It was amazing what a great feed of fish and oysters could be had in exchange for some high quality paint, even if the colour was grey.

The details of that final period have long since faded from my memory but there are certain things that come to mind when looking back. We were by this time very competent divers and this was in effect a week or so of practical examination as all training had been well and truly completed.

A Clearance Diving officer, Lieutenant David Lees, was along to judge whether we had earned the right to join the ranks of Clearance Divers. The class of Ord CDs that had come together seven months earlier was no longer a class. We had evolved into a close-knit team, which by jointly supporting every member of that team, could handle anything the instructors cared to throw at us. No one had to be told what to do. When we were given a task, we got on with it in a timely and efficient manner with everyone knowing and doing what was required.

Our instructors continually pushed us to our limits but we survived and eventually came to the end of it. There were two things that stand out vividly in my memory from Port Stephens. One was the incredible number of large jellyfish which moved into parts of the bay with the incoming tide. At certain times of the day it was not possible to jump into the water without spearing through a dozen or more of these ugly and unpleasant creatures. During compass swims it was difficult to concentrate on the task in hand as you were constantly trying to dodge the biggest of them. Eventually you just ignored them and ploughed on through. Our diving sets and suits fortunately protected us most of the time but we all suffered from stings to the neck, hands and feet. I used to take a morbid pleasure in watching the boat's propeller shred them into a thousand pieces.

The other incident of note was the most enjoyable compass swim I have ever experienced. The incoming tide surged into Port Stephens at a great rate of knots and one afternoon we were to conduct a deep compass swim from the mouth of the bay during the peak of this flow. The water depth was around 80 feet and visibility was good with a clean undulating sandy bottom. We were dressed in dry suits and using CDBA with a 60/40 mix. Fortunately, our compass heading corresponded with the heading of the incoming tidal flow and it was the ride of our lives.

On approaching the bottom, we could see that the current was already tearing us along at 5 or 6 knots so with very little effort we were literally flying over the sand dunes at 7 to 8 knots. It was totally exhilarating and we made the most of it. We were doing everything from barrel rolls and forward somersaults to kamikaze style dives at the tops of the dunes, missing them by inches. I felt I knew what it was like to be a bird.

We were very disappointed when it came time to surface but that one dive confirmed to me that I had chosen the right profession. From that point on my approach to everything in life became *'can do easy'*. Although it was never mentioned, I believe the instructors had planned that particular dive as a form of relief or reward, I'm not sure which. The memory of it however has stayed with me these past 48 years.

On our return to Rushcutter we all knew we had passed. It was just a matter of the formalities such as final individual theory and practical examination results. I was very pleased to find that I had topped the course. Alex Donald's faith in me had been justified.

We were very proud young men when on that day in February 1967, we approached the Commanding Officer's table to be presented with our gold CD badges and formally promoted to Able Seaman Clearance Divers. We had joined an elite and very proud band of men. In addition, I had the satisfaction of looking the CO square in the eye while thinking *'What do you think about this shithead, I not only made it, I topped the course - in spite of you..."*

From that day forward we would be referred to by the rest of the Navy as *'Bubblies'*.

My classmates were posted off to various jobs. Some went to diving teams, some became second dickeys to ship's diving courses and I became the assistant to the Ship's Diving training officer, a cocky little fellow by the name of Lieutenant Terry Jones. For the next few months I learnt about the administrative side of training and occasionally filled in as a second dickey when someone was sick or on leave. Fortunately, this was only a fill in period while Navy Office decided where my first posting would be. Postings were published every three months and I anxiously awaited my first draft as a CD.

It was during this period that I received the first real shock of my life. I had become close friends with one of the fellows on my course, a very laid back quiet sort of bloke who always just got on with the job at hand. His name was Jeff Hales and he had been posted to CDT2, the Branch's trials and evaluation team which also had the responsibility of exercising the Fleet in defence against swimmer attack.

Most of these exercises were conducted with ships at anchor in Jervis Bay, 100 odd miles to the south of Sydney. It was normal for the attack team to have an exercise *'window'* from sunset to sunrise, they being free to choose the timing of their attack while the ship's defences had to remain on full alert throughout the night. Pairs of divers would swim a compass course wearing oxygen rebreathers to the target from as far as a mile or so away with dummy limpet mines strapped to their backs.

Even though these O_2 sets left no tell-tale trail of bubbles, the best time to conduct an attack was on the blackest of nights with no moon, which also meant the most dangerous conditions for the divers. Once the divers descended into the black depths of the bay, they were completely lost to everyone on the surface, including the man responsible for their safety, the Diving Supervisor.

Each set carried a sea cell light which could be activated by a conscious diver when in trouble. Normal procedure in those days was for the *'driver'* to concentrate on navigating to the target while his *'buddy'*, swimming slightly above him and to his right, would carry the depth gauge. Both would be connected to each other by a light nylon 15-foot buddy line which was secured to a right arm band on each diver.

The buddy was responsible for maintaining the agreed depth, normally between 15 and 20 feet. He would control the driver's depth via hand signals *(called Bells)* on the buddy line. Two light taps meant that the driver was a little deep, three meant a little shallow, and one indicated he was spot on. A worked up pair of divers who have been swimming together for a period of time could easily maintain their depth without reference to the depth gauge. Their ears became so sensitive to changes in pressure that they could detect a change in depth of as little as one or two feet. Unfortunately, on this particular occasion the Boss of CDT2 paired Jeff up with Bluey Hislop, another young and relatively inexperienced diver who had only just qualified on the course before ours. Neither of them were what would be considered worked up and it was their first real night ship attack. Normally a relatively inexperienced ship attack diver would be paired with an old hand as this was a serious business. For some unknown reason this did not happen.

To make matters worse it was particularly bad weather with winds gusting to 33 knots (61 kms/hr) and one of those very black nights where it is possible for a perfectly weighted diver to suffer from vertigo to some extent, particularly when both are swimming hard and focusing on hitting the target on time.

I was sound asleep in the diver's accommodation block at HMAS Watson when the duty officer woke the entire block at about 3 AM and called for all qualified CD's to be ready to board a bus for Rushcutter in five minutes' time. All he could tell us was that there was a general recall of all Clearance Divers in the Sydney area as there had been a diving accident in Jervis Bay. I knew Jeff was down there on his first ship attack so I was dreading the worst.

My fears were confirmed when we arrived at the diving school. Two divers were missing from the night's attack and there had been no sightings or response to emergency surface calls. It was Hales and Hislop.

As divers began arriving at Rushcutter they were immediately put to work preparing all the necessary diving and search equipment to mount a massive seabed search operation. We were told that the remainder of Team 2 were continuing to search throughout the night and the target ship HMAS Stuart, had rigged and turned on all her underwater lighting. Unfortunately, her ship's divers were of limited help in the search as the depth in the vicinity of her anchorage was around 80 feet; beyond their 66 feet limitation.

I was picked as part of the immediate response team to get to Jervis Bay as quickly as possible as CDT2 had limited personnel and equipment to conduct anything other than a quick sweep of the area immediately under the keel of Stuart.

We were loaded up and on our way south before dawn. During the 2 or 3-hour bus ride we all assured each other that they had probably just screwed up and perhaps swum a reciprocal course and instead of hitting Stuart, had hit the beach.

They were perhaps at that very moment walking back to the Naval college situated on the bay.

When we arrived at HMAS Creswell we were hoping to see their grinning and embarrassed faces waiting for us. Alas it was not to be. There had been no trace of them. Navy helicopters were out searching every square inch of Jervis Bay and its surrounding beaches but it was as if they had been swallowed by the ocean. We bent to the task of preparing grid pattern bottom searches in the area of Stuart's anchorage. The visibility on the bottom was quite poor and I was dreading the thought of seeing two wetsuits appear out of the gloom. During our course we had visited the Sydney morgue to become accustomed to seeing corpses, as recovering bodies from the water is one of the less than pleasant occupations carried out by divers. It had not however prepared me to meet one of my best mates on the seabed. We continued searching until we were rested by a larger and more organised search team and after two days I was sent back to Sydney. Teams rotated constantly keeping up the search and it was not until the eighteenth day that their bodies were finally found. It was never determined exactly how they had died as 18 days in the water had taken its toll. Why and how they were both lost will never be known. The ironic part was that they were found very near Stuart's anchorage so they had been right on their target. Perhaps they thought they would bounce a little deeper at the last minute to ensure they would avoid detection and suffered oxygen poisoning. We'll never know. I have always felt that had one of them been more experienced they would be alive today. The surging tide had been moving their bodies backwards and forwards through the search area for almost three weeks.

For the following few months Rushcutter was a gloomy place. Moves were instigated immediately to prevent a similar occurrence happening again. Eventually a system of battery powered pingers and portable passive sonars were developed so that divers could be kept track of constantly throughout an attack. If divers were suspected of being in trouble and didn't respond to an emergency call-up, a diving boat could be in their immediate vicinity within a few minutes and a pair of rescue divers could home in on their signal using the hand held sonar.

Back at Rushcutter things gradually got back to normal as we all tried not to dwell on the tragic loss of our two mates.

Media reporting during this sad period of our history was particularly annoying to all serving Clearance Divers and must have been extremely stressful to the families of our two mates. Newspaper reports varied from them getting lost *(CDs might be off course but never lost)*, taken by sharks, going absent without leave, drinking alcohol prior to the dive and that they could only survive for 12 hours in the water if lost *(they were both wearing wetsuits)*. All the media reports were completely absurd and typically ignorant sensationalist reporting.

Unfortunately, the standard of media reporting in Australia has not improved in the slightest since that time.

6
HMAS YARRA – 1967/69

When my posting finally came out to join HMAS Yarra on the 21st August '67 I was more than pleased, as not only was it my brother's old ship, she was a real warship to boot. She was the third Australian warship to carry the name and in the late '60's was one of the most advanced anti-submarine vessels in the Western world. With a crew of 250 men, she displaced 2,750 tons, had a top speed in excess of 30 knots, carried twin 4.5-inch guns, a 3 barrelled anti-submarine mortar, a Seacat sea to air missile launcher and the advanced Ikara anti-submarine missile system.

I knew that it would be an interesting posting as I was certain that in Mike's two years aboard he would have made many friends and just as likely a few enemies. I was somewhat taken aback when the first person I met on climbing the gangway was one of the latter category. To make matters worse, he was the Executive Officer (2nd in command), Lieutenant Commander 'Dicky' Bird. As I stepped onto the area known as one deck aft, I saluted and reported "Able Seamen Ey sir, drafting onboard". Dicky replied, "No relation to ABRP (Radar Plotter) Ey I hope". I replied proudly "Yes sir, we're brothers". There was deathly silence and I could see a faint twitch developing in the corner of his mouth. Then in a high pitched voice he said "We didn't see eye to eye", with a very heavy emphasis on the 'We' and then he laughed in a deranged sort of way and abruptly departed, leaving me wondering what I should do next. 'Bloody wonderful' I thought, my home for the next two years and the XO is a loony who has it in for me already. I reported to the Coxswain's office and fortunately completed my draft-in procedures without any more negative reactions. Actually, a lot of people were quite friendly when they discovered that I was Mick Ey's brother. The skipper was also new so I hoped I could at least start on a clean sheet with him. After all, I was to be the ship's front line of defence against swimmer attack and sabotage.......

I was allocated a bunk in the after seamen's mess of '3 Papa', located at the very stern of the ship and directly beneath the Ikara loading station. This was the mess deck of the real sailors, the UC's (sonar operators), UW's (underwater weapons) and a few overflow gunnery rates from the forward seamen's mess. Billy Creedon, a good mate who had been one of the unlucky ones to have been told by POCD Badger Dall early in our CD course that his future lay in being a Sonar rate was already part of Yarra's ship's company and living in 3 Papa.

Finally, I was at the sharp end of the Navy. I was a 'sea going sailor' with a right arm rate (badge denoting branch of service) and aboard a real warship. My timing was perfect as Yarra was preparing for a six-month deployment to the Far East in company with her sister ship HMAS Stuart, also an anti-submarine Frigate. Yarra's captain was 'Fox One' which meant that we were the senior ship of the 1st Frigate Squadron. This meant certain perks like first into harbour and getting the plum berth when alongside. The down side was that everything aboard Fox One was a little more formal and Captain A. J. Robertson proved to be an absolute stickler for formality, much to the disgust of his crew. Whilst at sea he would often wander the upper deck with a large brass telescope tucked under his arm. I wasn't sure whether he lacked faith in the ship's radar or perhaps he fantasised that he was a descendant of Drake or Nelson.

During our short work-up period off the coast of NSW I became familiar with my Action and Defence stations. Whilst the ship was closed up at Action Stations my job was to man the ship's anti-submarine mortar, a rather large three barrelled weapon which fired 300 odd pound explosive projectiles at any submarines silly enough to allow us to get within range. More often than not we fired dummy mortar rounds which had to be recovered for re-use. They were painted yellow and floated, so with a little fancy manoeuvring by the officer of the watch, they were generally easy to recover using grappling hooks. Only occasionally did I have to jump over the side to pass a line for retrieval. It was a lot of fun watching a two and a half thousand-ton warship being manoeuvred around like a speedboat. With incredible power being delivered from Yarra's steam turbines to her large twin screws, it was pretty to watch a competent driver in control on the bridge. Every seaman officer was regularly given the opportunity to sharpen his handling skills however some were naturally better drivers than others.

My defence station was tucked away in the loading bay of the IKARA (Australian developed) anti-submarine missile system. All I had to do was fit the stabilising fins to the missile as it came out of the magazine and prior to it being loaded into the launcher. My job was the only manual part of the entire load and launch procedure.

At anchor in Jervis Bay I learnt what it was like to be on the receiving end of an attack by my fellow Clearance Divers. I was responsible for working up the ship's diving team to where they could quickly and efficiently search for and find any mines placed on the ship's hull by potential saboteurs, day or night. The ship's divers would enter the water from the bow of the ship and move aft in a 'half necklace' search pattern. The number 1 diver would control the pace of the sweep while following the keel which was distinguishable by a white painted line. (Warship's don't have keels as such. They have two bilge keels which are positioned partway between the centreline and the waterline). The rest of the team were individually linked to a swim line which connected the keel swimmer to the surface. Strung out at set intervals, there was sufficient overlap between the divers so that in theory the hull from keel to waterline was searched effectively. On the surface a swimmer would follow the float searching above and below the water line and relaying hand signals from the dive team back to the diving supervisor in the boat. As the ship's CD my job was RMS (Render Mine Safe) diver. Should a diver find a mine, he would signal up and down the line to his buddies to halt the sweep at which point I would enter the water and swim down and behind the necklace line until I came to the diver who had found the object. I would then send the team on their way while I inspected and marked the device with a small magnet tied to a marked line and float that I carried. When the small float broke the surface the surface team would read off the depth from the waterline and pass the information topside where damage control parties would swing into action and isolate the compartment adjacent to the charge and shore the area with sandbags. This procedure would continue until both sides of the hull had been searched. It was then up to me to decide if I would attempt to either remove the device or render it safe. Invariably the attacking CDs managed to place several charges on the hull and escape undetected. This was more a reflection of the Clearance Divers' stealth and diving skills than of the ship's level of defence. The ship however was somewhat restricted during exercises, as in a genuine threat situation such as at anchor in Vung Tau in Vietnam, (Sydney and her escorts regularly entered Vung Tau to re-supply the Australian Army contingent) the ship would be operating extra defense measures including active sonar; which will stun a diver at close range, and throwing one pound explosive charges into the water at regular intervals from the ship's circling boat to help deter any would be aggressors.

Back alongside at Garden Island it was time to store ship ready for our long awaited departure for the Far East. It was 'clear lower deck of all hands' to form a daisy chain from the wharf up over the gangway and down the passageways into the ship's fridges, freezers and storage spaces. When the pipe - 'in beer' (announcement over the ship's broadcast system) was made, I and a couple of the ship's divers arranged to be on the gangway while the cases of 26oz cans of beer were passed inboard. Unfortunately, a couple of cases inadvertently slipped out of our hands and dropped over the side. Naturally, as the ship's CD, I was called upon to recover these lost items. We had it all planned well in advance. With all attention focused on the wharf side of the ship, a couple of our messmates lowered a rope sling over the outboard side. I quickly secured the cases of beer and signalled to hoist away. After giving them sufficient time to haul up our catch, I surfaced from under the gangway to report that the mud and visibility were so bad that it was impossible to find any trace of the beer. As it was only a couple of cartons no one was too concerned – shit happens. However, as I came back onboard I noticed our ancient Chief Coxswain (the senior sailor responsible for law and order on the ship) eyeing me rather suspiciously. He obviously didn't trust Clearance Divers. We hid our little cache in the tiller flat (the compartment at the very stern of the ship which housed the hydraulic steering motors) ready to supplement our beer issue during the first few nights at sea.

Finally, on the 5th September '67 we slipped the berthing lines and the tug eased us away from the wharf. There was an air of excitement around the ship as the entire crew was anxiously looking forward to heading for the Far East. This was what the Navy was all about; adventure on the high seas and travel to the four corners of the globe. In company with HMAS Stuart, we had goodwill stopovers in Cairns and Darwin which gave us a short respite from the day to day routine of sea watches and exercises. While in Cairns a drunken sailor from the Stuart decided that he would slip the lines of his ship for a bit of a laugh. Unfortunately for him he was caught while still struggling with the bow line. In Darwin it was my turn to play up a little and a couple of us staggered back on board just as leave expired at 0630. We had enough time for a quick shower and change and then it was time to fall in for leaving harbour. I thought, no worries, I would be okay as I could grab a nap at lunch time. When I checked the watch-bill I found that I had the afternoon watch which meant that I was watch on deck from 1200 - 1600. Watch on deck is pretty boring at the best of times and especially in the middle of the day when the ship is under normal steaming conditions on a flat calm sea. Those who weren't keeping Lookout or Helmsman duties just sat around the Starboard boat space. Having just completed lunch and feeling a little weary, I asked the PO of the watch on deck if I could catch up on a bit of work in the Diving store, located less than 20 paces away on the opposite side of the one deck superstructure. He agreed and said he would call me if I was needed. Several minutes later I was sound asleep on the workbench in the store and so it came to pass that the XO, Dicky Bird and I were to fall out for all time. Less than 30 minutes into my much needed rest the door swung open and I heard Dicky screaming at me to report to the Chief Coxswain's office. I was charged with sleeping on watch and thus made my first appearance before the Captain. I was given 21 days' stoppage of leave with 14 days of extra work to be completed during what would normally be my off time. This form of punishment was referred to as 'chooks'. What bothered me most about the stoppage was that the ship was due in Singapore in a few days for 2 weeks alongside. It didn't take long for me to realise that I would be next eligible for leave just a few days after we sailed for a 2½ weeks stint at sea, having not been ashore in Singapore.

For the first few days I watched my mates coming and going and listened with envy to their stories. When they returned on board in the early hours of the morning, they would often wake me to proudly show me the cold greasy egg, onion and tomato sandwich (known as an egg sanga or egg banjo) which they had carried back just for me. Hot, they were delicious, cold, they were very ordinary. They would then proceed to tell me what a great run ashore it had been and that I should have been there. Just what I needed at 2 or 3 o'clock in the morning when I had to get up at 6 AM to start chooks. One night two good albeit drunken mates decided that I would appreciate a beer or two. Billy 'Bunk' Baird and Lance 'Fox' Foxon stuffed several bottles into their socks thinking their bell bottom trousers would hide them from the view of the Duty Petty Officer on the gangway. As Billy staggered up the ship's brow making a distinct rattling sound, it didn't take an Einstein to figure out what he had tucked away under his 'bells'. Fox being the more cunning of the two managed to slip past while all the attention of the gangway staff was focused on poor old Bill. So I had a couple of Anchor beers from Fox and Billy joined me on chooks.

After several frustrating days of listening to my mates' wild stories, I thought there had to be a way to get ashore. I approached LCDR John D. Foster, the Torpedo Anti-Submarine officer who was also the ship's diving officer, with a request. I told him that my physical condition was suffering because of the lack of opportunity to do any exercise whilst confined to the ship. It was not an unreasonable request as he was certainly aware of my responsibility to stay fit, plus he was a damn good officer. He said he would put in a word to the Chief Coxswain and between the two of them they agreed that I could go for a run and a swim every evening after 'rounds'- about 7pm. Of course I emphasised that I was a very keen runner and would need at least a 2-hour workout. So each night I would run down the wharf until out of sight of the ship, grab the first taxi I could find and race up to the dockyard junior sailor's club where my mates would have my civvy clothes waiting for me. I would change while knocking down my first pint and we would then all jump into the waiting cab and tear out into the bars of Sembawang for an hour and a half of drinking and partying. On my return to the club I would change back into PT gear, jump in the pool to get wet, grab a taxi to the wharf and then race flat out to the ship's gangway so that I arrived puffing and dripping wet. Somehow I managed to get away with this routine for the rest of our stay in Singapore. All in all, I did quite well. As I was a member of the ship's first Rugby 15, I was also allowed ashore to play in all football matches.

The following 2 weeks at sea were particularly uneventful and routine apart from the fact that when I became eligible for shore leave again the nearest land was about 200 miles away. On our return to Singapore the ship was put into 'tropical routine'. This was normal when the ship was due to spend some time alongside in the Far East and Yarra had some unexpected maintenance problems which had to be repaired. The positive side to this routine was that leave began at about 3 o'clock in the afternoon. The negative side was that leave expired at about 0600 in the morning with work starting at 0700. On the first night back alongside in Singapore my mates decided that they should help me celebrate my first night of legal liberty in about 5 weeks. We hit the downtown high spots including Bugis Street and enough bars that we lost count. Somehow we were split up and I woke up the following morning at about 0800, still in downtown Singapore with a murderous hangover and a 45-minute cab ride ahead of me back to the Naval dockyard. I told the driver to hurry but it didn't really matter. What were a few minutes either way when I was already over 2 hours adrift. As I walked down the wharf past the ship towards the gangway at about 9 o'clock on that bright sunny morning everyone on the upper deck stopped work to cheer me on. The mongrels were actually clapping. They all knew it had been my first night ashore and would probably be my last again for a while. Even the Chief coxswain waiting for me at the gangway had a grin on his face. I knew that Dicky Bird would not be smiling. As I fronted the Captain's table later that morning the skipper said to me "Not you again Ey?". I must admit JD Foster did a great job of defending me. He told the skipper that because of my long stint onboard without any alcohol, I had obviously succumbed to the evils of booze and that the extenuating circumstances deserved some leniency as I was normally a very sober and sensible individual. I believe even the Captain felt some sympathy for me as he let me off with only 2 or 3 days' stoppage of leave. As I departed his table I could see Dicky giving me his evil eye. I knew he was not going to forgive or forget so easily. We stayed in Singapore for a few weeks and a great time was had by all. My entire Mess was moved ashore into Royal Navy barracks for a week or so while work was carried out in the after part of the ship. It was great to be living in large roomy open air accommodation with purring overhead fans. We even enjoyed the change of diet - English food prepared by Chinese/Malay cooks. The only problem with the Pommie barracks was that many of the showers were rusted up and blocked through lack of use. We used to watch in absolute wonder as Pommie sailors, after a day's work in the humid Singapore climate would only have a bird bath at a hand basin, put on a clean shirt and then step ashore. Most Aussie sailors showered at least twice a day. The 'fresh water tanky' (the stoker responsible for producing the ship's fresh water) aboard an Australian warship was considered one of the most important sailors in the crew.

Each Mess had its favourite bar in Sembawang and there were many to choose from. One of the most popular was the Melbourne Bar, however my mates and I preferred the smaller and quieter bars, my favourite being the 'Ship Inn' The girls were friendlier and a little more genuine. At least they remembered our names when we went back. Normally we would drink outside the dockyard gate until after dark and then head into town. After a meal somewhere and a few more bars it was standard practice to finish the night in Bugis Street which came alive after midnight.

In those days we were allowed to wear civilian clothes ashore but sometimes we would decide to wear our white fronts and white bell bottom trousers. Being in 'rig' still had its advantages.

Underway once again the ship headed up the west coast of Malaya with stops in Penang, Langkawi and Port Jessleton - the port of Kuala Lumpur. They were great places in those days, unspoiled by the invasion of Western tourists and American soldiers on R &R leave out of Vietnam. One afternoon my mates and I were just settling into a cosy little bar in Penang when the shore patrol came through the door to announce that there was a general recall for the crew of Yarra. We were to return to the ship immediately and just to make sure we did, they took our names. Much to our disgust, Stuart's sailors were told they could stay put. When we arrived back on board we were informed that a Royal Air Force Shackleton bomber had crashed into the sea somewhere off the NW coast of Sumatra and we were going to the rescue. Our crew understood the seriousness of the situation however we could not help wondering why Fox One had to go and not the junior ship Stuart. Probably the best part of 5 percent of the crew had gotten wind of the recall before the patrolmen found them and they had gone into hiding knowing that the Stuart was not a part of the recall. If they hadn't been told, they couldn't get into strife. Had they known it was a rescue mission they would certainly have returned to a man. It was presumed by all to be just some harebrained recall exercise thought up by Dicky to piss the sailors off. Those left behind returned to the wharf that evening with looks of shock/horror on their faces asking "where's the Yarra?". The lucky devils spent another couple of days in Penang before sailing with Stuart to re-join us in Singapore.

Sport has always had a high priority in the Navy so we managed a few hard games of Rugby against the Brits along the way. The New Zealand Navy also had their A/S frigate HMNZS Waikato deployed to SEATO at the same time and whenever we met in port there would always be a fierce game of football followed by several fights in the bars afterwards. The Kiwis could play Rugby but they hated to lose, particularly to Australians. It was rumoured that when they deployed to the Far East the ship's crew was selected on the basis of football ability alone. Rugby is a religion to them and every game became a matter of national honour. In every port there were always several games organised, especially in Singapore and Hong Kong as the British presence was still very large in that part of the world. Interest ran high on Yarra with at least two and sometimes three teams being fielded. Even the skipper would come along to cheer us on, especially when we were playing the Kiwis. During one particularly dirty game my opposing Kiwi prop gave me a quick uppercut as the scrum broke up. The referee didn't see it but everyone on the sideline did. As the next scrum broke up, I beat him to it and flattened him. A cheer went up from the Yarra supporters and I heard our skipper Captain Robertson say loud enough for all to hear - including the Kiwi Captain, "Well done Ey". That was probably the only friendly thing he ever said to me in two years.

The more serious side of life at sea continued with our participation in regular exercises alongside the member Navies of SEATO. We always finished particularly well overall however we maintained a lot of respect for the professionalism of British and Kiwi sailors.

During some joint Navy exercises it was not uncommon to exchange technical observers with ships of our allies. In one such exercise Yarra was to conduct a live firing of an Ikara missile against the British nuclear submarine HMS Warspite and my old mate Billy Creedon, being a 'Sonarman' was to go aboard the target Sub as an observer for the firing. The object of the exercise was to firstly find the sub within the designated exercise area and then launch a fully operational Ikara missile at it, minus the explosive warhead of course. The purpose of the exercise was to prove the capabilities of the system to the Royal Navy prior to them making a decision to purchase Ikara for their A/S surface ships. We also had a group of Brits aboard to observe the acquisition and launch procedures. Ikara was unique in the world of A/S weapons in that it was the only delivery system that was guided post-launch. The guided missile itself had a Mark 44 homing torpedo strapped to its belly and it was controlled in flight up until the point of release whereupon the torpedo descended to the ocean surface beneath a parachute. On contact with the water, the torpedo released the chute and immediately began its deadly spiralling search pattern seeking out its unsuspecting target with its own onboard active sonar. The real beauty of the Ikara system was that the launch vessel's computer could be linked to other ship's and even helicopter's sonar (A/S helicopters carried sonar which could be lowered from the hover and dipped regularly thus ensuring the target could not escape). This meant that any sonar equipped vessel which acquired a submarine target could instantly downlink the data to the launch vessel which could be many miles away and completely out of sonar range. After launch, the control of the missile would be transferred across to the sonar control centre of the target tracking vessel or helicopter. Meanwhile the missile would receive constant updates of the exact position and track of the target so that at point of release the torpedo was directly above the ill-fated submarine. This capability gave convoys a huge radius of protection as A/S helicopters could dip their sonars at random over a very wide area and with great flexibility and speed. The test firing was a great success and when Bill returned to Yarra he told me of the stunned reaction of the Brit crew. Prior to the launch they had all been very sceptical about this new weapon developed in the 'colonies'. They had a lot of faith in their skipper and his ability to remain undetected and they knew they were many miles away from Yarra. Bill said the sub was running with a very low noise signature and was attempting to hide under thermal layers when their passive sonar identified a splash directly overhead. Immediately thereafter followed the sound of high speed torpedo propellers. Bill said there was a deathly quiet throughout the boat as the sound of the propellers grew louder and louder until finally the inert torpedo impacted the hull of the submarine.

    Part way through our deployment we were ordered to steam south to rendezvous with the Australian troop carrier HMAS Sydney, inbound to Vietnam fully loaded with Diggers and their equipment. Stuart and Yarra were to escort her on her remaining leg into the port of Vung Tau. We decided to give the Aussie soldiers something to tell their grandchildren about, so while the 'Vung Tau Ferry' was still approaching us on a reciprocal course from over the horizon, we loaded the triple barrels of the A/S mortars with food and vegetable scraps and whatever other colourful concoctions we could lay our hands on. As we came abeam of Sydney our skipper increased revolutions, accelerating and turning in towards the carrier. All the Diggers were on the flight deck waving and cheering and madly taking photographs as Yarra quickly closed the gap from astern on a parallel course which would take us to within 25 or 30 metres of Sydney. What we hadn't suspected was that they were prepared for us. As Yarra's bow drew amidships, the Diggers let fly with eggs and a number of various toiletry items. Our skipper added more revolutions and as we began a power turn away, we let loose with all 3 barrels. For those several hundred soldiers laughing and waving on Sydney's flight deck, their day quickly changed from brilliant sunshine to an albeit short heavily overcast day.

Things settled down to a more serious note as we neared the coast of South Vietnam. Due to the threat of possible swimmer attack the time spent at anchor in the port of Vung Tau was kept to an absolute minimum. Even though CDT3 was now operating there permanently, all ship's Captains were very nervous about the safety of their multimillion dollar charges. It was the only time I remember the ship being closed up at maximum readiness while still at anchor. Both propellers were kept turning slowly as a deterrent to underwater attack, armed sailors patrolled the upper deck and of course the ship's diving team were on full standby. I spent my time in the ship's seaboat making large sweeps around Yarra. Trailing astern of the boat was a weighted wooden beam which maintained a depth of 20 odd feet below the surface. This was connected by lengths of barbed wire to a towing beam secured just behind the stern and hanging from the submerged beam on wire traces were a number of extra-large shark hooks. My job was to toss one-pound explosives charges with short fuses overboard at regular intervals to deter any would be sapper-swimmers. All in all, Vung Tau anchorage was probably not the best place to take a relaxing afternoon swim. My responsibilities to Yarra's swimmer defence kept me from any opportunity to say hello to my fellow CDs in Team 3 who were assisting with the defense of the Sydney. As I watched the last of the Aussie soldiers disembark from the Troop Carrier I was saddened by the thought that not all of them would be coming home. Little did I suspect then that I would be returning to South Vietnam as part of CDT3 in less than two and a half years.

The minute the unloading and loading was completed all ships weighed anchor and were speeding seaward. Once well clear of the coast, Sydney turned south towards Australia and we headed north for another welcome visit to Hong Kong. As we steamed north along the coast of Vietnam the crew were kept fully closed up at Defence stations. Sitting in my Ikara loading station, I couldn't help but wonder; if we came under attack by the North Vietnamese, what good was my anti-submarine torpedo carrying missile going to do.

Entering Hong Kong was becoming a little like coming home. In those days it was a great place although US servicemen on R&R from Vietnam were starting to drive the prices of everything skywards. They would arrive with a few thousand dollars in their pockets and only seven days to spend it prior to heading back to the war zone. They were desperate for female company and in too many cases, drugs as well. It was best to stay well shy of them as some were pretty screwed up.

From either the Peak or the harbour at night, Honkers was probably the most beautiful harbour in the world and we never tired of the place. Both sides of the harbour were alive with bars, tailor shops and restaurants, although Kowloon was still a little quiet then, unlike today. All the tailor shops were desperate to get anyone to order their handmade suits and they would entice potential customers in with the offer of free beer. We took advantage of the situation and often went on tailor shop 'runs'. Several of us would allow ourselves to be reluctantly dragged off the street and into the shop where the owner would eagerly show us examples of his workmanship and samples of his cloth. They could all rattle off the names of several sailors from various ships who had already purchased suits at their shop. We would show sufficient interest over the course of several free beers until we had worn out our welcome having not placed any firm orders. It was possible to fill in a very pleasant and cheap afternoon in this manner. Eventually most of us did buy a suit with bright red or blue or green silk lining complete with embroidered Chinese dragons, as back home it was the badge which showed you had been to 'Honkers'. These suits were generally made of quite good quality material however the cotton stitching was always rubbish and the suits would fall apart within a few months of arriving home. This was not a major concern because even though they seemed a great idea at the time, back in Australia you tended to be a little reluctant to wear them in public with their gaudy silk linings.

We continued to cruise the length and breadth of the Far East taking part in numerous exercises which were regularly punctuated by port visits. Apart from Singapore, where we often spent a week or two at a time, most of our visits were limited to three or four days. Just enough time to get to know a few girls and like the place and away we would go, back to sea to suffer the rantings and ravings of our XO. Somebody had said that Dicky was originally a navigator in the Fleet Air Arm and had once been responsible for an entire squadron of aircraft getting lost. It was possibly an exaggeration however where there's smoke, there's fire. Knowing Dicky Bird, anything was possible. How the man became the Executive officer of an Australian warship was something that most of the crew pondered daily.

At regular intervals of about 3 months all seamen were rotated through the various parts of ship. Probably at Dicky's suggestion I was given the demeaning job of PO's Messman. The wardroom, or officer's mess, had trained stewards who had chosen as their career to wait on and serve officers. The senior sailor's messes had junior sailors delegated to keep their living spaces and mess areas clean. Messman duties also included serving meals, clearing up afterwards and washing the dishes. Some sailors thought this was a great job as they only really worked around meal hours and had a lot of time off. In those days the Navy recruited newly qualified tradesmen who underwent 3 months' basic instruction at HMAS Nirimba and then they were pushed out into the fleet as Petty Officers, much to the dismay of regular sailors. They were known in the Navy as '90-day wonders'. A regular sailor could look forward to a wait of 6 to 10 years before reaching Petty Officer rank so obviously there was some resentment towards these instant POs. In most cases they were reasonable types however many were not. In my case, I had been in the Navy for two and a half years at that stage and I most certainly resented serving food to, and cleaning up after, someone who had been in the Navy for only a 'dog watch' (referring to the two 2 hour watches during the afternoon). That aside, I also felt it was beneath the dignity and responsibilities of a Clearance Diver. The Navy had spent a lot of money training me and to my mind it wasn't to be a waiter. As a consequence, I informed the President of the PO's Mess that I would work in the scullery washing dishes but I was not serving food to arrogant little 90-day wonders. He was an old gunnery Petty officer and didn't take very kindly to an Able Seaman telling him what he would and wouldn't do. Actually, he almost came apart at the seams and after a heated argument he marched me up to see my Divisional officer, JD Foster. Fortunately for me JD could see my point of view. It was obvious to everyone that I was not suited to being a waiter, so common sense prevailed. I was transferred to another part of ship and discretion being the better part of valour, I stayed well out of the way of the President of the PO's mess for the rest of the cruise.

Despite my ongoing personal dramas with the Yarra's hierarchy, the ship continued its cruise, heading west out into the Indian Ocean to conduct exercises with the Royal Navy. After visiting Gan on Addu Atoll, the southernmost island of the Maldives, we spent a few less than pleasant days in Ceylon (now Sri Lanka). The beer there was so bad that no one could drink it. I'll never forget the name – it was called 'Three Coins'. The worst beer I have ever tasted.

From Ceylon, it was back to Singapore for a break before heading north again for a final 4-day visit to our favourite port, Hong Kong. En-route we transited the coast of Vietnam with the crew being closed up at Defence Stations for 2 days, much to our disgust.

With our commitment to SEATO pretty much over, we headed across to Cebu in the Philippines to show the Flag.

We were told that Cebu had not seen an Australian warship since WWII, and the locals treated the crew like royalty. Unfortunately, I only saw Cebu from the wharf as Dicky Bird had once again taken his revenge. The day before we arrived in Cebu, he managed to have me charged again.

Every working day, all seamen not on watch fell in on 1 deck aft at both 0800 and 1300 for 'both watches of seamen' (a muster referring to the Port and Starboard watches). This little ceremony was presided over by the Buffer (Chief Bosun's Mate) and the XO (Dicky) during which time everyone was accounted for and given their particular work responsibilities. On the dot, the Buffer would call both watches to attention and anyone not fallen in at that point of time was considered adrift. It was normal for most sailors to emerge from their mess decks with only seconds to spare. On this particular day I was casually climbing the quarter-deck ladder and probably within only five paces of my allocated spot when Dicky Bird spotted me. I knew I had about 30 or 40 seconds to spare and there were still several sailors coming up the ladder behind me. The moment Dicky saw me he screamed at me to stay where I was and then ordered the Buffer to *"call both watches"*. The poor old Buffer looked at his watch and stammered *"But sir, it's not 1300 yet"*. The XO raised his voice a tempo or two and repeated the order. With little choice in the matter, his order was obeyed. The second that formality was out of the way he told the Buffer to 'run in' (charge) all the stragglers. It was at that moment that it dawned on me, and half the crew, that Dicky was completely insane. To get at me he was prepared to charge a half a dozen other sailors as well. The Buffer was the senior seaman aboard and not a particularly friendly character but he actually apologised to us for the injustice that had been done. Nevertheless, none of us stepped ashore in Cebu. According to the rest of the crew we were missing the best run in the Far East. One of the other fellows under punishment, 'Occa' O'Connell, decided that he was not going to miss out. After the last muster for the evening was over, he put some clothes in a waterproof plastic bag and as I kept watch he quietly slipped over the stern into the water and disappeared out of sight under the wharf. The next morning at 0600 as I hauled him in over the quarterdeck, he looked very tired but was sporting a grin that stretched from ear to ear. I thought the man deserved to be made an honorary diver for his outstanding display of initiative.

Finally, we were heading south on our way home. Our last ports of call were to be Jakarta and Surabaya in Indonesia. We were in fact to be the first Aussie warship to visit that country since the Indonesian confrontation had ended several years earlier. Jakarta was a very basic city in those days and about the only place you could get a cold beer was at the Australian Embassy, and after our first visit we were not invited back. There was one international standard hotel and of course that was too expensive and not exactly suited to young sailors anyway. We had no regrets about leaving Jakarta and we pushed on to the port city of Surabaya, which also happened to be home port to the Indonesian Navy. For the last few miles of our run into our berth we were escorted by what had once been two Soviet missile carrying patrol boats. Both were un-seaworthy rust buckets that belched black diesel exhaust all over our clean white uniforms. While President Sukarno was in power the Soviet Union had provided equipment and aid to the pro-Communist Sukarno forces. I think the size of the Indonesian Navy surprised us all however it was all junk and very few ships were capable of putting to sea. Our berth was right astern of their flagship the 'IRIAN', a former Soviet cruiser. At first glance it was a very impressive looking ship with its scrubbed wooden decks, fresh paint and flags flying. She even had smoke drifting from her funnel giving the impression that she was ready for sea. Obviously all for our benefit as our Engineering officer noted after a closer inspection that the smoke smelt suspiciously of oily rags.

It turned out that we had quite a good time in Surabaya even though it was impossible to get a cold beer, unless you were prepared to use ice which was full of flies, mosquitoes, sticks, grass and most probably loads of hepatitis. The main attraction in town was a very long street that consisted of houses which doubled as bars and houses of ill repute. It was rather obvious as every house always had several girls sitting outside trying everything possible to entice every sailor who happened to walk past to go inside their house. In the locals' broken English it was hard to decipher whether the area was actually called the 'Jungle bar', which it certainly sounded like, or 'Young Girl bar', which made a lot more sense. Whatever its real name, it was a very popular spot with the sailors.

One of the most popular pastimes in any port of call was the inevitable 'Brewery Run', on this occasion to the Dutch brewer, Heineken. After a short but compulsory tour of the brewery floor it was down to some serious sampling which proceeded well into the afternoon. During the trip back to the ship, Lance Foxon, a TAS rate and ship's diver, asked the local bus driver to open the door as he needed to answer the call of nature. Fortunately for Fox the driver slowed down considerably as he drove along the grass verge of the road. I can still remember the stupid shit grin on Fox's face as he stood on the lower step relieving himself out the door, and as if it were a perfectly natural thing to do, he slowly tilted forward in his drunken stupor and disappeared out the door. If he had been sober, he would most probably have broken his neck.

On our last night in town a few of us were going back to the dockyard in pedal powered trishaws and this very same 'Fox' had conned his driver into allowing him to pedal the contraption while the Indon sat nervously in the passenger seat. These civilian drivers and their vehicles were not allowed inside the confines of the dockyard however Fox decided that as it was still a long walk from the gate to the ship, he was going to ride all the way. He sailed through the main gate laughing to himself and totally ignoring the guard who was madly waving for him to stop. He had probably gone some 20 or 30 yards past the gate when we decided we should bring it to Fox's attention that the guard had drawn his .38 calibre handgun and was sighting in on the centre of Fox's back. Fortunately, he realised that 'death before dishonour' was not what it was cracked up to be and the trishaw came to a rapid and screeching halt.

From Surabaya it was a relatively straight run south to Fremantle, our first port of call on Australian soil. As we eased up the river towards our berth I was pleased to see that the Fleet tanker HMAS Supply was also in port and our berth was going to be directly astern of her. I knew my brother was part of her crew so as soon as we were secured alongside I requested permission to go aboard to see Mike. It was great to see his grinning face wandering up to the gangway with his outstretched hand. He took me below and introduced me to the characters who shared his cabin. It just happened to be 'stand easy', or morning tea time and I was surprised at the relative comfort they enjoyed. While part of the British Navy, Supply had been manned by a civilian crew and they demanded comforts that the Navy did not allow its regular sailors. This included four-man cabins whereas aboard a warship like Yarra, I shared my mess deck with forty or fifty other sailors. Mike had a few other surprises in store for me; first and foremost, he had become engaged since I had left and secondly our younger brother David had enlisted in the Navy as a Junior Recruit and at that time was actually undergoing training in Fremantle at HMAS Leeuwin. During our stay we attempted to see David however as a brand new JR he was not allowed visitors. Fremantle was a very friendly town and we were pleased to be back on Australian soil. One night Fox suggested we stop in and say hello to his Uncle who was a Sergeant at the West Perth Police station. He turned out to be a great bloke and sent out for several cases of beer, so we made ourselves at home and spent an hour or two sitting in the cells of the Police Station drinking beer and telling lies to all the local constabulary about the mystical Far East.

Fox's parents had invited a few of his mates to their house for a welcome home party and he told me on the side that his mother was absolutely petrified of the potential consequences of having over a dozen sailors, recently returned from the flesh-pots of Asia, running amok in her house. We all arrived in our flash Hong Kong tailor made suits looking and behaving like a million dollars. Fox had invited his favourite cousin and a number of her friends to the party and likewise, they were unsure of what they were letting themselves into. By the end of the evening Mrs. Foxon thought we were the most charming young gentlemen she had ever met and most of the girls soon lost their hearts to a sailor. In fact, for many years after, Fox used to tell me that his Mother never stopped talking about "those fine young men from the Yarra in their flash suits". She did say however that she had never met anybody who could talk as much as Billy 'the Bunk' Baird. Some of the girls from the party, including Fox's cousin, later travelled all the way to Sydney to see us again. In those days before the advent of cheap international travel, there was something that most girls found irresistible about a young sailor in bell bottom trousers who had seen half the world before he had turned twenty-one. I must admit there was something special about the Navy. The discipline was tough and our living conditions left a lot to be desired, but amongst sailors, it was like being in a big family. Your home was always on the move and your mates stood by you through thick and thin, unlike many of the lost and flighty civilian generation of our day who just wanted to break away from and protest against every convention that our parents stood for and believed in.

We departed Fremantle in company with Supply for the final run to Melbourne. On arrival at Williamstown dockyard the ship went into dry-dock for her mid cycle refit and most of the crew proceeded on annual leave.

I went back to Adelaide to see my parents and after a short spell at home it dawned on me that I now had very little in common with my civvy mates. I had travelled from Cebu to Ceylon and from Manila to Macao and had seen things that most people don't experience in a lifetime and my old mates still had the same girlfriends, still went to the same pubs and still hadn't left the confines of suburban Glenelg. They were good blokes but we had nothing much to talk about. I realised that I had become completely 'Navy' and I found from that point on that it was very difficult to relate to anyone who had not shared the same worldly experiences that I had already been exposed to at the tender age of twenty.

When I returned to the ship from leave, a lot of the older crew had posted off to begin their two year cycle ashore and fortunately that included my old adversary Dicky Bird. He was replaced by a younger more professional officer by the name of LCDR Paul Berger.

After leave I was made a Quartermaster which meant I was responsible for the gangway security during my watch. I had to ensure that everyone who left and re-joined the ship were legal to do so. Routine pipes over the ship's broadcast system were also my responsibility. I was assisted by an ordinary seaman who made the tea and hot cocoa and ran errands for me. Being the quartermaster of a warship high and dry in Williamstown dry-dock in the depth of a Melbourne winter is not the most exciting job on earth. As we were so far from downtown Melbourne we tended to frequent a couple of favourite pubs located just outside the dockyard. One such establishment was owned by a very pleasant spinster who took our motley bunch under her wing and we spent many a cold wintry night in the warmth of her pub playing darts and shooting the breeze. She was an ardent St. Kilda football supporter and woe betide anyone who spoke badly of her team. At closing time, she would toss out everybody who wasn't from Yarra's 3 Papa mess and we could kick on for as long as we wanted.

A warship in dry-dock is a little like a sedated lion. At sea or even alongside a warship feels like it has a heart and a soul and is ready to pounce at a moment's notice. It lives and breathes 24 hours a day and it is a life support system for its entire crew. So after several months of watching Yarra being subjected to oxy torches, sandblasting, welding and a host of other indignities inflicted by dockyard workers, it was heart-warming to finally see her afloat again and looking like a new pin.

On completion of our refit, with a new Skipper aboard, Captain J.D. Stevens, we returned to Sydney for work-up periods before heading off for a visit to the 'Land of the long white cloud'. New Zealand was a country high on my list of places to visit as I had grown up with the ANZAC legend and I had heard it was a beautiful country with lots of friendly girls. However, my first impression as we steamed into Auckland harbour was a little disappointing. After Sydney harbour, Auckland on a dull overcast day was a little lack-lustre to say the least. The natives quickly made up for the bleak weather and we settled down for an enjoyable visit. Our warm welcome almost came to a sudden end when on our first day ashore, Billy Creedon and I both wandered into a pub in the main street of Auckland. We ordered two beers from the friendly young maiden behind the bar and then watched in complete amazement as she poured two 8-ounce glasses from a beer gun that looked awfully like a draft horse having a leak. The beer looked extremely flat and lifeless and to some extent very much like the by-product of the aforementioned horse. Even the price of 8 cents per glass didn't make up for the appearance of the beer. I knew we might be in trouble with the patrons of the pub when Bill took his first mouthful. Like a man who suspects someone has just tried to poison him, Bill immediately spat it out and said "What's this piss?" All conversation ceased and the whole pub took on a very hostile atmosphere as everyone stared daggers at the two Australian sailors in uniform. I quickly said to Bill in a very loud voice, "Are you okay Bill? I know you've been a bit crook lately". The pub slowly returned to normal as I patted him on the back and said aloud, "Another beer will fix you up Mate". He realised the delicate situation we were in so he said aloud "Thanks mate, I'm okay now. Something must have been stuck in my throat".

After a few weeks in Kiwi land we almost adjusted to the beer which we discovered to our horror was delivered to pubs in what looked like milk tankers. While in the nation's capital, Bill and I met a couple of lovely young ladies from quite well to do families who had access to their 'Daddy's' car and they showed us a great time. Within 12 months of our NZ visit Bill was to meet and marry a Kiwi lass and I followed suite two years later.

From Auckland we headed south east down the East coast to the country town of Napier in Hawkes Bay. This turned out to be another great sailor's run and we had a ball. We were almost asked to leave by the Mayor when one of our Leading Seaman, a wild and woolly character by the name of 'Shiner' Wright decided to show the old folks at the local RSL the infamous ritual known within Navy circles as 'the dance of the flaming arseholes'. They didn't know whether to laugh or cry, call the police or just pretend it didn't happen. Surprisingly Shiner became something of a celebrity for the rest of our stay in Napier.

Invitations flooded into the ship on a daily basis for sailors to attend everything from flower shows to debutante balls. If no-one volunteered, a number of the poor old duty watch were ordered to represent the Aussie flag. Fox and I were volunteered to 'accept' an invite to a function put on by the local Deer-hunters club. It was a family affair and the two Aussie sailors in full dress uniform were definitely the centre of attention with most of the fathers keeping a very close eye on their daughters. As they were obviously all crack rifle shots, we behaved ourselves. These fellows were mad keen hunters of the superbly antlered Wapiti deer and they invited us on a deer hunting expedition into the high country. As the ship was due to leave the following day, we had to get a snappy approval from the Captain. To our surprise he agreed, and we were told to re-join the ship several days later in New Plymouth on the West coast. My vague memories of this experience consist of a few days of wandering the scrubby hills in extremely cold, wet miserable weather in return for the brief sighting of one deer on a distant hill which escaped unharmed. We did however enjoy a couple of good home cooked meals of venison.

Back in Sydney we were told that we would be heading back to the Far East again for a short visit as a sister ship, Derwent, had a gun mount problem and we would be taking her place as part of the SEATO commitment until she was ready to sail.

So back to Singapore, much to the delight of the crew, before heading across for a visit to Tacloban on the island of Leyte as part of the 24th anniversary celebrations for General Douglas Macarthur's return to the Philippines during WWII.

Unfortunately for us, Derwent was by then on her way north so it was homeward bound again.

For the next several months the ship continued her never ending work-ups and exercises including hunting for an unidentified foreign submarine lurking off the NSW coast.

Finally, on the 5th May 1969 I posted off to CDT2, which along with the entire diving school had by then been re-located from HMAS Rushcutter to HMAS Penguin.

7
CDT 2 -1969/70

My new posting was to CDT2, the trials and evaluation diving team. While I had been away keeping the sea lanes open, constant pressure from self interest groups both within the Navy and outside had seen the Diving school relocated from its outstanding prime location at Rushcutters Bay to the less than exciting Naval establishment of HMAS Penguin at Middle Head, a place which had few pleasant memories for me.

I soon found that Team 2 had its share of characters, from the Chief of the team down to the youngest CD's just off course. Chief Petty Officer CD Sandy Brennan was one of the old originals of the diving branch and he was as comfortable in the water as a pod of dolphins. He was a wiry little bloke who could never sit still and no-one had ever known him when he hadn't had a crewcut. I don't think Sandy had an enemy in the world and he was well known throughout the Navy for his big shit grin, his very relaxed attitude towards Naval discipline and the fact that he hated to wear shoes. He was also probably the most popular Chief in the Diving Branch. Whereas most Chiefs and Petty Officers rarely got their head wet, Sandy would always take along an extra supervisor on diving jobs so that he could get into the water at every opportunity, often telling the younger divers that they had to wait their turn as he wanted the first dip of the day. I'll never forget the day he surfaced after a 60-foot dive on the clump of a mooring buoy in Sydney Harbour. As his head broke the surface, he let his demand valve drop from his mouth and said with a big smile, *"I've got morning tea for you boys"* and he held up his right hand to reveal a large Leather Jacket (fish) that he had actually speared with his diving knife. In my 20 years in the Branch I never saw that feat bettered by anyone. There were stories that Sandy, after a few too many beers in the Chiefs' mess, would jump on a late train to head home to the western suburbs of Sydney and immediately go to sleep. He would then wake up a few hours later as the train pulled back into Central station – right back where he had started.

Noel 'Stewy' Stewart was a wild and slightly crazy Leading Seaman who eventually went on to become a LCDR in command of a Minehunter. Had the Selection Board for officer candidates seen the side of Stewy that I had, it is unlikely that he would have gone past Leading Seaman. Another fellow diver on Team 2 with whom I was to become a life-long friend was a young newly qualified CD by the name of Larry 'Digger' Digney who went on to become the senior Warrant Officer of the CD branch. In those days he was a wild young larrikin who had great difficulty staying out of trouble.

The Team's responsibilities rotated through the mundane fleet maintenance diving tasks to the more interesting, although less common, sonar dome changes and submarine propeller changes. These were sometimes done by CDs while the vessel remained in the water, thus saving the considerable time, cost and delays of dry-docking.

I had only been with the team for a week or so when the Boss decided we should begin working up for ship attacks. As I had only just returned from two years at sea and not used an O_2 set in that entire time, he decided unwisely – in fact it was sheer stupidity - that I should have my very first night compass swim using CABA (Scuba air) and not oxygen. Diving Officers rarely got in the water and were often completely out of touch with hands on diving. To make matters worse we had a ship's diver attached to the team as a working hand and our young officer in all his wisdom thought he would let him swim with me so that he would feel 'part of the team'. This fellow had never done a compass swim in his life. We were to use SCUBA air for the swim and he was given the responsibility of keeping my depth - at night. There were two major problems with this situation. Firstly, as the relatively large air cylinders are breathed down their buoyancy changes considerably, and secondly, as a CD I had routinely practised controlled breathing while using air *(a breath of air is held a little longer than normal to help conserve the air supply by utilising more oxygen from each breath)* and it was a habit which was difficult to break. It would have been a disaster in the making putting two worked up CD's on SCUBA for a compass swim at night let alone an out date CD and a ship's diver. Being right out of touch, I had to rely completely on my so called 'buddy' to keep our depth and he unfortunately had no idea. He thought he was along just for the ride. After perhaps 30 minutes into the swim it was becoming increasingly difficult to maintain a steady depth due to the changing buoyancy of the set and I began to feel some chest pain and initially put it down to my deep breathing. When the pain persisted I realised that I had a problem, so we surfaced and I signalled for the safety boat to come over to pick me up. By the time I had climbed aboard and removed my equipment, my normally deep voice had risen by several octaves. Sandy told me to describe the steadily increasing pain while he carefully felt around my neck. He then immediately got on the radio and called for a Navy ambulance to be waiting at the wharf as we headed back to the Diving school at full throttle. I was in considerable pain by that stage and I had begun to breathe pure oxygen from the Oxy-Viva resuscitator. I remember being quite fascinated by the soft crackly feeling caused by the escaping air bubbles forming in my neck tissue. I knew what had happened to me. In medical terms it was called a *Pulmonary Barotrauma* which resulted in a *Mediastinal Emphysema*, or to a layman, I had burst part of a lung and air was leaking into the chest cavity surrounding my heart. Fortunately, the Naval hospital at Penguin was kept on alert while night diving operations were in progress so I had a reception committee waiting for me at the end of my 2 minute ride up the hill in the back of the ambulance. I was rushed into X-ray and kept on my left side to help keep any air bubbles from collecting around my heart. From there I was put into an oxygen tent and checked over by a doctor while they discussed my prognosis. Surprisingly they then left me for the remainder of the night under the concerned and watchful eye of a young junior nurse with instructions to report any change in my condition. I then spent the most uncomfortable and painful night of my life with my chest feeling like it was about to explode. I survived the night no thanks to the diving school's senior U/W medico who didn't feel it was serious enough to interrupt his evening's cocktail party. He finally found the time to see me at about 1000 the next morning and I felt like saying to the arrogant bastard, *"Thanks for your concern Doc"*. This doctor actually went on to become a Rear Admiral - incredible. Once I got over the worst of it, there was not a lot that could be done for my condition, so it was just a matter of waiting for my lungs to heal themselves. They kept me under observation for about 2 weeks so I spent my 21st birthday in the Naval hospital flat on my back, after which I was discharged on sick leave and sent to my parents' home in Adelaide. My compressed air buddy had avoided my fate because he would have been quite anxious about his first night swim and had been breathing quite rapidly, making no attempt to conserve air as I had. I did not bear any grudge towards him, only towards the stupidity of the team OIC. Unfortunately, the Military often place less than competent officers in charge of sailors who have far greater experience. Once qualified, very few officers ever got in the water and consequently had no real diving experience other than that gained on course and from a text book.

I was made unfit for diving for 6 months while my lungs slowly healed and scarred so I spent the time as the Team storeman and driver.

Not too long after the accident my old mate Billy Creedon asked me to be the best man at his wedding. Most of the old 3 Papa Seamen's mess of Yarra were there, all dressed to the nines with Billy and I dressed in tuxedos for the first time in our lives. Bill's wife had decided that she would play Cupid for me and did her best to match me up with her bridesmaid Kay, also a Kiwi. At the wedding reception I was introduced to the bridesmaid's younger sister and that was that. Antoinette Taylor and I were married a little over two years later. We didn't get off to the best of starts when after the reception I volunteered to drive the bride and groom, the bridesmaid and her friend, and Antoinette, back to the girls' flat at Coogee for a continuation of the party. I had consumed my share of alcohol as every best man is obliged to do and may have exceeded the speed limit by just a tad when Kay said from the back seat, "*Tony, there is a car with a blue flashing light following us*". After I had pulled over and the policeman had taken a look in the window, he obviously didn't have the heart to book me with a pair of newly-weds sitting in the car so he wished them good luck and told me to get to where I was going via the most direct route possible. It turned out to be a great party with Billy *Bunk* Baird and I upholding the best traditions of the Yarra, even though Bill did require a little encouragement from me – in the form of, *'we'll just have one more Bill'*, much to the disgust of a young lady who fancied him. Billy and I slept in the girls' lounge room in our tuxedos, only because we were not in any condition to find our own way home. I was quite surprised and so was everybody else when Antoinette agreed to go out with me a couple of evenings later. We had managed to get a couple of miles down the road from her place when my car's clutch master cylinder decided to throw it in. Antoinette was not impressed. We continued to go out together while all her friends warned her that it couldn't last any longer than a few months because *'he's a sailor'*.

The Team had what we called a *'brass old box'* and as the months went by, we collected all the non-ferrous metals that we had managed to 'acquire' – borrow, find or steal - from our various expeditions around Sydney Harbour. When this collection became too heavy to lift, we would take it to a local scrap metal dealer and trade it for cash. The money would then be deposited into our team bank account ready to subsidise our regular social functions at the local pub. One unsuspecting source of brass was HMS Jaguar, a visiting Royal Navy frigate. During her most recent exercise she had lowered her long, slender and very heavy solid brass Pitometer Log and it had obviously impacted something sufficiently large to bend it so that it could not be fully retracted back into the hull. Our job was to recover the probe after it was disconnected from inside the hull and allowed to drop free. Sandy was the dive supervisor and instead of securing the probe to the recovery line provided by the ship, we secured it to our own line which was hanging outboard of the diving boat. As the probe was released it very neatly swung down directly below the outboard side of our boat. The pair of divers then surfaced and explained that the probe had slipped through their knot and speared off into the muddy bottom. Sandy proceeded to dress down the two divers in a loud voice telling them that they weren't *"divers' assholes"* and to get to the bottom and find it. After 10 or 15 minutes of fruitless searching, Sandy apologised to the Poms with his usual shit grin for his divers' incompetence by saying, *"Bloody dickheads, I can't trust them to do anything right"*. He then told the Poms there was nothing else we could do. I could see the look on the face of the Royal Navy Chief Bosun's Mate and I knew he was thinking, *'You bastards, you're divers and I know what you're up to'*. With a friendly wave we flashed up the engine and idled around the corner until out of sight, all the while with the Brit Chief never taking his suspicious eyes off us. We couldn't go any faster than idle as we didn't want to lose the probe a *'second'* time. Our substantial addition to the CDT2 slush fund was then hauled inboard and we departed for Penguin, quite pleased with our day's work.

After numerous tests had been carried out on my lungs by civilian specialists at various hospitals, I was finally cleared *'fit to dive'*. This was a great relief to me as I was bored stiff and anxious to get back into the water again. Initially I was limited to a maximum depth of 66 feet until they were certain that my lungs were functioning normally. As a result, I spent a lot of time on oxygen working up for ship attacks and this suited me fine as I much preferred the CD oxygen set over any of the air diving rigs.

I thoroughly enjoyed swimming on oxygen and practising the art of ship attack. There was an intense feeling of freedom swimming like a fish below the surface with no tell-tale bubbles and no one above knowing where you were. Clearance Divers were trained to carry out a huge variety of tasks using a large inventory of equipment, but swimming on O_2 at night while attacking a multimillion-dollar target was what I considered to be the core business of being a CD. It came down to the skills of you and your buddy, alone in the far from friendly depths, pitted against a ship or ships carrying hundreds of professional sailors, all intent on preventing us from reaching our objective. We were acutely aware that during training, detection meant no more than the end of the exercise, however if we ever became involved in the real thing, it could result in something much more permanent. With this in mind we took our profession very seriously. I believe that most other elite forces such as the Army's SAS and the US Navy SEALS have a similar attitude, as when you are trained to penetrate and operate in the opposition's *'territory'* in very small numbers, it all comes down to just you and your buddy's ability to apply the well-practised skills acquired from constant training and repetition. There is generally no backup or support available and in any difficult or deteriorating situation, you know it is just you and your buddy. This awareness made for a high level of camaraderie in small specialised units such as Clearance Diving Teams.

Most of our work-ups for ship attacks were done in Sydney Harbour with the bulk of the actual fleet exercises being conducted in Jervis Bay, to the south of Sydney. We always enjoyed our trips to the Naval College in those days as Jervis Bay was alive with fish of every variety, from Garfish to Grouper and large patches of the seabed were literally covered with scallops. Those were the days before the professional fishing trawlers systematically swept the bay clean of every last shell. We would take one of the College's 40-foot work boats out into the bay and using surface supplied breathing apparatus, or *hookah* as it was then known, place two divers on the seabed while the boat drifted slowly across the bay. A 112-pound concrete shot was lowered to the bottom with a wheat bag secured to the shot line. While holding onto the drifting shot with one hand the two divers could easily fill the bag with the biggest scallops within 30 minutes. The scallop beds migrated back and forth across the bay but we always seemed to find them in about 60 feet of water. While in Jervis Bay we usually camped in a large timber cottage which was not too far from the Captain's house. It was fully self-contained and included a gas oven which was the perfect size for a few dozen scallops. We would place these in the hot oven until the shells opened and then a dollop of garlic butter and a squeeze of lemon juice would be added to each one before another few sizzling minutes back in the hot oven. Along with a good cask of Coolabah red wine or a few beers it was a meal fit for a King.

When it came time for the more serious business of conducting the actual ship attacks, the mood amongst the team changed immediately to one of professional concentration. Once the attack swimmers had been designated and the entire team briefed on individual responsibilities, very little was said. Everyone settled down to the task of ensuring his own equipment was perfect and nothing was forgotten or overlooked. Clearance Divers are amongst the most team oriented men in the Military yet they are also total individuals, as their wives will certainly attest to. Each man's equipment is his responsibility alone. His life will depend on it.

The ideal night to carry out an *'Operation Awkward'* as it was officially known, was when the sky was under heavy overcast or even drizzling rain with a light chop on the water and a steady breeze blowing. Nothing dulls the alertness of a sentry more than gusting rain on a cold miserable night and the last thing he wants to do is be exposed to the direction of the weather, and of course we always attacked from the weather side. Surprising as it may sound, on such nights it is very pleasant to be underwater. Just knowing it is cold and miserable on the surface adds to the enjoyment of being in the ocean's *'dark embrace'*. Under these conditions visibility can sometimes be quite exceptional below the surface. On our approaches from a mile or so away, it was normal practice for the *'driver'* to just barely break the surface long enough to check his bearing to the target. This was done every fifteen minutes or so and was the only time an especially alert sentry had any chance of spotting the attackers. A properly weighted diver can surface so covertly that he would not be seen or heard from as little as ten metres away. It is done in a similar fashion to the way a crocodile breaks the surface. As we neared the target we could usually hear the clanking of the ship's anchor chain, as it is incredibly quiet underwater at night with the only sound being the steady hiss of the set's reducing valve as it supplied its life giving oxygen to the diver. The closer we approached, the louder the hum of the ship's machinery - the noise acting as a beacon in the night. Finally, the huge dark shadow of a 3,000-ton warship would appear menacingly out of the gloom. At that point in time we would normally descend to make our final approach at a depth of about 30 feet, just to minimise the chances of an alert sentry spotting something. Some ship's rigged underwater lighting and at irregular intervals would switch it on, lighting up the hull like centre court at Wimbledon. This was a risk as there was the possibility that we could have already been in and laid charges with light sensitive initiation. Even though we carried dummy Limpet mines, we often put small black powder charges in them just to remind the ship's divers that this was a serious business. Mostly we just fitted basic pressure release devices which would activate when an attempt was made to remove them from the hull, but occasionally we made up time pencils with sufficient delays which we intended would go off just as the ship's diving team was making its regular sweeps of the hull.

Once during an '*Awkward*' in Sydney Harbour while we were attacking ships alongside at Garden Island dockyard, '*Mumbles*' Aldenhoven and I placed a Limpet mine on a merchant ship that for some unknown reason to us was tied up at G.I. She sailed that same night with a mine on her hull which was activated by a pressure release device. At some stage as she was gathering speed down harbour, the mine would have most likely been torn off the hull and the crew would have heard an unexplained bang echo throughout their ship.

One particularly black night in Jervis Bay as we arrived at the keel of HMAS Stuart, we heard the overhead splash of the ship's diving team entering the water. We thought we might have some fun so we descended several metres and waited in the shadowy depths below the keel. As the *'half necklace'* of divers passed above us we swam up and behind them and withdrew our diver's knives, which looked about the size of Bowie knives underwater. Just grabbing hold of one of the diver's fins would give them enough of a fright, but when they turned and saw our gloomy outline their hearts would have been in their mouths. We knew that dressed in black wetsuits and hoods, with the matt black UBA and its single corrugated black rubber breathing hose disappearing into a black full facemask gave us the appearance of an alien life form from another planet. The fact that our sets gave off no bubbles at all made the sight even more eerie to a young shallow water diver who just wanted to get back to the warmth and comfort of his mess deck as quickly as possible. It was enough to completely ruin their already uncomfortable and miserable night.

As in any military outfit, if someone has a natural flair for a particular role he tends to gravitate to that position as a matter of course. So it was that I became a regular *'driver'* on ship attacks. This ability to steer an accurate compass heading came in handy a number of years later when I obtained my Pilot's licence.

Life in Team 2 continued with a mixture of the more mundane harbour diving jobs and ship's U/W maintenance to the more interesting EOD and demolition tasks. Our trips away were particularly enjoyable as we always managed to fit in a lot of diving and lived quite well. Promotions came and went and I still remained an Able Seaman - due to my bad PP1a's resulting from my regular confrontations with the XO of Yarra. *(PP1a's were six monthly reports submitted to Navy office by your superiors. One bad report could set a sailor's promotion back by years).* I was gradually working my way towards the dubious honour of becoming the senior Able Seaman in the diving branch. Most sailors had their *'Hook'* (Leading Seaman) after about 4 years' service. It had some advantages for me as the younger sailors felt they could trust a senior AB whereas Leading Seamen were already *corrupted* by power and couldn't be trusted to the same degree. The downside was the lower pay.

During this period I was awarded my 1st good conduct badge for four years' service and henceforth became a *'badgeman'*. This entitled me to wear a gold wire flat V shaped stripe on the left arm of my dress uniform and this brought with it a certain increased level of respect. The military quite wisely encourages this visible elevation in status as it has serviceman always aspiring to the next level. This always visible display of position in the hierarchy may partly explain the difference between the military and civvy street, where a lack of respect often exists between different levels of management. To a large extent in the civilian world, people are advanced through who they know rather than actually earning advancement. Servicemen are very proud of their rank and take it very seriously as it is known to all that each and every step takes a minimum time and numerous qualifications.

As my first year in Team 2 drew to a close the entire Branch was anxiously awaiting the news as to who would be selected for the next Clearance Diving Team 3 - the Navy's Special Operations team serving on active duty in South Viet Nam.

8
CDT3 VIETNAM – 1970/71

The eagerly awaited Postings notice from Canberra announcing the names of those selected for training and subsequent deployment to South Viet Nam as the 8th contingent of CDT3 came out in May 1970. The Diving Regulating Chief at Penguin, CPOCD Vic Rashleigh, actually informed me on my 22nd birthday that I had been selected for the team and it was the best birthday present I could ever have hoped for. By the time the sailors' postings were announced it was common knowledge who the Boss was to be and the rumours were already running thick and fast as to who would be the Senior Sailors of the Team. The entire CD Branch of approximately 100 odd Divers held their breath hoping that they had been selected for what was the most sought after posting in the diving branch. To a man, it was comparable to winning the Lottery. Most of the civilian population at that time would have found this to be a very curious attitude, but we were a very proud and dedicated band of professionals who were anxious to put our training to the test. I don't believe any of us thought too much about the politics or the rights and wrongs of the war, only that we were to have the opportunity to do what we had been trained to do. Viet Nam was to be our proving ground and we were all worried that it might be over before we had a chance to get there.

Hindsight is a wonderful thing and perhaps many of us might now agree that Australia should not have sent combat troops to South Viet Nam, however we were sent and nothing can erase the past, or the fact that Australia tragically lost over 500 of her finest young sons.

The 8th team to serve in SVN was officially formed up on the 3rd of July 1970. We posted into HMAS Waterhen, which was to be our parent establishment for administrative purposes during our work-up period as members of CDT3.

It was normal for each replacement team to be made up of seven divers. Six would eventually be selected to deploy to Viet Nam on completion of the three-month work-up period with the seventh member remaining behind as a standby replacement in case he was needed. The previous team had already needed their replacement; John Aldenhoven, after the accidental death in country of Able Seaman Bobby Wojcik. Normally the diver left behind was guaranteed a slot on the following team with the poor devil having to go through the full work-up period twice. Who would remain behind was not announced until the completion of our work-up and just prior to us all proceeding on pre-embarkation leave. So we *'Indians'* all sweated for 3 months and hoped like hell that we would not be the one left behind.

Our new boss was Lieutenant Edward (*Jake*) Linton, already something of a legend in the branch. One of the very first Clearance Divers to qualify in the RAN, Jake had earned a BEM (*British Empire Medal*) for a particularly deep and dangerous diving operation in the icy waters of Lake Eucumbene in the Snowy Mountains. Our second in command was CPOCD John (*Speed*) Gilchrist with POCD Phil (*Narra*) Narramore taking up the number three slot. The remaining four 'Indians' were LSCD Tom McNab, ABCD Larry (*Digger*) Digney, ABCD Brian (*Blue*) Furner and ABCD yours truly.

Our pre-deployment training began with a diving refresher, not that we really needed it, but it started us thinking and working together as a team. The old *'Bomb & Mine Disposal Section'* had been moved from HMAS Rushcutter to HMAS Watson and had a name change to *'EOD Section'*. It was mainly staffed by veterans of earlier Vietnam teams with Lt. Alex (*Tiger Man*) Donald in charge. This training quite rightly focused on weapons, ordnance and booby traps which had been discovered by previous teams.

We were immediately put into the swing of things by exchanging our Navy working dress for Army greens which became standard dress from that point on. This early stage saw us in the normal round of training venues including the Army School of Military Engineering at Liverpool, the demolition ranges at Marangaroo in the Blue Mountains and the underwater training area off Clark Island in Sydney Harbour.

We also attended a week of training at the Army's Intelligence Centre located at Woodside near Adelaide. This quiet little break proved to be very interesting as we learnt a little about the history, culture and religions of Viet Nam with a detailed operational brief on enemy activity within Phuoc Thuy province. We did wonder about the value of that as we already knew we would be operating 600 miles to the north, totally separated from the Australian Army presence.

Later, after we had arrived *'in country'*, I did sometimes wonder what the Viet Cong's D445 battalion was up to at that particular point in time, far away to the south of us in Phuoc Thuy…. Nobody ever bothered to tell us who was operating in our backyard. I suspect no-one knew.

At the completion of the Woodside course, the troops returned to Sydney while our three fearless leaders remained behind and were subjected to a week of the Army's *'Code of Conduct'* course. This far from pleasant little sojourn was meant to introduce selectees to the adventures and pleasures of being a Prisoner of War of the communists in Viet Nam. It was to be a rude awakening for 3 relatively naive matelots. I was to have the dubious honour several years later and it was the most unpleasant experience of my life; something I will never forget. When I was finally released, I had a changed perspective on the human race. I presume we lowly sailors were left off the course at Woodside because the powers that be thought we had no knowledge that would have been useful to the enemy even if we were captured. The stories we were later told made us feel lucky that we were not considered worthy.

Our work-up continued with a specialised weapons training course which much to our surprise was conducted by the Navy's own weapons specialists at the Naval Air Station at HMAS Albatross. The seven of us learnt how to field strip and reassemble, with our eyes closed, every small arms weapon in the Australian Military inventory. We all became excellent shots with everything from the M60 machine gun through to the M79 40mm Grenade Launcher and down to the 9mm Browning pistol. On the range with the M60, we would fire at targets until the barrels became red hot. During one morning session with our 9mm handguns, the seven of us fired well in excess of a thousand rounds. We all felt we could have taken on Wyatt Earp and his crew at the 'OK Corral' and have won easily.

As it turned out, on arrival in Vietnam we were all issued with the much heavier US issue Colt M1911A1 .45 calibre handgun as a personal weapon.

While we were at Albatross, we spent some time flying with the Navy's *'Helicopter Flight'* which was also working up in preparation for deployment to South Viet Nam. It was great fun to be chauffeured around at low level and it gave us some insight into what the operational flying would be like once we arrived in country. We were to eventually spend so much time in choppers that we took them for granted as most people take their family car or taxis for granted.

One interesting little sidelight to our visit to the Naval Air Station occurred the night before we were due to leave. Digger, Blue and I had spent the evening consuming a few quiet beers in the nearby town of Nowra. After being kicked out of the White Ensign Club, we headed back to base where a vote was taken and it was unanimously decided to pay a visit to the WRANS quarters - strictly off limits to all male sailors. I had driven my big red Ford V8 down from Sydney and when we were finally chased out of the Wrans' quarters by the duty *'Crushers'* (Naval police), we made our getaway in my red beast. It didn't take an Einstein to track down the owner of the only Candy Apple Red Ford V8 on base, so at 0800 the next morning I was piped to report to the gangway. I was promptly marched in to see the Regulating Lieutenant who was infamous throughout the Navy; especially for his hatred of Divers. His nickname was *'Swoops'* and he was considered an absolute pig by every sailor who had the misfortune to come in contact with him. When he finally rounded up the three of us, he rubbed his hands with glee as he told us we were going to be charged with breaking every rule in the book, and if he had his way we would all serve a good long spell in 'cells'. He then ordered us to be locked up awaiting Commander's Defaulters set for later in the day.

Meanwhile Jake got wind that his boys were in jail and had a little chat with the Base Commander. We later discovered the meat of the conversation was basically that the team was due in Canungra within two days to start our Jungle Training/Battle Efficiency course and half his team in cells was not Jake's preferred option. As we were in preparation for deployment to a war zone, official charges were definitely not on his agenda. The Commander readily agreed after Jake told him that he would not hesitate to get on the telephone to his boss, the Fleet Commander, if further explanation was required. The Admiral would not have been overly amused to see half his operational Diving team locked up over such a petty matter. When Swoops was ordered to drop all charges and release us, he almost had a fit. He had us marched into his office and with no witnesses present, started to froth at the mouth as he swore that one day he would have his revenge on us all. He spat and dribbled and prattled on for ten minutes about how his memory was long and one day we would meet again. Standing at attention listening to the ravings of this lunatic, it was difficult to suppress our grins. This made him spit and froth even more until he screamed at us to get off his base and never come back.

Going to war certainly had some advantages although Jake made it very clear that he didn't want to have to bail us out again. Narra just had a quiet chuckle to himself and muttered to us on the side, *"You bunch of dickheads"*.

We knew we were in for a tough time at Canungra. It was talked about far and wide as a particularly hard and demanding 3 weeks. Almost all personnel posted to Viet Nam had to complete the Battle Efficiency (BE) course at the Jungle Training Centre (JTC) as it was then known.

We had heard a rumour that the US Military had sent some of its Special Forces instructors to do the course with a view to sending some of their troops over for training, but they had gone home saying it was too tough.

Situated in the middle of the hilliest country in Queensland, it was ideally suited for its purpose. It had near vertical mountainsides, tropical jungle, rivers, creeks, lots of mosquitoes and snakes and some very professional instructors. I think to a man they had all served at least one or two tours in Vietnam. It was very comforting to know that these boys were not teaching just from a text book. They had been there and survived, and when they spoke, we listened.

From memory there were about 90 on our course. Our day began with us getting roused out of our tents just before sunrise and it was straight into a nice little morning run in typical Army fashion - neatly fallen in, keeping in step and wearing ruddy big clod-hopping Army boots. This was followed by a session on the muscle toughening course. After a quick shower and what was the Army's excuse for breakfast, it was straight into the day's sadistic training program. Numerous classes were held in the field so that we could go from the theory straight to the practical. Regular infantry troops – all Vets - would give demonstrations prior to us practising the real thing.

In Canungra they didn't play games. While we were practising the skills of *'Fire and Movement'*, they were actually firing live ammunition just over our heads from an old water cooled .303 Vickers machine gun. They told us it was to encourage us to keep our heads down. We didn't need any reminding after that.

We spent a lot of time patrolling and learning how to stay alive army style, day and night. On the occasional rare night that we were in the main camp, evening lectures were the norm with updated briefings direct from the war zone - VC tactics, map reading and a hundred other things that were designed to help keep us alive.

When we finally arrived in Viet Nam we were quite shocked to find how ignorant our Americans allies were about the country and the people they were sent to fight. We were certainly well prepared and it was a credit to the professionalism of both the Australian Navy and Army. Some US troops arrived in Viet Nam not even knowing where the hell to find the country on a map of the world.

We were split into 9-man sections with Tom McNab and I being put together. Each section consisted of two men on *'point'* carrying US M16s which had the capability of being easily flipped into full automatic mode (*850 rounds per minute*), a handy function if you were the first to make contact with the enemy. One man carried the M60 machine gun with the remainder of the section carrying 7.62mm Self Loading Rifles (SLRs). As Tom and I were the fittest, we seemed to gravitate to sharing the *'Gun'*, day about. As it weighed about 30 pounds/13.6kgs with a 100-round belt of ammunition, most of the Pongos (soldiers) shied away from it. After a full day's humping an M60 along with the rest of your kit, you came to appreciate a break as point man carrying the very light M16 (8.8lbs/4kgs loaded with 20 round magazine), even though the life expectancy of this forward position was not great. Interestingly enough, the M16 was quite new to the Australian Army at that time and it turned out that our intensive weapons training with the Navy had us one jump ahead of the Pongos and the instructors actually asked us to run the M16 training sessions for our sections once they realised our proficiency with the weapon.

After two weeks of hell we were all given a day's leave in Surfer's Paradise. It was a major relief to see that civilisation still existed.

The final week focused on applying our training to all-night ambushes and combined manoeuvres. After many sleepless nights in the bush, the grand finale for the course was a forced march of several hours back to camp via *'Heart-break hill'*. On arrival at the camp we were put through the obstacle course for the last time. It was rumoured that one of the water pits on this course was regularly used by the Sergeants Mess as their latrine.

John Gilchrist best described the various phases of Canungra training in an article he later wrote for 'Navy News': -

"Weapons Handling -

This consists of learning the methods by which a soldier carries, strips, cleans, fires, cleans again and sleeps with the firearm which he has been issued with.

Contact and Ambush Drill (Fire and Movement) -

What to do if one is confronted by the enemy. Contrary to general belief, one does not turn and run or shout some battle cry and charge headlong into the affray. Instead the well trained soldier carries out a precise drill designed to put him and his companions into the best tactical position from which he can engage and ultimately defeat the enemy. The drill consists of everyone shouting out what he thinks has happened, running in various directions and diving headlong into the ground which can be either soft bog grass, short hard grass, small sharp stones and gravel, large blunt rocks, a variety of tropical vegetation or mud and stagnant water.

Harbour Drills -

Any similarity between the harbour which sailors have grown accustomed to entering from time to time and the JTC harbour are purely coincidental. After having marched, doubled or stalked us through miles of South East Queensland, the Platoon Commander decided that the time for relaxation had arrived. He gave a sign akin to a flight deck officer telling a Chopper pilot to start his rotor turning. The platoon of some 30 men, breathed a sigh of relief and commenced a strange ritual which finally resulted in everyone laying down in a large circle facing out, weapon at the ready waiting for the enemy to arrive. The skill required for a Platoon Commander to select a suitable site for a harbour is immense. He must select an area some 50 yards in diameter, the terrain such that Platoon headquarters, the centre of the circle, must be on level ground, well grassed and preferably under a shady tree. The remainder of the circle around the circumference of which he places his platoon in pairs must be sloping so that when the soldier faces out, his head must be lower than his feet. The ground must be covered with small stones, large boulders or ant hills, and in the obvious course of streams of rain water. It is in this harbour that troops will remain for a short period or overnight. Should the stay be overnight, the soldiers' comfort is greatly improved as he is allowed to erect his HOOCHIE, which is a six-foot square of moth eaten waterproof material which he strings between two trees about two feet from the ground. Beneath this he prepares his bed, consisting of another waterproof sheet on top of which is placed a sleeping bag, best described as two ultra-thin blankets covered by two almost sheer sheets of silk. All this clips together, blankets on the inside and into which the soldier crawls. Considering the amount of sleep the soldier in the field receives, I sometimes considered this to be over-complicated.

Ambushing -

This is the art of being strategically placed on the ground so as to trap an unsuspecting enemy. Once again the skill required and the thought that goes into the selection of the site is paramount. In practice, what happens is that a section is positioned on the ground, invariably at night, facing a track or road - weapons at the ready, and there you wait. You are not allowed to move, flinch, scratch, pass wind, cough or talk. This may sound easy. However, consider the case of two sailors together in a mass of bushes for camouflage, the presence of flies, ants and a variety of bush animals, having marched halfway across Queensland, not had a decent meal for days to complicate matters further, not having been allowed the use of a latrine for hours. Eventually, when you least expect it, the enemy arrives. All Hell breaks loose; blank ammunition is expended in profusion all around you. You blink, allow yourself the luxury of a cough, a scratch and all the normal body functions you have been deprived of and then discover that you have forgotten to load your weapon, the enemy by now had disappeared and you had not fired a round.

Miscellaneous -

Under this heading we were taught such subjects as the Confidence course, best described as a dozen or so objects such as pools of stagnant water into which you jump, barbed wire to crawl under, mud, tunnels of wind and water to negotiate, slippery logs to walk across and a variety of obstacles crossed by ropes.

Muscle Toughening -

Designed to exercise those few muscles which the remainder of the course has not tortured.

Obstacle Course -

This is the conventional course we have all either experienced or known about.

We spent nine days of the course living in the bush. On these days one carried on his back all he could eat, wear, sleep in, on and under, drink etc.

The average day's food (24 hours) was: -

Breakfast: cup of instant coffee; one or two cereal blocks. These are best described as extremely tough.

Lunch: Cup of instant tea or coffee; a packet of biscuits (these are pre-broken and are completely devoid of taste and possess an odour akin to cardboard); a small tin of Kraft cheese.

Dinner: THIS IS THE MEAL OF THE DAY!

Cup of instant tea or coffee; a selection of the following: -

Vienna Sausages - like valve rubber.

Luncheon meat.

Tuna in oil - use your imagination.

Sausages and veges - two 2 inch sausages, the remainder carrots.

Corned Beef ration - standard fare since World War I.

Added to this there were such things as curry powder, soup powder, instant rice (takes 10 minutes to cook), condensed milk, sugar, a 10 cent chocolate block, a packet of fruit drops (recently included for National Servicemen) and last but not least, six sheets of 4x4, polished one side, matte the other.

    In conclusion, I feel that the main points to be learned from this course were: -

    1. Do not join the Army.

    2. If you do, do not become a foot soldier.

    3. If you are thrown into battle, quickly become Platoon Commander, otherwise you will find survival difficult.

4. All the mountains in Australia are in the south-east of Queensland."

When we finally departed Canungra after three very long weeks, I had decided beyond any doubt that I had made the right decision when I had joined the Navy. Our training as CDs was much harder but at least we were able to stay reasonably clean and free of ticks.

This completed the final phase of our pre-deployment training prior to pre-embarkation leave. As we sat in the Brisbane airport waiting to return to Sydney, Jake made the dreaded announcement as to which one of us would not be deploying with the 8th Team. Digger was most definitely going because he had trained with the previous team and Tom was a Leading Hand, outranking both myself and Blue. Much to my relief, I was going.... It was to be Tom who remained behind as standby. We all knew how disappointed he must have felt however we were going and that was uppermost in our thoughts. It was to be a bitter disappointment for Tom as we were destined to be the last Clearance Diving team to be sent to Viet Nam.

While at Brisbane airport awaiting our flight to Sydney, Jake spotted the then Minister for the Navy, James Killen. Without the slightest hesitation Jake walked over and introduced *'his team'* to the Minister. We were to see more of the Honourable Jim after that as he was to visit us in our humble abode in Viet Nam on Christmas Eve 1970. After the war Sir Jim graciously became, and remained until his death, the Patron of the Clearance Diving Association.

With the work-up over we all proceeded on 5 days' pre-embarkation leave. Everyone went home with the exception of Digger. He came home with me to Adelaide.

On our last night in Sydney before starting leave, there was a general farewell to the team at one of the local pubs in Cremorne with most of the Diving school showing up to wish us a safe tour. We all had a little too much to drink and once again I had my big red V8 with me. On my way home I was obviously a little heavy on the foot and after crossing the Sydney Harbour bridge heading south, I was pulled over by a Policeman in a Morris Mini who said he had clocked me at 80 miles per hour (130kms/hr) down the Cahill expressway and over the harbour bridge. He said it had taken him the length of the expressway and bridge to catch me. I thought I was in a bit of strife for a while until we told him we had just attended a final farewell prior to leaving for Viet Nam. Much to my relief he immediately backed off and said, *"Piss off home via the shortest route at the speed limit and get to bed — and best of luck in Vietnam".*

At home in South Australia, Digger and I made the most of our leave. We visited my relatives in the country with the highlight, in Digger's opinion, being a visit to a relation's winery called Bleasdale. We proceeded to taste every wine they produced, and in his less than sober state Digger complimented my uncle by saying it was the best *'brewery'* he had ever been to and the best *'plonk'* he had tasted.

We finally departed Sydney's Mascot Airport late in the evening of the 14th October 1970 aboard a chartered Qantas 707. Destination: Saigon - in friendlier times known as the *'Pearl of the Orient'*.

Our departure was delayed by three or four hours due to some radio problems aboard the aircraft so the airport bar remained open and the farewell gradually took on a party atmosphere. Once airborne our friendly Qantas crew (all male) opened the in-flight bar for their 120 or so Military passengers. The stewards found to their surprise that the majority of their passengers were more interested in sleeping than drinking. Even though it was after midnight, the Naval contingent of six Clearance Divers and one Chief Petty Officer Writer were the exception. *('Googer' Gent was returning with us on our flight to Saigon from his R&R leave in Sydney. Googer was responsible for looking after both the Diving Team's and Helo Flight's pay and allowances in Vietnam).*

As Navy Divers we felt compelled to uphold the best traditions of the *'Senior Service'* however we weren't quite up to the large volume of free beer on offer. By the time the aircraft landed in Darwin to refuel we were beginning to think that sleep may have been our better option. The early morning Darwin to

Singapore stage of the flight passed far too quickly for seven very tired and very hung-over sailors.

During the Viet Nam War era the Singapore Government allowed Australian military flights a brief stopover at their airport whilst en-route to South Viet Nam but they insisted on keeping the visits as inconspicuous as possible because of the ever increasing public opposition to the War. To remain relatively unnoticed, we had been ordered to carry a civilian shirt with us onboard the aircraft and these had to be donned prior to disembarking for breakfast in Singapore. It was quite absurd to think that 120 fit young men with identical short haircuts arriving on a Qantas flight dressed in regular Army boots, identical khaki trousers and a variety of colourful flowery shirts would fool anyone. We were instructed not to leave the confines of the airport and to ensure we complied, Military Police were stationed at strategic exit and entry points.

Jake obviously thought this ruling did not apply to Naval Officers as he decided to make a surprise visit to one of his old flames in Singapore and this presented an opportunity not to be missed. Unfortunately for Jake, within minutes of his going 'AWOL', we were advised over the airport's public address system that our planned two-hour breakfast and fuel stopover had been shortened to one and a half hours.

While we sat in the aircraft watching the ground staff preparing to remove the stairs, John Gilchrist was frantically trying to invent a plausible excuse as to why only five of us instead of six would be arriving in Saigon. At the last possible moment, we saw the stocky figure of Jake sprint from the airport terminal at a speed to behold. Another 30 seconds and it would have been too late. We could hear John mumbling and muttering obscenities to himself. He didn't expect that sort of stress so early in the trip. We hadn't even arrived in the war zone and his Commanding Officer was already giving him grey hair.

We were met at Saigon's Tan Son Nhat Airport by the Senior Australian Naval Officer in Vietnam, the always smiling Commander Rang Hall. CPOCD John Dollar, the Chief of the diving team we were to relieve, had flown down from their home base in Da Nang to organise our first few days *'in-country'* and arrange our subsequent movement north.

After being welcomed by the US Navy's Saigon based EOD team at their villa in Cholon (the old Chinese quarter of Saigon), we were completely kitted out with US gear, including Cammies and the famous and much sought after *'K-Bar'* knife. We were then invited to participate in the traditional EOD welcoming ceremony which consisted of sculling a very large boot-shaped glass filled to overflowing with Budweiser beer. The earlier stress of Singapore had obviously taken its toll on the Chief as he alone failed to make the grade. He was we presumed distracted by the thought of *'what if'* the Boss had missed the flight.

Narra was conned into an American EOD ritual new to us all. After we had consumed several beers, one of the US Chiefs asked Narra if he thought he was *'pretty strong'* and if he had heard of *'the 3-man lift'*. Naturally Phil hadn't, but when he confirmed in the positive regarding his strength, they knew they had him hook, line and sinker. The US Chief said one of his fellows could lift three men with one hand. Narra naturally replied *"bullshit"* and numerous beers were bet on the outcome. To allow the Yank EOD strongman to perform the lift, Narra was told to lie on the floor with arms and legs spread. Two Americans were to lie on either side of him with his arms under them and their legs extended over the top of his. The process was explained to Narra that he was to hold them very tight so that the US superman could lift Narra by his belt with one hand, and Narra would at the same time lift the other two. After this detailed explanation, Narra was all ready to go, albeit a little suspicious. It hadn't yet occurred to him that in this position he was in effect pinned to the ground by the two big blokes on either side of him. After much ado, with the Yank standing astride Narra, deep breathing while giving instructions for him to grip the two accomplices very tightly, the lifter as quick as a flash undid Narra's belt, unzipped his fly and pulled down his trousers. The rest of the Americans, waiting in the wings and ready with copious quantities of iced water, proceeded to pour gallons of very cold water and ice over Narra's bare crotch. It gave him such a shock that he actually lifted the two other blokes clear of the ground as he tried to struggle clear. When we had all finally stopped laughing, the Yanks announced that he was in fact *'pretty damn strong'*, as he had managed to lift two 200 pounders off the ground. He was considered a worthy member of the EOD community.

Our American counterparts decided that time was not to be wasted sleeping and we should visit the hot spots of downtown Saigon beginning with that very infamous street of bars, *'Tu Do'* Street. Larry Digney, about 19 years of age and on his first trip beyond Australia's borders, did his utmost to buy every bar-girl in Tu Do Street a *'Saigon Tea'* (expensive coloured water).

The following morning, John Dollar informed us that Typhoon *'Louise'* was intensifying over the central coast near Da Nang and we would have to remain in Saigon until it had blown over. This unexpected bonus enabled Larry to revisit Tu Do street that evening and catch up with the bar-girls he had missed the previous evening and gave him the opportunity to buy all their sisters, mothers, daughters and cousins numerous drinks as well. It was an expensive introduction to Asia for Larry but I'm sure he thought it a very enjoyable lesson. We certainly had a lot of laughs watching him.

I managed to lose my beret in some dark and seedy bar. Most probably souvenired by a Yank. The remainder of us old *'Asia hands'* kept our hands in our pockets and the bar-girls noting this, gave us our introduction to the first verse of the infamous ditty sung by all Saigon bar-girls when referring to Australians (Uc Dai Loi): -

> "Uc Dai Loi, cheap Charlie,
> He no buy me Saigon tea,
> Saigon tea cost many many Pi,
> Uc Dai Loi, he cheap Charlie.

For posterity; the rest of the verses are:
> Uc Dai Loi, cheap Charlie,
> He no give me MPC,

MPC costs many many Pi,
Uc Dai Loi he Cheap Charlie.

Uc Dai Loi, cheap Charlie
He no go to bed with me,
Bed with me costs many many Pi
Uc Dai Loi him Cheap Charlie.

Uc Dai Loi, cheap Charlie
Make me give him one for free,
Mama-San go crook at me,
Uc Dai Loi, he Cheap Charlie.

Uc Dai Loi, cheap Charlie,
He give baby-san to me,
Baby-san costs many many Pi
Uc Dai Loi, he Cheap Charlie.

Uc Dai Loi, cheap Charlie
He go home across the sea,
He leave baby-san with me,
Uc Dai Loi he Cheap Charlie."

Charlie: pronounced char-lee.

Cheap Charlie: a 'round-eye' who was stingy or unwilling to spend money on the bar-girls.

Uc-Dai-Loi: Vietnamese term used for Australian military (pronounced *'ook die loy'*). *Uc* means Australia.

Saigon Tea: served to bar girls as whisky and coke at inflated prices when a 'round eye' was paying. It was never alcoholic and was usually just cold tea.

MPC: Military Payment Certificates which replaced American dollars. It was an American attempt to get US currency out of the system. MPC was of no use to the

NVA or VC and could be changed by the authorities regularly to maintain currency control. All Allied troops had to use it.

Pi: Piastre – the major unit of currency of French Indochina and South Vietnam. MPC was equivalent to about 1,000 Piastre (or more) on the black market. The official Vietnamese currency was, and still is the Dong (VND).

Mamasan: female bar/brothel owner.

Baby San: Baby.

(the ditty is sung to the tune of Nick, Nack, Paddywack, Give the Dog a Bone.)

After our hectic but enjoyable few days in Saigon, we finally boarded a US Air Force C-130 Hercules and headed north to a waiting reception from the team we were to relieve. With a welcoming barbecue of spare ribs and steak complete with endless quantities of icy cold Victoria Bitter beer, we were all beginning to assume that our tour of duty was going to be somewhat of an extended round of piss-ups.

This early complacency was soon shattered rather dramatically. Within three days of our arrival in Da Nang the new team experienced its baptism of fire.

As part of the hand-over procedure, two members of the incoming team accompanied two members of the old team on a *'routine'* sensor implant mission assisting a US Jungle Surveillance Group. With an ARVN unit as support, the group were to conduct the operation to the south of Da Nang, on Cam Thanh Island. A Viet Cong bunker system was soon discovered and as expected, it had been booby-trapped. A member of the Surveillance Group, keen to find a few souvenirs, triggered a booby-trapped 105mm howitzer round and sustained massive injuries to both legs. After the detonation, the Viet Cong, who had been lying in wait, initiated their ambush and the group came under heavy small arms fire. True to form, a number of the ARVN support group dropped their weapons and departed the area rather hurriedly. During the ensuing fire-fight, LSCD John

'Mumbles' Aldenhoven and ABCD *'Blue'* Furner crossed open ground to recover the wounded US Adviser and carry him to relative safety, recovering several of the dropped weapons in the process. The first 'Dust-off' *(Medical Evacuation)* chopper attempt failed as a result of the heavy VC ground fire, but after a number of strafing passes by US Army Cobra helicopter gunships, the second Medivac attempt succeeded.

Unfortunately, the Adviser died whilst in transit to the nearest Military hospital. He had been within one week of completing his tour and going home to the States. The remainder of the team was extracted by chopper to Da Nang and John Aldenhoven was subsequently awarded the British/Australian Distinguished Service Medal (DSM). His Citation stated that he had *"displayed personal courage of the highest order"*. I clearly recall (Chief) John Dollar saying that he was only able to recommend one award for bravery. As Mumbles was going home and Blue had a full tour left in which to earn an award, Mumbles got the recommend. Because of the pathetic inconsistencies of the bureaucratic British modelled Australian awards 'quota' system, Blue received absolutely no recognition then or since for the equal part he played in that same action.

Over the next few days, events continued to remind us that we were now smack in the middle of a war zone. On the 24th October 1970, a radio call was received from US Harbour Security informing us that a large ammunition barge, having broken adrift during Typhoon Kate and run aground on a sand bar in Da Nang harbour, appeared to have been sabotaged. Security personnel reported seeing a small but intense fire burning on the upper deck, so three members from the *'new'* team were immediately dispatched to investigate. The old team having said they were *'too short'* (going home) to take any more risks, the task fell to the new crew. I was driving the vehicle and took several wrong turns in trying to locate the Harbour Security wharf. None of us had been there before. This turn of events fortunately delayed us by several minutes. As we were boarding the waiting security skimmer boat to proceed to the barge, the barge's cargo detonated in a massive blast that shook the whole of Da Nang.

While watching the mushroom shaped cloud forming from the fireball, I remain convinced to this day that I saw a body soaring skywards amongst the flying debris. We were later advised that two male VC suspects from the nearby village had disappeared without trace.

Had any of us been familiar with the most direct route to the wharf area, or had one of the old team accompanied us to show us the way, CDT3 would without a doubt have lost at least three of its members that day.

Approximately half of the 154 tonnes of mortars, rockets and projectiles on board the barge had detonated and the remaining 70 odd tonnes were *'throw-outs'*. We found one intact pallet of 105mm howitzer rounds in a village, several hundred metres away from the blast.

The team had *'ARRIVED'*.

The process of recovering and disposing of this ordnance kept us busy during our quiet days for the next few months.

Several days after the barge episode, John Gilchrist flew south to Saigon. That night the VC saturated the area in which he was staying with 127mm and 140mm rockets. Within a week of surviving the rocket barrage, John returned south again aboard a US Marine Corps DC3 to pick up, among other things, three pallets of Australian beer from Vung Tau. On their return, the aircraft suffered serious mechanical problems and diverted to Saigon. John was asked if he wished to parachute from the aircraft or accept the risk of a crash landing. He chose to stay with the aircraft which then limped to a belly landing at Tan Son Nhat Airport. Fortunately, John and the crew walked away unhurt, and the beer was undamaged.

When the news reached Da Nang that the Chief's plane had crashed, the three AB's asked in shock horror, *"What about the beer?"* When John finally arrived back in Da Nang, he was mumbling out loud about whether or not he should stay in bed for the remainder of our tour.

The US Marine EOD detachment at Da Nang airfield very kindly arranged a Marine DC3 on an *'as required'* basis to re-supply us with Aussie beer from Vung Tau, about 1,000 kms to the south. The only condition to this arrangement was that we sold them one pallet of beer from each trip at our cost price. To the best of my recollection, there were about 84 cartons of beer to the pallet and the beer only cost us 11c per can.

A lot of favours could be arranged with promises of *'Uc Dai Loi'* beer. Unfortunately, we had to arrange our own resupply of beer as the Australian Army system was not the slightest bit concerned about 6 Navy divers in faraway Da Nang. Fortunately, we were used to looking after ourselves.

A week or so after we arrived, I had what is officially known as an *'accidental discharge'*. I was in our workshop cleaning my .45 when Jake wandered out from his office, saw what I was doing, pulled out his .45 and asked if I would clean it as well. It was standard procedure to clear all weapons on entering the hooch and I made the mistake of assuming Jake had done so. I removed the magazine and got the shock of my life when it discharged a round into the workbench. The bullet struck a steel punch, blowing it in half, and then buried itself in the wall. Fortunately, training and habit had me pointing the weapon away in a safe direction as I began the stripping procedure. The noise was deafening and it was pretty to watch how quickly everyone responded to the sound of gunfire within the hooch. Digger mounted the spent cartridge behind the bar with the inscription *'Tony's first shot fired in anger'*.

The old team had all departed for home after a fortnight and the realisation that we new boys were on our own began to sink in. Routines were quickly established. While two members of the team remained on duty for 24 hour stretches, another two were on stand-by and the remaining two on stand down.

It is interesting to note for posterity that two Able Seamen (the most junior rank in the team) were regularly on duty together, and if a call for EOD assistance was received, the two AB's responded on their own and without supervision. This would not and could not happen in a peace-time Navy, and it speaks volumes for the responsibility, maturity and professionalism instilled into the team during its pre-deployment training and the very high standard of Clearance Diving training in the 60's. It also shows how peacetime regulations can and need to be bent, and in many cases ignored through necessity in time of war. Had we strictly adhered to Navy regulations, it would have been impossible to fulfil the role we had been sent to perform.

South Viet Nam was divided into four Military Regions which were also known as 'Corps'. We were to spend our entire tour based in I Corps. This was very fortunate from an experience point of view as Vung Tau in III Corps, where previous teams had been based, had become relatively pacified because of the large Australian Army presence. I Corps was still regarded as 'Charlie country'.

The northern limit of our area of responsibility was the DMZ (*de-militarised zone*) and our range of operations included normal hull searches in Da Nang Harbour as required and an ever increasing number of surface EOD and other tasks throughout the length and breadth of I Corps.

Our *'hooch'* was located within Camp Tien Sha, a US Naval Support Facility located on Da Nang's Tourane peninsular. The hooch consisted of a workshop/lounge room complete with a 16mm movie projector and pool table, a fully self-contained kitchen, garage, outdoor barbecue and arguably the finest bar in South Viet Nam. The team's transportation comprised two Jeeps, a Dodge Pickup truck, a Dodge four-wheel drive Power Wagon, a Kaiser Jeep truck and a 16-foot skimmer boat equipped with the hottest 85 horsepower outboard motor in Da Nang.

We had a full time Mama San who was a Vietnamese lady of indistinguishable age with a very limited comprehension of the English language. She attended to our personal laundry, made the beds and maintained an impression of neatness about the place. Occasionally she was encouraged to cook a Vietnamese meal which always meant liberal lashings of the local fermented fish sauce, *'Nuoc Mam'* - which was very tasty, but unfortunately smelt exactly like rotten fish. (*Nuoc Mam is an amber-coloured liquid extracted from the fermentation of fish with water and sea salt. It is a staple ingredient in numerous cuisines throughout Southeast Asia and features heavily in all Vietnamese cooking. In addition to being added to dishes during and after the cooking process, Nuoc Mam is also used as a base for a dipping condiment that is prepared in many different ways. Vietnamese fish sauce is usually used in moderation because of its very intense flavour).*

The team had two able assistants, a mongrel affectionately known as *'Dog'*, and *'Fred'*, a female Rhesus monkey. Dog closely resembled a Queensland Blue Heeler cattle dog in both appearance and temperament and was an excellent watch-dog. With the exception of our Mama San, he would not allow an unescorted Vietnamese national within a 100 metre radius of our Hooch. I think he was aware that dog meat (*'Cho'*), was a favourite dish of the Vietnamese and as a consequence he hated them all.

Fred had to be watched constantly as she had an amazing appetite. On more than one occasion she had snatched a lighted cigarette from an unsuspecting visitor, flicked off the burning ash and eaten the entire cigarette in the blink of an eye. She also had a bad habit of scrounging through the empty beer cans every morning and after drinking the dregs of several cans would become quite aggressive in her half inebriated state, particularly towards poor old Dog. Her favourite party trick was to sneak up behind Dog, give his family jewels a quick tug and then squealing with delight, head for the top of the nearest banana tree with Dog barking in hot pursuit. Needless to say, Dog was not particularly fond of Fred.

Our team operated totally independent of Australian support. We wore US *'Cammies'*, carried US weapons, lived in a US compound, drove US vehicles, ate US food and were officially known as EODMUPAC Team 35. We answered directly to a Captain M.A. Horn USN.

The only other Australians in I Corps were the Australian Army Training Team (AATTV) and we saw little of them. We mostly associated with other EOD units and US Special Forces including Navy Seals and Underwater Demolition Teams (UDT). Most US Forces assumed that we were in fact the Australian equivalent of their SEAL Teams. We had a lot to do with these fellows and it is interesting to recall their motto: -

> *"Yea, though I walk through the*
> *Valley of the Shadow of Death,*
> *I fear no evil, for I am*
> *the meanest mutha-fucker in the Valley."*

Being the only fully operational Navy EOD team in I Corps, we had a large area of responsibility. The Air force and Marine teams looked after the Da Nang airfield and the Army team was responsible for Da Nang City. We virtually had the rest of I Corp.

A South Vietnamese Navy team under the guidance of four US Navy EOD Advisers was responsible for Cua Viet, located near the DMZ. However, this team was relatively ineffective due to its low level of competence and difficulty in retaining personnel. Vietnamese team members would disappear without trace for weeks at a time without explanation and reappear when it suited them. We would not have been surprised if they were part-time VC. When we first arrived they were using our hooch as a transit centre. After Narra had some money disappear, Jake changed the rules and they stayed elsewhere.

The US Advisors rotated in pairs between Cua Viet and Da Nang. Most of their off time was spent at our hooch. One of these Advisors, WO Gerry Dunn was quite an odd personality. He would spend his spare time and he seemed to have a lot of it, reading paperback Westerns with a cigarette in one hand, alternating between sips of hot coffee and cold beer, and carry on a conversation, all without ever lifting his eyes from his yippee *(cowboy)* book.

Jake became a particularly close friend of the Boss of the Marine EOD team and we consequently spent some quiet times socialising at their hooch. I have crystal clear memories of these two connoisseurs standing at the bar smoking huge American cigars and drinking generous helpings of Chivas Regal whiskey. Another frequent visitor to their mess was a US Marine Catholic Padre who had a very puzzling approach to what was normally expected of a *'man of the cloth'*. His steady stream of foul language was disconcerting to say the least and I believe even our Instructor Sergeants from Canungra would have been embarrassed by this man's constant stream of four-letter words. The war certainly affected different people in different ways.

Team members took every opportunity to gain additional experience by working with other EOD units. We all rotated through Cua Viet, a very busy place indeed, being the last friendly outpost on our side of the DMZ. *'Birdcage'* mines were a constant threat in the Cua Viet River with both civilian and military craft being sunk regularly with considerable loss of life. During December 1970, five Birdcage mines were recovered and 22 NVA/VC Sapper swimmers were killed in one operation. Sleep was always hard to come by at night because of the constant outgoing 81mm mortar rounds.

The trip north to Cua Viet was particularly interesting as the road passed through the ancient Vietnamese capital of Hue. During the Communist's *'Tet'* (Lunar New Year) offensive of February 1968, Hue, located on the Perfume River and surrounded by an ancient citadel, was overrun and held by North Vietnamese troops and local VC for 26 days before being recaptured by US Forces. It has been recorded by the Americans that during this period approximately 5,800 civilians, including a multinational medical team, were executed in reprisals by the Communist troops.

Further north, beyond Hue and Quang Tri, the road to Cua Viet became a very rough bush track meandering through small villages, rice paddies and finally sand dunes. This was a journey which we would undertake only during daylight hours due to the constant threat of ambush. During one trip, Jake was actually fired upon by South Vietnamese troops in broad daylight. Choppers were always our preferred means of transport.

Other detachments included Phil and Larry spending time with the US Air Force EOD team at Da Nang airfield, Speed with our friends at Marine EOD and Larry, Blue and I on separate occasions with the US Navy EOD team in Cam Ranh Bay. This superb harbour proved to be quite a different operation from Da Nang. During the day the team played beach volleyball followed by an afternoon of diving for lobster which were then barbecued fresh that evening for dinner. At night we conducted boat patrols during the curfew hours to try and catch small boats running VC and weapons across the Bay. Heavily armed and using Starlight scopes, we ambushed angry little people dressed in black pyjamas. On one of those night ambushes I was to discover first hand and up close that not all VC were male adults. I am haunted to this day by what happened that night.

As the sun was rising over the horizon, it was normal routine to pull into one of the team's favourite bars on the beach for breakfast and a few beers before heading back to base for a much needed sleep.

A vivid memory of their hooch was the massive python snake they kept as a pet. It lived in their darkened pantry and was fed about once a month. The Yank sailors would just throw a live duck into the pantry and close the door.

Cam Ranh Bay was also home to a US Navy top secret Dolphin training program where EOD divers taught Dolphins to attack underwater swimmers and recover ordnance from the seabed.

Another interesting deployment for me was with the 51st ARVN Regiment in Quang Nam Province, north west of Da Nang. This particular unit had an Australian Army Training Team Adviser, WO2 Vic Pennington, who at that time was based in an old triangular shaped French designed fort located on the high ground above the village of Dai Loc. Several large units of NVA regulars were dug in on the nearby ridge-line and one night after a patrol, I recall Vic and I relaxing with beer in hand on top of the fort watching a firefight with the red and green tracer rounds cris-crossing the rice paddies to our front.

Only days prior to my arrival in Dai Loc, an American Adviser to the 51st had stopped his jeep on the outskirts of the village after a group of children had flagged him down to scrounge cigarettes and candy. While he was digging through his backpack, one of the children threw a hand grenade into the back of the vehicle, killing him and his South Vietnamese counterpart instantly. The burnt out wreck of his vehicle served as a grim reminder that not all VC wore black pyjamas and carried AK47's.

This part of I Corps was referred to by the Advisers, rather sarcastically, as *'Marlboro country'*.

Most of our calls for diving assistance came between the hours of midnight and 3 am, usually after a sentry had reported swimmers or intruders at the nearby Deep-Water ammunition piers. We had to respond immediately to all calls, and many turned out to be false alarms. False alarm or not, it is an indescribably eerie and lonely feeling to be searching a ship in the middle of the night with the knowledge that it contains around 9,000 tonnes of high explosives and that a fanatically dedicated saboteur has recently been sighted onboard.

We all participated in the R&R program and with the exception of Jake, we all returned to Sydney for our short break. A memorable call occurred on my first night back from R&R. It was a black moonless night and a local watch-tower sentry had reported seeing silhouettes and movement prior to witnessing explosions on a nearby beach. Creeping warily along the beach, long after the event in almost complete darkness, Jake and I could not understand the constant squelching feeling underfoot. Having found nothing, we returned to our vehicle, switched on the lights and examined our boots to discover the reason for the mushy texture of the beach sand. The nearby village used that particular section of the beach as their latrine and relied on the incoming tide to dispose of it. We had unfortunately arrived before the tide had done its work. The cause of the explosions remained a mystery. Most probably a spaced out soldier high on dope playing games with hand grenades.

Our home became the most famous EOD hooch in South Viet Nam as our hospitality extended to all EOD teams from all four US services and our door was always open to US Navy UDT and SEAL teams. Large stocks of Victoria Bitter beer contributed to our reputation and an invitation to stop over with the Aussie Divers for a few days became much sought after.

A sign over our bar announced our extremely liberal *'Bar Hours'*: -

Saturday AM - 2359

Sunday AM - 2300

Monday to Friday was at Narra's discretion....

Occasionally when a visitor had worn out his welcome, Narra changed these hours at extremely short notice. Visiting USO tours, most of them Australians, usually managed to find their way to our hooch to free-load a few beers and a meal.

During our tour, the team was visited by many, but one of the most memorable visits was on Christmas Eve 1970 by the then Minister for the Navy, the Right Honourable Jim Killen whom we had last seen at Brisbane airport. The Minister succumbed to our generous hospitality and having failed to take advantage of the bed we had offered, left us on Christmas Day with his well known sense of humour still intact but looking somewhat the worse for wear.

Our tasks varied from dealing with booby traps through to major salvage operations. During the typhoon season in November 1970, a US Army YFU carrying 150 tonnes of 81mm and 105mm White Phosphorus shells had capsized off the coast to the north of Da Nang and was driven ashore on a remote section of beach near the village of Tan My. Four team members along with US Army Divers and a US Navy Salvage team, all under Jake's command, were immediately flown to the site aboard a CH47 Chinook helicopter to commence salvage efforts. Sadly, none of the eleven YFU crew members had survived.

Conditions were atrocious with typhoon Patsy still in full force. After numerous attempts in high surf conditions, tow lines were finally attached and passed to Naval tugs standing offshore. Repeated efforts to tow the craft to seaward were finally abandoned in favour of attempting to drag it further up the beach using bull dozers and tank retrievers. This too failed, so a ramp of sand was built by the dozers to afford easier access to the hull. With the weather abating, the hull was opened and the remaining ordnance removed, and I'm sure to this day that the wreck remains, embedded in the sands of Tan My.

I have a vivid memory of this task when after several days on site, we radioed for a re-supply of drinking water and rations. When the chopper finally arrived, it was loaded with C rations and cases of warm Budweiser beer. When we asked the crew chief, *"Where's the water?"*, he replied with a smile, *"We heard you guys needed a drink"*. Warm beer and cold C rations on a miserably wet cold day don't make for the best meal.

A friendly US Army Tank crew offered a couple of us a ride back to their base for a shower and a hot meal. Riding atop a monstrous Main Battle Tank thundering along narrow bush tracks, hanging on for life and limb while trying to dodge tree branches at every turn was quite a hair-raising experience. The tracks we followed were about half the width required for the tank to pass and as all tracks eventually led through villages, it created a problem, although this did not deter the driver. He managed to avoid most of the huts and chicken coops on his side of the 50 tonne monster, but flattened everything on his offside.

My observation to Blue was *"If we ever have to come back through these villages again Mate, we're dead"*. As Murphy's Law would have it, the track eventually petered out to a path that was too narrow, even for this would be rally driver, so we had no alternative but to turn around and head back to the beach the same way we had come in. On the return trip he managed to flatten everything he had missed on his first pass. Luckily for us, he drove at about twice the speed and no-one expected us to be foolish enough to return. Blue and I were expecting to be ambushed at every turn. By the time we arrived back at the beach, we were quite content to eat cold C rations and forget about the hot shower, even though the tanky insisted he knew another shortcut to the base. We suggested that he find it without us.

One evening a Negro gunner on another tank decided to test fire his .50 calibre machine gun. He didn't think it was necessary to tell anyone and unfortunately Jake just happened to be below and slightly in front of the weapon when this dickhead cut loose. The noise and shockwave from a .50 cal is rather severe to say the least. By the time Jake had finished with the happy shooter, he was under no illusion as to the error of his ways and where the final resting place of his weapon would be if he ever did it again. Not only did the idiot nearly burst Jake's eardrums, he put everyone unnecessarily on full alert as we assumed we were under attack.

Our eventual return to Da Nang was aboard a Chinook helicopter during a heavy morning sea fog. The pilots had to remain visual so we headed west at treetop level at about 100 knots through the swirling mist. I sat behind the pilots enjoying the low flying immensely. Eventually we came to Highway One, turned left and followed it home.

The following official *'Summary of Salvage Operations in Military Region One during the period 10 Oct. - 21 Nov. 1970'* was reported by Captain M.A. Horn, Commander US Naval Support Facility (NSF) Da Nang:

"During the period 10 Oct to 21 Nov 1970, the US NSF Da Nang was involved in several salvage operations which required extensive coordination of Army as well as Navy assets, and which demanded the dedicated and courageous efforts of many US Navy, US Army and Royal Australian Navy personnel. These salvage operation responsibilities were in addition to the normal mission requirements of the US NSF, Da Nang and were completed only through the exceptional efforts and devotion to duty of many individuals.

On 10 Oct 1970, the Vietnamese Navy MSC 116 went aground on an isolated beach just south of the mouth of the Cua Viet River. The USS DELIVER arrived on scene and commenced initial recovery efforts the same day. Two days later, upon being assigned as area support coordinator for the MSC 116 salvage operations, the Commanding Officer, US NSF, Da Nang, immediately inspected the salvage site and began making arrangements for a coordinated salvage effort using all available US and Vietnamese Army and Navy resources. Eventually a salvage force was assembled which included NSF Da Nang work forces and diving barge, USS DELIVER, USS COHOES, USS CONSERVER, and Army CH-47 and CH-54 helicopters. Two Army tank retrievers were obtained from the US Army at Dong Ha and delivered to the site. Units of Vietnamese Navy Coastal Group MID 92 also participated, and the 1st ARVN Division contributed a bulldozer, crane and security forces. Heavy surf and seas made the entire salvage operations dangerous as well as difficult. The USS DELIVER workboat had capsized outboard of the MSC 116 the first day, obstructing salvage efforts until it was removed. A unique combination of a CH-47 helicopter, a CH-54 sky crane and a tank retriever were used to move the craft from deep water to the beach. The salvage of the workboat and its return to USS DELIVER in good condition represented a monetary savings of approximately $37,000. The passage of two typhoons during the period 16-25 October, twice forced the temporary suspension of recovery efforts and eventually rendered the MSC 116 unsalvageable. However, during the period 12 Oct to 3 Nov under the direction and coordinating efforts of the Commanding Officer, US NSF, and by the untiring efforts, bravery and devotion to duty of salvage team personnel, all salvageable machinery, equipage, equipment and material were recovered from the grounded ship under the most adverse conditions.

Three other salvage operations were also conducted in the Da Nang harbour area by Commanding Officer, US NSF, Da Nang while the MSC 116 recovery effort was underway. During the passage of Typhoon JOAN on 16 Oct 1970, the Vietnamese Navy PCE 12 dragged anchor and grounded in Da Nang Harbour Commanding Officer, US NSF, as on-scene Commander, director of salvage operations and salvage support coordinator, assembled a salvage force. Using LCM-8's, pusherboats, US Army tugs, and with the USS COHOES standing by, the PCE 12 was successfully salvaged on 17 October, less than 48 hours after being reported aground.

On 25 Oct 1970, Typhoon KATE tore six US Army contract barges loose from their moorings in Da Nang Harbour, one of which, loaded with ammunition, exploded and scattered munitions throughout the inner harbour area. Using US NSF personnel, equipment and craft and assisted by US Army Support Command pusher boats, three of the remaining five barges were recovered and returned to safe moorings by 26 Oct 1970.

On 30 Oct 1970, the swollen debris filled Da Nang River, with a 14 knot current, forced the German Hospital Ship HELGOLAND aground near the mouth of the river. Commanding Officer, US

NSF boarded the stricken ship, surveyed the situation and after receiving the concurrence of HELGOLAND's Captain, assumed the responsibilities of on-scene commander of salvage operations. A water depth survey in the vicinity of HELGOLAND was completed, equipment's and material were readied and plans were made for extraction as soon as the swollen river and swift currents permitted. The timing of the extraction effort was critical; tugs had to be positioned as soon as the river current subsided to eight knots, but before the river level receded and left HELGOLAND more firmly aground. Four tugs were brought in on schedule and hooked in tandem to one tow line attached to HELGOLAND's stern. Radio was used to coordinate all evolutions and to ensure that the towing, deballasting and use of HELGOLAND's propellers properly maximised the salvage efforts. The swirling, treacherous current demanded expert seamanship to prevent HELGOLAND from being swept against the breakwater directly downstream from her position. Salvage team personnel met the challenge and their coordinated efforts pulled HELGOLAND clear, narrowly avoiding collisions on three occasions and safely anchoring HELGOLAND on 1 Nov 1970. In each of the recovery operations conducted in Da Nang Harbour, the rapid professional response, the untiring efforts of all personnel, and the close cooperation exhibited by US Navy and US Army personnel, in the face of extremely hazardous weather and sea conditions, were directly responsible for the success of these salvage efforts.

On 3 Nov 1970, as the MSC 116 salvage operation was drawing to a close, NSF personnel, returning by helicopter to Da Nang, observed an overturned YFU grounded near shore off Tan My. US Army Support Command, Da Nang confirmed that YFU-63 and its crew were missing and requested the assistance of Commanding Officer, US NSF, Da Nang. An initial investigation of YFU-63 on 4 November indicated there was no possibility that any of the eleven crew members were trapped alive in the compartments. Commander Seventh Fleet was requested to provide a salvage ship and salvage operations began on 5 November with the assistance of USS COHOES, a large fleet tug, a NSF diving barge, many salvage personnel, perimeter security forces, and much equipment, such as air compressors, pneumatic tools, cutting torches, tow wires and heavy lines. Efforts to pull YFU-63 off the beach and to right her were severely hampered by adverse weather and heavy surf conditions. Nevertheless, a helicopter, two tank retrievers and two bulldozers were added to the salvage forces and efforts to recover the craft continued until 15 November when, after Herculean efforts to re-float or par buckle YFU-63 were unsuccessful, it was necessary to cut into the hull to remove ammunition and other material and to search for bodies of crewman who might have been trapped in compartments. In spite of heavy seas constantly breaking over YFU-63 and perilous diving conditions, the salvage team recovered the ship's engineering log, quartermaster's notebook and other documents but discovered no bodies. On 21 Nov 1970, with a tropical storm imminent, Commanding Officer, US NSF, Da Nang determined further salvage efforts were no longer feasible and terminated the operation.

Throughout the period of 10 Oct to 21 Nov 1970, unusually severe weather conditions posed a constant threat to all salvage operation personnel. What would, even under the best of conditions, be difficult became extremely hazardous and complicated by high winds and seas, swift currents heavy surf and near-constant rain. Under these conditions exceptional performance and acts of personal courage were commonplace. These individual efforts and the close coordination of air, sea and land units from different commands and countries made it possible to save millions of dollars of assets without loss of life or injury to any salvage team personnel. The professionalism, self-sacrifice, initiative and devotion to duty exhibited under these hazardous conditions were in keeping with the highest traditions of the United States Naval Service".

This report is particularly interesting to read because it gives an insight into the way official military reports are written, i.e. - to make the Commanding Officer look extremely professional and competent, thus enhancing his future career prospects.

Phil Narramore and I had an interesting experience when a US Army Air Cavalry unit requested our assistance. Based near Phu Bai, they reported losing a Helicopter Gunship during one of their recent mission and it was presumed to have crashed into a shallow waterway in VC country as a returning crew had sighted part of a rotor blade protruding from the muddy water.

We arrived at the scene by chopper in company with US Army Rangers who immediately set up our security perimeter. Another chopper circled overhead keeping a sharp eye out for our old friend *'Victor Charlie'*. Narra *'pulled rank'* on me so I had to do the dive while he supervised. My first priority was to recover the bodies of the crew and then any ordnance or weapons. Diving inside a mangled helicopter searching for bodies, weapons and armed ordnance in zero visibility, is not what you would describe as pleasant or easy. The aluminium hull was extensively damaged with many sharp edges and I was very aware that it would be extremely easy to become entangled inside the wreckage. We only had one set of air cylinders and I was wearing them, so Narra could not come and get me out.

I was diving in what was literally liquid mud and it was as black as a goat's guts. The complete lack of visibility meant that I had to rely on feel alone. When I found what I thought to be the cockpit, I couldn't work out why there were no bodies. Having searched the aircraft reasonably thoroughly, I brought to the surface various bits and pieces which proved it was not their chopper, but a gunship that was eventually identified as one which went missing during the Tet Offensive of 1968, almost 3 years earlier.

That explained why I could not find the crew. After that length of time there would have only been bones. I often wonder if their remains were ever found and repatriated to the US. When I emerged from the water I was disgusted to see that I had a couple of dozen slimy leeches feeding on me.

Back at their base camp, our Army Ranger buddies had us join them in their ongoing *'rappelling'* training. We also had a couple of drinking sessions with the Air Cav pilots - an interesting experience because the average age of these young and very gung-ho gunship pilots was about nineteen - 2 or 3 years younger than me.

As a unit of the US Cavalry, their dress uniform still included hats identical to the ones worn in General Custer's day. They were kept on a hat rack at the entrance to their bar and when a pilot was killed, his buddies would take his hat from the rack, place it on the bar, solemnly toast his memory and proceed to get drunk, trying not to dwell on the fact that it could have been any one of them, or that they may be next.

The highlight of my stay with the Air Cav was a hands-on flight in the front seat of a Huey Cobra helicopter (AH-1) gunship, a very formidable weapons platform indeed. Its arsenal included 2.75 inch rockets with high explosives heads, white phosphorus heads and Fleshette heads, a 7.62mm mini gun with a rate of fire of 6,000 rounds a minute, and a belt fed 40mm grenade launcher.

This particular unit's aircraft inventory consisted of 6 Iroquois (Hueys/Slicks), 6 Cobra gunships (Snakes) and 6 Hughes 500s (Loach/LOH).

As the VC could never resist the temptation to fire at a chopper flying low overhead, the Loaches were paired with the Cobras for what were called *'First and last light missions'*. With only the pilot aboard, the Loach would be flown at treetop level over Charlie country attempting to draw fire, usually successfully. At the first sign of hostile fire, the pilot would toss a smoke grenade out the door and haul ass away from the area at best possible speed while radioing to the waiting Cobra above *"taking fire (colour) smoke"*. The Cobra, hovering at 2000 feet or so, would immediately enter a manoeuvre where it rolled onto its side, dropped the nose to almost the vertical and began a steep powered descent at about 200 knots towards the position marked by the coloured smoke, with mini gun blazing, belching rockets from its stubby wing pods and spitting grenades from its belt fed launcher. Nothing could survive this mini Blitzkrieg. Charlie never seemed to catch on to the set-up and continued to regularly take the bait. The downside was that it was extremely dangerous flying for the Loach pilots. They told us that if they managed to survive the first and last light missions for six months, their chances of surviving Viet Nam and getting home were *'looking good'*.

The amazing thing about these young pilots was their *'gung-ho'* attitude. They thought themselves bulletproof - in hindsight I believe we all did. The extreme manoeuvrability of the Loach was demonstrated to us when one evening Narra and I spent last light playing *'fox and hounds'* with several other Air Cav Loaches, low flying at max speed, chasing each other through the gullies of nearby sand hills - an ideal way to relieve the tension of flying for your life every day of the week.

Before we left, Narra presented the CO with a pair of Australian made GP *'SEAL'* boots. Sadly, only a few days after we returned to Da Nang we were told that the C.O. was killed when the chopper he was flying took a direct hit on the pilot's position from an RPG. He was wearing Narra's boots when he died.

To this day I often recall that most of these young helicopter pilots were not old enough to drink alcohol or even vote in their home States, yet here they were flying helicopters in the face of the enemy, risking their lives every single day. In total over 4,700 helicopter pilots and crewmen were killed in Vietnam. Most would have been under 21 years of age.

Occasionally our calls for assistance were closer to home. Located directly across the road from our hooch was the local Navy lock-up known as *'Correctional Custody'*. They once asked for our help after a disgruntled ex-inmate had returned to toss a hand grenade through the front door. Luckily for them, it had dud-fired. A simple pick up and carry away.

Our old Kaiser Jeep had a rough time of it. To my knowledge it was one of the few vehicles in Viet Nam to ever be shot at from within. Larry Digney and a US Navy EOD Adviser, PO3 Rick Watkins were once driving through the town of Quang Tri on their way north to Cua Viet when Digger carried out some unintentional target practice on the door of the Kaiser with Rick's sawn off M2 Carbine. Needless to say, Digger was right on target. By the time the story filtered back to Da Nang, Digger had supposedly rampaged through the main street of Quang Tri shooting at the local civilians with a Soviet AK47 assault rifle. Jake was not happy.

Digger did in fact have a captured AK47 which he had meticulously restored to mint condition. Unfortunately, he was not able to bring it home due to Australian Customs regulations forbidding the importation of automatic weapons.

A more serious incident occurred when Digger's Colt .45 handgun disappeared from the hooch. At the time we had two or three South Vietnamese Navy EOD personnel staying with us for a couple of days. One of these *'gentlemen'* was later arrested in downtown Da Nang after he had shot a Vietnamese civilian during an argument. The weapon he had used was traced by serial number and found to be Digger's missing .45. This same weapon had a second chance at notoriety when after a night of steady drinking at the nearby Special Forces camp, Digger and WO Gerry Dunn had a slight altercation over an overweight and particularly loud German female entertainer who was performing at the camp's club. She announced in a very guttural German accent that she was from Australia and when Gerry Dunn, who obviously fancied her, invited her over to our table, the trouble began.

Digger was feeling a little argumentative and when she repeated that she was from Australia, Digger said in a loud clear voice, *"Pig's arse"*. This obviously did not help Gerry's perceived chances of a romantic evening with the lady so he ordered Digger to leave the premises without delay. Digger replied by telling Gerry to *"Piss off"*, so they immediately invited each other outside to chat about their difference of opinion.

As we all left the premises, our side arms were returned to us and during the ensuing argument which followed in the carpark, Digger decided that his Colt 45 *'peacemaker'* was the best way to resolve the argument. Fortunately, I was close enough to prevent him from carrying out his objective and common sense finally prevailed before anyone was hurt in the looming showdown. Gerry, having missed the opportunity for a romantic interlude with the overweight Kraut entertainer made a beeline back to our hooch where he made demands to a very sleepy Jake that severe and immediate disciplinary action should be taken against our Able Seaman Digney. As I was the main witness to the altercation, Jake had me recount my unbiased view of the evening's events. Obviously my recollection of the incident favoured my old mate Digger and not the obnoxious WO, so I became the latest addition to Gerry's *'ass-holes list'*. Digger didn't get off quite scot-free and spent quite a bit of time on stoppage of grog from that point on.

One wet, dark and miserable night during the typhoon season, Blue and I decided to make a spontaneous social call to the US Army EOD detachment in downtown Da Nang. When it came time to leave in the early hours of the morning, we discovered that it was just as wet and miserable inside our Dodge Power wagon as it was outside. We soon discovered that some enterprising local had decided that he had a better use for our windscreen than we did. It wasn't a complete loss as the can opener which the thief had used to remove the windscreen was left on the dashboard.

On returning to our hooch, we found *'Murphy's Law'* had struck yet again. As always happened when the weather was at its worst, VC Sapper swimmers had been spotted at the Deep-Water ammunition piers and Digger and Narra had been diving for most of the night by the time we returned. Needless to say, Blue and I spent what was left of that long night searching ship's hulls and anchor cables for explosive devices. I believe 32 hulls was our final count. A sobering experience for both of us. As we had overlooked informing Jake as to our intended whereabouts that evening, our social life was severely restricted for the following two weeks.

Even though an after dark curfew applied to all US servicemen in Da Nang, there still existed the odd hotel, bar and dance hall which stayed open for civilians and ARVN soldiers. As EOD personnel, we were authorised by the US Command to be anywhere at any time, provided we were *'on the job'*.

To ensure that American troops complied with the curfew, their Military Police regularly patrolled the streets and the less than desirable spots of Da Nang. We were often pulled over by these clowns, not surprising as we were Caucasian, wore US Cammies and drove US Jeeps. The fact that we were Australians was usually enough to totally confuse them, but to save any argument we always carried a few dummy rocket heads in the vehicle. Once we had told them it was live ordnance they couldn't get away fast enough.

One particular night Speed, Narra, Blue and I were leaving a hotel bar and as we walked towards our Jeep in the parking compound, we spotted several *'White Mice'* police hassling a young girl. She was very distraught and seemed very frightened. Being Aussies, we decided to go to the aid of the damsel in distress. When we asked the police what was going on, they told us in very threatening and impolite terms that it was police business and we should leave before we were in trouble as well.

We knew that it was common practice for these *'official'* thugs to arrest young girls off the street on some ludicrous charge, take them back to the police station and gang-rape them. Discretion being the better part of valour, we quietly backed off and headed for our vehicle from where we waited and watched one of them force the girl onto the back of his motorcycle and take off, presumably heading for the police station. His mates remained, presumably to round up a few more young girls.

With the lights of our Jeep switched off, we tucked in about 50 metres behind the motorcycle and followed it until we were well clear of the hotel area. Speed was driving and once we reached a deserted street, he accelerated past the bike, cutting it off and forcing it into the gutter. The policeman immediately began screaming obscenities at us and making threats. Believing he had the upper hand, he reached for his .38 handgun, but before it cleared his holster he was staring down the barrels of four cocked Colt .45s, all of which had *'one up the spout'* and were aimed directly at a spot between the mongrel's eyes. I believe his bowels let go at that point, as with some justification it dawned on him that he might be about to meet his illustrious ancestors.

I have no hesitation in saying that if he had moved so much as a hair, four 45s would have barked as one. In hindsight we were all hoping he would give us an excuse as we really despised these corrupt and totally evil little bastards. We told the young lady to get into the Jeep and suggested to the police officer that he *'di di mau'* (leave very quickly). Needless to say, he took off like a cut snake. As we were quite close to the US Army's EOD compound, we stopped in for a beer and after explaining what had happened, we left the girl in their able care. Their officer's parting comment was *"crazy fucking Aussies"*.

We were to discover later that our damsel in distress was a member of the *'oldest profession in the world'*. After we had departed, she offered her services to the blokes at Army EOD. I don't believe they were even offered a discount. We had a bit of a chuckle about it, but we still felt we had done the right thing.

On another occasion we were drinking in an area known as Red Beach where there were several houses of ill-repute as well as a few small bars. Our Jeep was parked outside one of these and it obviously attracted the attention of some passing US Military Police. As quick as a flash, Speed was outside and went straight on the offensive. He asked the officer in charge what the hell did he think he was doing there. Didn't he *"know that booby traps had been reported in this area"*. Speed told the young officer that he was in charge of a delicate clearance operation and he (the MP) had better get his men and vehicles clear of the area *"now"*. Thrown by the Aussie accent as well as Speed's confident air of authority and unfamiliar rank badges, the MP officer stuttered and stammered, apologised profusely while addressing Speed as sir, saluted smartly and ordered his men *"You heard the officer, get your butts outta here"*.

We finished our beers and thought it might be a wise decision for us to leave before the young officer recovered sufficiently to check out our bullshit story.

Several weeks later Digger was back in the same area with a US Navy mate and had consumed enough *'Dutch courage'* to try the same line of bullshit. Being a little under the weather and only 19 years of age, his gibbering line of garbage fell on disbelieving ears. Later that night Jake received a phone call advising him that a young Australian sailor by the name of Digney was being detained in custody and would we like to come and pick him up at our convenience. Jake let Digger suffer the indignity for a few more hours before he sent one of us to his rescue.

Digger, Blue and I kept an assortment of US Officer's collar devices and occasionally for a change of pace, we three would promote ourselves to 1st Lieutenants or Captains, and visit an Officer's mess on one of the nearby US bases.

One night our accents gave us away and to absolve our sins, we were asked to mount the stage and sing *'Waltzing Matilda'*. After the first verse, there was a deathly silence as we looked at each other hoping someone remembered the second verse. We didn't, so we launched into the first verse again. The Yanks didn't know the difference, and loved it. We were welcome to go back anytime, with or without the collar devices.

We inherited a kangaroo stencil from the previous team and by the time we left, there was hardly an EOD vehicle in Da Nang that did not have several large red kangaroos painted all over it. To the EOD community, it became something of a status symbol and we were often asked to spray their vehicles with the famous Aussie's likeness.

Digger became an avid collector of rank badges and unit patches. On one occasion upon meeting a very senior US Admiral, a very junior Able Seaman Digney, without hesitation, told him he collected collar devices and needed an Admiral's badge for his collection. To everyone's surprise the slightly dumb-founded Admiral happily obliged.

During our quieter periods, we all assumed responsibility for various housekeeping tasks. Narra looked after the bar, Digger maintained the diving equipment, Blue took care of the victualling and I kept up the vehicles and the boat. Blue became a close friend of the on-base Chief Victualler so there was never a shortage of prime US beef, ribs, flavoured milk, dehydrated prawns and canned pacific oysters. We were very fortunate in one respect to go to war with the Americans as in some areas they spared no expense.

Our formidable private weapons arsenal included personal Colt .45 calibre handguns, 5.56mm M16's, 40mm M79 grenade launchers, a 7.62mm M60 Heavy machine-gun, CAR15's and a various assortment of captured weapons including Digger's infamous 7.62mm Soviet AK47 assault rifle. We did not leave our hooch without a .45 strapped to our side and whenever we left the camp, we carried at least one long weapon each, generally an M16 with 30 round magazines. Had the North Vietnamese Army marched into town during 1970-71, we were ready, or at least we thought we were.

One non-EOD American with whom we became firm friends was Petty Officer 1st Class Roger Smiley, a Navy Seabee. During some quieter moments Roger helped me to fulfil a boyhood ambition. He was a heavy equipment instructor and he taught me to operate a Caterpillar D-8 bulldozer at a local quarry. After completing his tour of duty in Viet Nam, Roger intended to emigrate to Australia. Unfortunately, we lost contact with him after our return home.

One of our sadder moments was the day we found Fred's body. Her appetite had been her undoing. Unbeknown to us, rat poison had been laid amongst some banana palms nearby and Fred could not resist eating anything which appeared edible. Jake reported in the December 'Monthly Report of Proceedings' that 'WRAN EOD FRED' had passed away on active duty. We buried her in our backyard with a suitable headstone over her grave. It read: -

"Here lies Fred,
the Meanest Monkey in the Valley
R.I.P."

Not all EOD tasks were completed. On the 11th January, Jake, Narra & myself were uplifted by Huey to the village of Loc Phuoc. A 500-pound Low Drag General Purpose bomb had been found by a farmer, not 50 metres from his village. He and his water buffalo had uncovered it whilst ploughing a rice paddy in preparation for planting.

We decided we had two options - attempt a Low Order (partial or incomplete detonation), or try to render it safe. The first option put the village at risk, if in fact we had a High Order (normal or complete detonation), and the second option put both the village and us at risk.

An interesting sideline to this situation was that had we had a High Order detonation and damaged property in the Vill we would be held personally responsible for the damage and be required by the South Vietnamese Authorities to pay compensation to the villagers. Incredible in a war zone, but nevertheless a fact of life. After this was pointed out to us by a local District official, a third option emerged. We left the bomb exactly where it was and told the official to contact the nearest ARVN EOD team. We weren't going to put up with that sort of bullshit. On departing the area for Hoi An, our chopper was diverted at the request of the 51st ARVN Regiment Advisors to take part in troop lifts and gunship operations against a group of VC caught in the open. The results of this action were 1 VC KIA and 1 VC POW.

One of the many fascinations I found in Viet Nam was the blending of the Vietnamese culture with the French/Catholic influence. Throughout the countryside were reminders of the French presence. Schools, churches and government buildings had the unmistakable imprint of French colonialism. There was a certain subdued elegance in some of the people and their towns. I was always amazed to see young Vietnamese schoolgirls heading off to school along the muddy roads, immaculately dressed in their beautiful white silk national dress, the *'Ao Dai'*.

Another legacy left by the French was their technique for making bread rolls – called 'Banh Mi'. I have not since tasted bread to match that baked by the Vietnamese.

During our training at Woodside South Australia, we had been introduced to the fascinating history, culture and religions of Viet Nam. Fascinating because, these people had been at war with their neighbours for a thousand years. Our war was to them, a continuation of hundreds of years of determined struggle against foreign invaders.

As a result of this small but valuable insight, I believe we had an advantage over the US troops, as we had a clearer understanding of the land and its people. To the US soldiers, they were just *'gooks'*. I like to think we had a little more compassion towards the Vietnamese.

The Australian Military Forces were in fact issued with 'Nine Rules' covering their conduct whilst in Viet Nam. They are worth repeating as they highlight traditional Aussie values, even though they may not have been followed to the letter: -

1. Remember we are here only to help; we make no demands and seek no special treatment.

2. Try to understand the people, their way of life; customs and laws.

3. Learn the simple greetings of the Vietnamese language and use them frequently.

4. Treat friendly people, particularly women with respect and courtesy.

5. Don't attract attention by rude behaviour or larrikinism.

6. Avoid separating us from the Vietnamese by a display of great wealth or privilege.

7. Make friends among the soldiers and people of Viet Nam.

8. Remember decency and honesty are the signs of a man and a soldier; bad manners are the sign of a fool.

9. Above all remember you are an Australian, by your actions our country is judged. Set an example of sincerity and fair play in all your dealings with Vietnamese and with other people who are assisting them.

Unfortunately, we, along with the Americans, were seen by the general populace as just one more foreign invader supporting an unpopular and extremely corrupt government.

Normally when we flew to points south of Da Nang, we utilised Air America, the CIA's private airline. They shuttled backwards and forwards on a regular basis between Da Nang and Saigon, and being EOD, with the highest travel priority, we were allowed to fly with them. They operated silver Curtiss C-46 'Commandos' with airline type seats which were a vast improvement over the uncomfortable webbed seats of the C-130 Hercules. What and who the airline carried besides us was not discussed. We didn't ask and they didn't tell us. I often sat next to stony faced Americans in civilian clothes. Presumably they were CIA on their way to subvert somebody. Air America also very kindly brought in our mail twice a week from Saigon.

The US Air Force operated shuttle services between all major bases and during the late 60's, Saigon's Tan Son Nhat and Da Nang airfields were among the busiest airports in the world. Da Nang reached an average of 2,595 air traffic operations daily.

All one needed for travel anywhere in Vietnam was a set of written orders from your CO and it was then a matter of waiting in line. When one aircraft was full, it departed and another moved in to take its place. For an Australian Serviceman, it was mind blowing to see the sheer size of the American Military machine in operation. In a country less than the size of Victoria, large transport aircraft had a choice of 75 tactical airfields.

We maintained a 24 hour a day radio contact with *'Derringer'* - our local operations centre and when we heard our callsign *'Cliffside'* on the net, we knew it was time to hustle. There was a Helo pad within 200 metres of our hooch and the Americans could usually provide a chopper for us at very short notice. Most helicopter flying was done either above 2-3,000 feet and out of small arms range, or at treetop level, to reduce the risk of taking ground fire. By the time the VC heard the chopper, it was over the top and out of sight. This was not always successful. Once, when returning to Camp Tien Sha at night, we took small arms fire through the aircraft whilst overflying Da Nang city. I was a little taken aback to see pinpoints of moonlight suddenly appearing in the fuselage. Luckily no-one and no critical components were hit. Charlie was everywhere....

After observing at length the attitude of the ARVN, (they avoided fighting, working, patrolling and everything else if possible) it was almost chilling to see the ruthless efficiency of the Korean soldiers, known to everyone as *'ROK's'*. Their vehicles, weapons and uniforms were always immaculate. They were without a doubt the most disciplined troops I have ever encountered and the Vietnamese were petrified of them for good reason. The ROK's regarded the Vietnamese as an extremely inferior race and treated them accordingly.

Once, when heading for the airfield to pick up the mail, I was halted at a roadblock which had been set up by disabled ARVN veterans on the main road outside of their compound. They were protesting against their appalling pensions and living conditions, with very good reason. They had moved onto the road enmasse on their crutches and in their wheelchairs and refused to budge.

After unsuccessful negotiations followed by threats, the ARVN MPs still could not move them, so the American MPs were called for. More negotiation followed by more threats and still they refused to move. This Mexican standoff continued until someone had the bright idea of calling in the ROK MPs. As word passed around the vets that the ROK's were coming, they became visibly agitated and I could see a genuine fear growing in their faces. At the mere threat of ROK intervention the Vets disappeared back into their compound as if the Devil himself was after them.

In the interest of keeping our souls pure, we had two brief visits by RAN Chaplains. One, the Reverend P. Ball, presented us with a verse composed by members of the Ship's Company of the Australian destroyer HMAS Perth, at that time serving on the Gun Line off the coast of Viet Nam. It read: -

> "O God in Heaven, hear our plea,
> for Clearance Divers 'neath the sea.
> While in the Ocean's dark embrace,
> keep us Thy sons within Thy Grace.
> And hear us Lord, o Thou who saves,
> for us Thy servants 'neath the waves."

We were impressed that our fellow sailors offshore had taken the time to think of us but none of us thought for a minute that prayers would make a scrap of difference to our survival.

During the final weeks of our tour, Jake and I visited the Australian Army bases at Nui Dat and Vung Tau, both of which were located far to the south in III Corps. Hoping to make some duty free purchases from the ASCO canteen at Nui Dat before we headed home, we were advised by the canteen manager that they had only just re-stocked with goods recently arrived from Australia *(courtesy of the Navy's troop carrier HMAS Sydney)* and he informed us that the canteen was only open to Colonel rank and above on that first day. Even after explaining that this was our first and only opportunity to take advantage of Australian canteen privileges during our entire tour, this typical tiny minded REMF (*rear echelon mutha-fucka*) would not bend his pathetic little rule. I cursed myself for not bringing our box of collar devices.

We were extremely disappointed to hear the news that our relief team would not be coming. Our Team was in fact the first token unit withdrawal (albeit only 6 of us) from South Viet Nam by the Australian Government.

Jake made a last minute effort to have us return to Australia via Hawaii to *'hail and farewell'* the US Navy's EOD Group which had overall responsibility for us while we were in Viet Nam. As we expected, the Canberra paper shufflers rejected that idea out of hand, even though the Americans had offered to cover all transportation and accommodation costs.

Mama San was particularly upset to find that we were leaving and that her employment was coming to an end. We dug into our slush fund which had been saved from our beer sales over the bar and gave her the entire amount as a parting cash gift, although even this failed to cheer her up to any great degree. I believe that she sensed things were only going to go downhill for the South and our leaving brought that realisation to the surface.

She had agreed to take Dog to her home and look after him but we all felt very sad about leaving him as we knew life was going to be pretty tough for him. On the day we finalised our packing, Dog was quite noticeably agitated. By the time we arrived at Mama San's house, he was shaking and yelping like a pup. The poor old fella knew we weren't coming back.

With mixed feelings of regret that it was all over and relief that we were all going to make it home in one piece, we departed Da Nang on the 21st April 1971 courtesy of a RAAF *'Wallaby Airlines'* Caribou. Our first stop was Pleiku in the Central highlands where we landed for fuel and then it was on to Saigon.

A South Vietnamese team was assigned to take over our responsibilities in I Corps, but they had failed to materialise by the time of our departure from Da Nang.

In hindsight, our withdrawal coincided with the beginning of the end of the war as *'Vietnamisation'* was proving to be a dismal failure as subsequent events showed, culminating in the fall of Saigon to the Communist Forces on April 30, 1975.

Less than a fortnight after our departure, we were informed that the only Vietnamese EOD technician whom we had ever regarded as being anywhere near professional, had been killed by a *'Birdcage'* mine in the Cua Viet river. Our departure had left I Corps with very little surface EOD and absolutely no underwater EOD capability whatsoever.

Before we departed from Da Nang, the US Naval Commander in 1 Corps awarded a number of individual US Navy Citations to Team members, including the following Unit Citation: -

"For meritorious service during the period October 1970 to April 1971 while attached to and serving with the Royal Australian Navy Clearance Diving Team 3, Explosive Ordnance Disposal Mobile Unit, Pacific Team 35 at the United States Naval Support Facility, Da Nang.

You provided an invaluable service to all branches of the United States Armed Forces and other Free World Military Assistance Forces in Military Region One by engaging in explosive ordnance disposal, channel clearing and salvage operations. Your exemplary professionalism, endurance and devotion to duty were particularly evident during the extremely hazardous salvage of a United States Army logistic craft which had capsized with a full load of explosives aboard.

Your consistently outstanding performance of duty contributed to the successful accomplishment of the mission of United States Naval Support Facility, Da Nang in support of Free World Military Assistance Forces in the Republic of Viet Nam. Your exceptional achievements under arduous working and living conditions and constant threat of enemy rocket and small arms attack were a credit to the Royal Australian Navy and were in keeping with the highest traditions of the Naval Service".

We spent two weeks winding down with the US Navy's EODMUPAC Team 33, located in Cholon. They were still living in the delightful old French villa that we had stayed in on our arrival seven months earlier. Tu Do street was revisited and on one occasion Narra and Blue arrived at one of our favourite bars to find it completely ablaze - flattened by a satchel charge only minutes prior to their arrival, courtesy of two local Viet Cong on a motorcycle.

After Da Nang, Saigon was a wild town and we thoroughly enjoyed driving down the tree-lined boulevards in tiny old French Renault and Peugeot taxi-cabs looking for new bars to enjoy a beer and female company, preferably bars that didn't attract the attention of VC sappers.

On Anzac Day 1971, the Australian Embassy held a formal dawn service with each of the three services being represented at the Cenotaph ceremony. I was detailed to represent the Navy and spent several days practising for the ceremony at *'Free World Headquarters'* in Saigon. After the formal service was over, we mixed with the dignitaries and enjoyed a traditional Anzac breakfast complete with Bundaberg rum and Australian sausages freshly flown in from the *'Land Down Under'*.

Prior to leaving Viet Nam we received the following signal from the Australian Naval Board: -

"On this, the eve of the withdrawal of Clearance Diving Team 3 from the Republic of Viet Nam, the Naval Board congratulates all who have served in the team since its inauguration and also all those who were instrumental in the training of the team members for service in Viet Nam.

Throughout the four years of deployment in Viet Nam CDT3 has done extremely well.

Their dedication to duty in trying and hazardous circumstances has brought great credit to the Royal Australian Navy and to Australia.

This was the first occasion that a unit of the RAN has been employed on extensive land orientated explosive ordnance disposal tasks and the success of CDT3's operations and the lessons learned there from have been invaluable to the Clearance Diving branch as a whole."

Finally, on the 5th May 1971, after almost four and a half years' service in South Viet Nam, the RAN's Clearance Diving Branch closed the chapter on its first exposure to active duty.

With mixed emotions, the last Team boarded the Qantas *'Freedom Bird'* and departed Saigon to the south, back to the *'real world'*.

A total of 49 Clearance Divers had served in South Viet Nam during the period February 1967 through to May 1971. Our casualties were surprisingly light with one killed in a motor vehicle accident and one wounded during a firefight.

As our pilot fire-walled the throttles and I felt the Boeing 707 begin to accelerate down *Tan Son Nhat's* runway, I was thinking of the words of the popular Peter Paul and Mary song of the 70's, "*I'm leaving, on a Jet Plane, don't know when I'll be back again.*" We were on our way home. At the exact moment the pilot lifted the nose wheel of the aircraft from the runway and we began our climb through the humid haze blanketing Saigon, a loud cheer erupted throughout the entire length of the cabin. One thought only was in everyone's mind; we were leaving Viet Nam and going home. No more monsoons, no more humidity, no more rice paddies, no more incoming *(the term applies to mortar rounds, rockets etc which are heading in your direction)* and no more 'Charlie'. It was over and we were leaving it all behind us forever. Or so I thought. Not in my wildest dreams would I have imagined that I would ever return to this war-ravaged land.

As the euphoria began to settle down, lunch was served by the cheerful Qantas stewards and more importantly from our point of view, cans of beer were passed around. This was a time to celebrate. There can be no doubt that every passenger onboard that aircraft felt very relieved to be going home alive. Too many mates had left Vietnam in body bags.

Our flight was direct to Sydney with no stops. My main recollection of the trip was about two hours out of Sydney's Kingsford Smith International airport when the Captain apologised that the beer service was being terminated due to the toilets being near full to capacity. I suspect the Captain had ulterior motives. He probably just wanted to get his charges home in a reasonably sober condition. A very sensible move I thought. We landed after the Sydney airport curfew so we were the only passengers in the entire terminal. I'm sure this was deliberate. Servicemen returning home from Viet Nam were not exactly welcomed back as conquering heroes.

As Murphy's law would have it, the Diving team's baggage was the very last to be unloaded from the plane so we were the last group through Customs. When we finally emerged to waiting families, friends and sweethearts, they were all beginning to suspect that the Team had found a bar tucked away somewhere inside the immigration area.

On our arrival back on Australian soil, Clearance Diving Team 3 was officially disbanded, with the proviso *"to be reformed again at the discretion of the Australian Naval Board"*.

It was great to be home again, but after a few short weeks leave to catch up with family, it was back to work for all of us. We returned from leave to report to our new postings in the diving school, Team 1 or Team 2. It was back to work as if Viet Nam had never happened. Curiously enough, Team 3 was not discussed much by anyone. Those that went probably felt it was *'big-noting'* themselves to talk much about it, and those that didn't go, weren't interested. They were extremely disappointed to have missed out, as it was now relegated forever to the history books. To this day there still remains a very noticeable undercurrent of resentment and jealousy from some CD's of the 70's towards those who served in Team 3.

The lack of understanding and in many cases outright animosity displayed by the Australian public at large towards returning Viet Nam servicemen still haunts many a veteran to this day. We didn't deserve to be shouldered with this misplaced blame brought about by the folly of our political leaders.

> *"No event in American history is more*
> *misunderstood than the Vietnam War.*
> *It was misreported then, and it is misremembered now.*
> *Rarely have so many people been so wrong about so much.*
> *Never have the consequences of their misunderstanding been so tragic."*
> Richard M. Nixon

It wasn't until many years later that the stigma attached to being a Viet Nam Vet was finally eased for some of us by the *'Welcome Home'* parade through the streets of Sydney in October

1987. The crowds lining the route of the march reacted as if we had just returned from the beaches of Gallipoli. I think that most Australians felt secretly embarrassed that it had taken so long to *'bring us home'*. By then we were all middle aged men, but better late than never. I remember the Prime Minister, Bob Hawke, was taking the salute at the march past - the same Bob Hawke who was the Australian Council of Trade Unions (ACTU) boss when the unions refused to allow the delivery of mail to servicemen in Vietnam. To show the absolute and utter contempt we felt towards this politician, all CDT3 veterans deliberately stared straight ahead instead of giving him the customary courtesy of an *'eyes left'* as we passed the official dais. We couldn't believe the man had the gall to stand there pretending that he gave a damn about us. Just goes to show how two-faced politicians can be.

The opening of the Viet Nam Forces memorial in Canberra on the 3rd October '92 and the march and reunions that followed further helped to heal some of the psychological wounds left over from the war.

In hindsight, there is no doubt that the lessons learnt in our *'first'* war had a significant impact on training syllabuses for the years that followed and heavily influenced the direction the Diving Branch since has taken.

After the Vietnam war came to a close, it was decided by a majority of Team 3 vets to form a Clearance Diving Team 3 Association so that we could stay in touch over the years via Anzac Day marches and the occasional reunion, just as veterans of previous wars had done. I remember as a young lad seeing what it meant to my father when he would head off to the odd Anzac Day march in Adelaide to catch up with his old mates from the war. Sadly, in his later years he was to lose contact with the few remaining survivors of his squadron.

From this ex CDT3 association evolved the Clearance Divers Association to include all ex Clearance Divers and especially veterans of more recent conflicts. It has continued to grow from strength to strength.

In addition to receiving many individual awards for gallantry in Vietnam, CDT3 was awarded the following: -

the **Republic of Vietnam**
'Cross of Gallantry with Palm Leaf' Unit Citation,
the **'US Presidential Unit Citation'**,
the **'US Navy Unit Commendation'** (twice) and
the **'US Navy Meritorious Unit Commendation'**.

The three US awards are the highest Unit awards in the US Military and CDT3 is the only foreign Unit to be ever awarded all three.

"We were young, we were proud, we were all that we could be."
author unknown –

"In the creeks and swamps of the Rung Sat and along the Cua Viet, the fishermen have returned. Sometimes in the tree roots or sandbars they find shattered wood and twisted metal fragments: sampans, junks, patrol boats, helicopters....
The young boys listen to the recollections of their grandfathers, of the old days when the foreigners fought the Vietnamese in these very streams, rivers and bays."

Lex McAulay
'In the Ocean's Dark Embrace'

Diver in dry suit and CD Breathing Apparatus. (CDBA) rigged for mixed gas – circa 1965.

Drager 9608 mixed gas rig - 1973.

Diving workboat at HMAS Rushcutter – late 60's.

HMAS Yarra – my home from '67 – '69.

Yarra & Stuart with HMS Warspite in the Indian Ocean - 1967.

Author's Team - Da Nang, South Vietnam - 1971.

Remains of the ammunition barge, Da Nang harbour. - 1970.

PBRs, channel clearing - near Hoi An – 1971.

Cua Viet river, DMZ - VC Birdcage mine in foreground.

Narramore, Furner and Ey back from the 'Boonies'. Da Nang, 1970.

Advanced CD Course – HMAS Penguin – 1973.

Promotion ceremony to E8 Senior Chief - US Navy, Hawaii – 1978.

CDT1 unit, Honiara - Solomon Islands.
CPO Harmon Slappy (USN exchange) in khakis – 1981.

'Specwarex' in Philippines. Wet deck launch & recovery training.
USS Grayback - Special Forces submarine - 1974.

'The Chiefs'.
Joint exercises – CDT1, US SEAL Team 1 & RNZN CDs - 1980.

Mike Ey and author with ABCD Jason Ey – receiving
2 US Navy Unit Commendations (NUC) – 2010.

Classmates from my original CD course of '66 who all
served as members of CDT3 in South Vietnam.
L/R: author, Ray Cocks, Jeff *'Cowby'* Garrett, Jim Henry & John Branch.

Back from Vietnam. CDT2 – 1971.

Jungle Training Centre, Canungra – 1970.

Willy & the author - Ouray, Colorado – 2013.

Author with Kimberley and Jason.

The author and Antoinette – wedding day 1971.

9
CDT 2 - 1971

On completion of my post-Vietnam leave, I drafted into CDT2 and spent the remainder of 1971 on general diving duties operating from Team 2's base within the Diving school at HMAS Penguin. During this period two important events in my young life were to take place.

The first, and the one which obviously had the greatest impact on my life, occurred on the 4th September. Antoinette and I were married in the Naval Chapel at HMAS Watson. Sitting atop South Head at the entrance to Sydney Harbour, it is a spectacular piece of real estate and has the most incredible views of this world famous harbour. My older brother Mike was the best man and Antoinette's older sister Kay was bridesmaid. My parents came over from South Australia as did my two favourite uncles. One of my old compatriots from Team 3, Phil Narramore, was the Master of Ceremonies and was the perfect host for the wedding reception; except that once he got started no-one could shut him up. Phil loved to talk. He read out a number of telegrams but the one which raised the most eyebrows was from *'Saigon Rose'*, supposedly a young Vietnamese lass who accused me of being *'Number 10'* for having left her heartbroken, destitute and pregnant in Saigon. It received a good laugh but I did worry a little about the look on Kay's face. Her sister was marrying a sailor, and perhaps she was thinking *'where there's smoke, there's fire'*.

The second, although perhaps less important event for the year, was my promotion to Acting/Leading Seaman Clearance Diver on the 30th September. In those days' promotion was initially to *'acting rank'* for 12 months after which, if recommended, the sailor was confirmed in the rank of Leading Seaman. So for a year I had to put up with being called an *'A stroke'* Kellick by my mates. My rise in the ranks was accompanied by a small salary increase which came in handy as Antoinette and I were living in a small flat at Bondi while we waited our turn to be allocated a Navy flat. This was a big move as the rent for a L/S was less than $10 a fortnight. Antoinette remained at her job with a major Japanese import/export company while we saved for the day when we could buy our own home.

During this period, I consolidated my general diving experience in the Fleet maintenance role, being a large part of Team 2's responsibilities. In late '71 we were introduced to the RAN's new mixture breathing set, the 9608 FGT1-A Drager. We called it the *'Volvo'* set because it was rumoured that the rig cost about the same as a new Volvo motor car. Compared to the old set it replaced, I thought it was heavy, cumbersome and uncomfortable.

One of the team's more interesting and unusual tasks during this period was changing the sonar dome on HMAS Queenborough while she was alongside. This quite major task would normally be carried out while the ship was in dry dock at Garden Island Naval dockyard. We also carried out the first 'wet' propeller exchange on one of the Oberon class submarines while it was alongside at HMAS Platypus.

Another unusual job was the recovery of a World War II torpedo from Moreton Bay in Brisbane. A fishing trawler had hauled it up in its nets and the team was called in to check it out and ensure that it was safe. As it turned out, the torpedo was traced back to a departing US Navy Destroyer which dumped it in the Bay, minus the warhead, at the close of WWII. The remainder of '71 was quite uneventful - just more ship attacks and the usual diving tasks in and around Sydney Harbour.

10
CDT 1 - 1972

Much to my delight I received my next posting effective January '72 to the Mobile Team. CDT1 was the branch's 12-14 man mobile team which had diving and EOD responsibilities throughout Australia and the near north. The team also participated in numerous exercises with our SEATO allies in South East Asia. The team, along with the RAN's minesweeper and minehunter squadron, was based at HMAS Waterhen, a peaceful little out of the way Naval depot situated at Balls Head Bay on Sydney Harbour.

In those days Team 1 was a 12 month posting so a completely new team was formed at the beginning of each year. The early months of the year were spent working up as a team in all forms of diving, EOD and demolitions. The Team comprised Lieutenant Ian (Mac) McConnochie as OIC, Lieutenant Bruce (Bruco) Thompson as XO, Petty Officers Harry Brankstone and Phil Tonks, two Leading Hands - myself and Graeme (Johhno) Johnson, and seven AB's including Larry Digney & Blue Furner, both team mates from CDT3 in Vietnam. We also had an underwater medicine sailor attached to us who was responsible for the Team's day to day health and kept us in-date with vaccinations and inoculations, ready for any overseas deployment at short notice.

Our first major deployment for the year was to Papua and the Territory of New Guinea, in those days still two separate territories administered by Australia. Each year the team conducted a 2-month long sweep throughout the islands disposing of unexploded ordnance still remaining from WW II. Australian *'Patrol Officers'*, based throughout Papua and NG, would forward to the Australian authorities in Port Moresby lists of unexploded ordnance discovered in their local areas. They in turn would prepare a suggested itinerary for the Team's next annual visit.

On May 1st the team loaded our recompression chamber, boat, outboard motors, Land Cruiser, personal equipment and all necessary diving equipment at Richmond RAAF base for the noisy and uncomfortable flight to Manus Island, courtesy of a RAAF C130 Hercules transport. HMAS Tarangau, the Naval Base at Manus Island was our destination.

On arrival we were met by the resident POCD, *'Bluey'* Johnson, and with his friendly assistance we enjoyed several days acclimatising at the best of the local diving spots. We dived on WW II aircraft, cargo ships and some of the best reefs I have ever seen anywhere in the world. In the evenings under swaying palm trees while watching spectacular sunsets from the beach, we barbecued fresh crayfish and sampled the local South Pacific Lager.

The memory of one particular dive near Manus Island has stayed with me because of the incredible visibility. A lot of off-shore reefs such as the Great Barrier Reef have poor *'vis'* due to the constant wave action over the shallower corals and sand. This dive was on what was known as a *'drop off'*, where a sheer wall descended vertically for 200-300 feet and beyond. While the diving boat hovered overhead, two or three of us dropped over the edge and sank down to about 100 feet. From that depth as I looked up, I could clearly see my mates in the boat as they peered over the side. The water was absolutely crystal clear and I felt as if I was suspended in space. It was fascinating watching my bubbles from that depth slowly rising to break the surface over 100 feet above me. Looking below, the sheer wall continued on downwards disappearing out of sight into dark blue inky depths. After several years of diving in relatively dirty water, that was a dive to be remembered as I never again encountered sea water of such clarity. Blue took us to the WW II Mokorang airstrip on Manus. It had been built by the Americans during the second world war and since then it had been completely reclaimed by the ever encroaching jungle. However not all was as it appeared.

The thick cover of trees was growing in a very thin layer of humus which covered the runway and on closer inspection all the roots were found to be growing horizontally. Incredibly the runway surface was still very much intact and Blue said the airfield could be operational again in the space of a few days with the use of only one or two bulldozers to push the trees to the side.

Before too long our transportation arrived at HMAS Tarangau. It was the *'MV Arcturus'* which would be our home for the next two months. She was an ex British whale-chaser which had been built for the Arctic circle. Belonging to the PNG Administration, she was skippered by one of life's real characters. His name was Bill Tebb, an Englishman who from our point of view was quite a legend.

In October 1942, Bill was selected as one of ten charioteers to train for a planned attack on the huge German battleship Tirpitz (sister ship to the *'Bismarck'*), which at the time was moored in Trondhelmsfjord in Norway *(a chariot was about 6 metres long, driven by an electric motor and carried a 600lb detachable warhead. It was manned by two crew dressed in diving gear. The plan was for the crews to steer the chariots under the Tirpitz, release and attach the warhead to the hull and make good their escape)*. Bill and his mates were kept from reaching the mighty battleship by an array of submarine nets and mechanical problems with their chariots. After their aborted attempt to sink her, Bill and his buddies had to escape overland through German held Norway. He was a tough man and we enjoyed listening to his stories over a few beers. During his escape he shot and killed two German policemen who had tried to arrest him and his two mates.

Bill ruled his boat with iron discipline. His native crew both loved and feared him. If any of them stepped out of line, it was a size 10 boot fair up the backside. One incident we witnessed had the diving team doubled up with laughter. Bill had caught one of the engine room crew frying eggs on the hot engine exhaust manifold. We heard a yell from below and the unfortunate native erupted through the hatch with Bill hot on his tail. Round and round the deck they went with the blackfella letting out a yell every few metres as Bill's boot connected with his rear end.

Our explosives arrived at Tarangau aboard a small coastal freighter and after transferring all onto the Arcturus, it was time to start work. It was well and truly time to leave Manus as we had worn out our welcome at the naval base. In addition to out-drinking the Tarangau sailors every night in their bar, we had upset some of the base officers. One Sunday afternoon a fast ski boat had roared past us rocking our diving boat. ABCD Bob Speed took it upon himself to find the offender and *'word him in'* about his lack of seamanlike courtesy. Later that day the Boss was *'worded in'* by the Commanding Officer of Tarangau to the effect that he didn't appreciate Able Seamen Clearance Divers verbally abusing and threatening his Executive Officer.

Our first stop was Kar Kar island, an idyllic little spot just north of Madang. From there it was on to Wewak to inspect a downed WW II USAF Airacobra *(a single engined US Fighter)* which still had a live bomb on board. It turned out that the aircraft was the favourite dive site for the local expatriate dive club and they were not at all happy that we may have to dispose of the bomb, and perhaps the aircraft with it. They didn't seem overly concerned about diving in the vicinity of 250 pounds of potentially unstable high explosives which may one day detonate while they were diving on the wreck. *'Ignorance is bliss'* they say. What they did not appreciate was the fact that the TNT based explosive fill was nearly 30 years old and that it was deteriorating with age, crystallising and becoming increasingly more sensitive to shock.

The whole team had the opportunity to dive on the wreck prior to a decision being made as to how to handle the bomb. The Airacobra appeared to be in quite good condition. She was sitting on a sandy bottom with one wing clear and the other partially buried in the sand. The story was that the pilot had bellied it in and escaped before it sank. Beneath the exposed wing there was the corroded remains of a .50 calibre machine gun. It stood to reason that there would be another one under the other wing so after carefully scavenging away the sand we found the other weapon was still in place and in excellent condition. Why this had not occurred to the civilian dive community was a mystery. We were always on the lookout for trophies to add to the team's collection back at Waterhen, so using detonating cord we severed the mounting bracket and took it back onboard Arcturus to have a closer look. We stripped the weapon completely, washed it in fresh water and then kept it immersed in diesel while we cleaned every single component back to bare metal. When we reassembled the WW II .50 cal it was as good as new. The action functioned perfectly and the weapon was ready to fire. After returning to Australia, we had the weapon treated with gunmetal blue and added it to the CDT1 trophy collection.

The fusing on the bomb was completely corroded so any attempt to render it safe was ruled out. Knowing that the wreck was a favourite dive spot we decided we would attempt to shift the aircraft leaving the bomb exposed for disposal. We were prepared to make every reasonable effort to save the aircraft but any risk to members of the diving team from the bomb was totally unacceptable. After scouring all the sand away from over and under the partly buried wing, we attached two mine lifting bags to the aircraft's lift points and began to slowly inflate the bags. Every precaution was taken to ensure an even and steady lift, but unfortunately the almost 30 years the airframe had spent in a salt water environment was against us. The Airacobra separated neatly into three sections as the buoyancy of the bags took charge, but once we had started there was no turning back. With the bulk of the aircraft removed to a safe distance, albeit in 3 pieces, the bomb was disposed of by detonating it sympathetically with a smaller charge of plastic explosive. Our only remaining hiccup was the wrath of the expatriate dive community. Their influence extended to Wewak's senior Australian government bureaucrat who less than politely informed the Boss that his team might like to *'move on'* as soon as possible. These turkeys failed to appreciate that we had probably saved several lives.

A little aside in Wewak made everyone laugh. One night we were all wandering down the hill from the pub heading back to the boat when one of the younger members of the team became a little obstreperous. After being told by the Boss several times to pull his head in, Chris Balven soon discovered that Mac was serious about his directions being complied with. In the blink of an eye, Chris was lying flat on his back rubbing his bruised jaw. I seem to recall Chris saying afterwards, *"Thanks Boss, I deserved that."*

Not slow to take the local administrator's hint, we weighed anchor and chugged off down the coast towards Madang and Lae. Madang was mostly a brief social visit with the real work beginning in Lae. Earlier in the year an Australian Naval Patrol Boat had visited the Lae Yacht club and had run aground on an *'uncharted'* reef. When a ship's diver had been put over the side it was discovered that the *'reef'* was in fact a pyramid of dumped WWII high explosive ordnance. The ship was safely floated off on the next high tide and the discovery reported for the attention of CDT1.

During WWII it was not an uncommon practice for the Americans to ditch excess ordnance and equipment over the side of a vessel. One of the incredible things about New Guinea is that a ship can be alongside a wharf with the water depth on the inboard side being 40 feet or less and the outboard side being 200 to 300 feet or more. As a consequence, they probably believed they were dumping surplus ordnance into sufficiently deep water.

The Lae *'dump'* consisted mainly of anti-aircraft ammunition, piled up the slope from a depth of about 80 feet. For this we needed to use our 60/40 mixture diving equipment working on a muddy 45-degree slope. The search area was covered in a very fine silt and not only did this make it a particularly unpleasant job, but sediment in the tropics can cause divers all sorts of problems. I quickly came down with severe ear infections which have continued to cause me problems throughout my life. After a few days of diving in the bacterial contamination of the silt, a number of the team had *'boils'* (abscesses) breaking out on their arms.

As the ordnance was recovered, we headed about 200 metres offshore and dumped it over the side – in about 500 metres of water.

Our stopover in Rabaul was at the request of the Seismic station where they were constantly monitoring the volcanic activity throughout that part of the world. We were asked to drop 40 pound (18 kg) explosive charges into deep water while they measured the shock wave reflections on their measuring equipment. From memory, it had something to do with calibrating their more delicate instruments.

While in Rabaul, we were asked to check out a local backyard where a home gardener had uncovered a suspicious looking metal drum. We recognised it immediately as a WWII Japanese depth charge. With a little careful digging we soon discovered 15 more neatly laid out in two rows. This family had been living with a potentially catastrophic time bomb in their backyard for over 25 years. We had no choice but to physically remove them to a safe location for disposal. A major concern was the sensitivity of the filling. The Japanese used Picric Acid explosive in most of their ordnance and this became extremely unstable with age. As there was nowhere locally to detonate such a large quantity of explosives, we decided to dump them in deep water. Fortunately, there is no shortage of that in PNG. From memory they are now sitting in over 1,000 metres of water.

With a couple of days to kill, we took the opportunity to dive on some of the Japanese merchant ships lying on the bottom of Rabaul harbour in about 180 feet of water.

At every port of call the local Australian Patrol officer was waiting to show us his collection of old ordnance. This varied from an unexploded 16-inch naval shell, obviously fired from a US battleship, through to Japanese land mines.

When we examined a dozen or so Japanese JE anti-boat mines it appeared that most of the explosives had been eroded away by time and weather. Assuming this to be the case, Blue Furner and I lit the safety fuse and retired to a large tree no more than 50 metres away. We couldn't believe what happened next. The concussion from the blast was bad enough but the shrapnel that hit our tree was unbelievable. All of the bark on the exposed side was completely stripped away and it seemed to rain metal fragments for several minutes. These mines when new each contained 21kg (47 lbs.) of high explosives so that we may have been messing with close to 600lbs of Picric acid. A valuable lesson about assuming anything to do with old ordnance.

As we moved up through the islands of New Britain and New Ireland, we visited some of the most idyllic places on the planet. Just palm trees, beautiful white sandy beaches, magnificent coral reefs and crystal clear waters which were alive with crayfish, shells and fish of every description. Everywhere we went the diving was spectacular. Most of the bush airstrips had the remains of numerous old Japanese aircraft parked alongside the runways.

Another of our regular tasks was to blast channels through reefs to allow better access for the local villagers' canoes. This was achieved by placing obsolete Mk 10 anti-submarine mortars at set distances across the top of the reef and detonating them all instantaneously at high tide. This always resulted in a very symmetrical sandy bottomed channel about 5 or 6 metres wide and 2 metres deep.

These mortars weighed in at 400 lbs and contained 207 pounds of *'Minol'* explosive. The locals happily volunteered to help us carry them across the reef and place them into position. We stressed to them not to drop the mortars and as they were very eager to impress, they took their task very seriously. Once while I was watching 6 locals gingerly stepping across the reef (in bare feet) with their mortar, they all disappeared from sight as they stepped off the edge of the reef. One mortar and 6 natives gone.... We thought no big deal as we could recover it easily enough. As time went on and no natives reappeared on the surface, we realised how seriously they were taking their instructions. One of our team had to jump in and signal that it was OK to let go of the mortar and come to the surface.

In the main the natives were very friendly and happy people although we often laughed about the need to *'retrain'* them each day in the simplest of tasks. They lived an idyllic lifestyle which had changed very little for thousands of years.

The old *Arcturus* was not built for the tropics and there was no way any of us could sleep in the cabins, especially while underway. The heat rising from the engine room was unbearable.

We all slept under a canvas awning just for'ard of the bridge. This was fine while the weather was warm and balmy however it wasn't so good during the severe rain squalls which regularly came out of nowhere. Fortunately, we were used to being wet. It was what we did for a living.

One of our last jobs was on a remote island quite a distance from the main islands. While enroute, the old tub caught fire. A bucket brigade soon brought things back to normal and we reflected on what might have happened had we not been able to beat the fire. We were at least 100 kilometres from the nearest land and the chart showed that we had close to 3,000 feet of water beneath us.

Suntanned and fit, we eventually worked our way back to Manus Island to await our RAAF flight home. As a result of our earlier misadventures we thought it wise to spend our last few days away from the Naval base. We had found a beautiful beach not too far away and spent our time there snorkelling, eating crayfish and drinking beer.

I had a serious fright one day after having consumed my share of the old South Pacific Lager. We were just climbing into our Landcruiser for the trip back to Tarangau when I discovered that I couldn't breathe. As much as I tried, nothing happened. It was as if the muscles of my diaphragm had completely seized. Harry Brankstone was belting me on the back thinking something was stuck in my throat. Thoughts were rushing into my head about my burst lung and I thought it had finally caught up with me. I really thought it was all over when just as suddenly I was able to breathe again. The medics were unable to explain what had happened and it was to hit me again several years later while on leave in Adelaide. It gave my uncle quite a scare as we had been drinking at his local country pub and he thought I was having a heart attack. Touch wood, it hasn't happened since.

We were no sooner back from PNG when we were advised that we were off to the Far East for exercises with the Poms and the Yanks. The team was to be embarked aboard HMAS Stalwart as all the exercises were to revolve around mine sweeping and mine countermeasures, and she was to be the mother vessel for the Aussie minehunters participating in the joint exercises off Malaya and the Philippines. Stalwart was designated a Destroyer Tender and was basically a huge floating repair shop. She was a relatively new ship with the best of accommodation and had huge storage facilities with cranes to lift our vehicles and boats on and off as required. We knew it was going to be good trip as each accompanying minehunter carried several CDs and the senior skipper of the squadron was a Clearance Diving officer. Not only were my two old team mates from Vietnam, Blue and Digger, with me on Team 1, Narra was on one of the Minehunters.

It didn't take long before we were in trouble. The ships spent a couple of days in Darwin on our passage north. Stalwart had to anchor out in the bay while the smaller ships were alongside the wharf. Staggering back along the wharf one-night heading for where the liberty boat from Stalwart would pick us up, we noticed that the Hunters were having an officer's cocktail party on the outboard vessel (all three ships were secured abreast of each other with only the inboard vessel being tied to the wharf). Divers hate to see officers having a good time so without any further ado, Blue Furner casually slipped the lines on the inboard vessel. By the time the quartermaster realised that the entire Mine hunting squadron was no longer secured to the wharf, we were on our way back to Stalwart. L/Cmdr. Burns (*Lumpy Bum*) was not impressed. Being a diving officer it didn't take him long to arrive at the conclusion that CDs had to be responsible for slipping his boats and disrupting his cocktail party. Mac was told in no uncertain terms that his team was being watched very closely and none of us should cross paths with Lumpy Bum for a considerable time.

By the time we arrived in Singapore, beards were all the go. No sooner had Stalwart tied up alongside at the Sembawang naval dockyard than we had our Landcruiser unloaded and ready to go. First *'official visit'* was to the Singapore Navy's diving base. We all knew most of their divers as they had all been trained by the RAN.

Once onboard their diving tender, it was out with the Anchor and Tiger beer. As the morning wore on we had divers being tossed over the side and generally behaving as divers often do after a few drinks. By the time we left our hosts, most of us were wearing Singapore Navy shirts and those of us who were actually wearing caps, weren't wearing RAN issue. Unfortunately, we timed our return to Stalwart very badly. Just as we pulled up to the gangway and literally all fell out the back, the Captain of Stalwart was just coming down the ship's brow to his waiting car, on his way to attend an official luncheon. It was obvious from the look on his face that we (the Boss most likely) were in a bit of trouble. We scrambled onboard and most of us headed for somewhere to get our heads down. Jock Kingston woke up about 11pm that night spread-eagled in our Hercules aluminium boat which was stored in a forward hold. He had no clothes on and didn't have a clue where he was. Our mess was located at the opposite end of the ship but no one took much notice as he tiptoed back to his bunk as that sort of thing was *'par for the course'* for Jock. Definitely a crazy man. By that time the rest of us had already showered, eaten and descended on the bars of Sembawang.

From memory we spent about a week in Singapore and a book could be written about the trouble we got into. As if Mac wasn't in enough trouble after bringing his team back drunk and out of uniform in the middle of the day, one night he took the team vehicle ashore on the grog. On our return to the ship, with most of the team in the back, I remember sitting in the front giving Mac directions to avoid driving into the storm drains as he was in no shape to see them. He definitely would have failed the breathalyser that night.

I think that was the same night the shit hit the fan in the *'Melbourne'* Bar. The entire team plus every CD from the minehunters were drinking in the bar and were having a great time when a number of Maoris from a Kiwi ship came in. Had they known the bar was full of Aussie CDs, they might not have stayed. A band was playing and when they stopped for a break, Johnno Johnson decided he would show us all that he was a better drummer than the bloke in the band. He climbed up onto the stage and began belting away. Within 30 seconds he had tripped arse over head, knocked over the entire drum stand and fell clean through the base drum, completely destroying it. We thought this was hilarious but apparently the Kiwis took exception to it and the largest Maori in the group decided to give Johnno a bit of a biff. As he moved in to thump Johnno, who was too drunk to fight the neighbourhood cat, Narra stepped up to the big Maori and said *"If you want to fight my mate, you'll have to fight me first and I'll give you a two hit start"*. The Maori couldn't believe that anyone would be so stupid. He took a swing at Narra and before he knew what had happened, Narra had him on his back and was punching the living shit out of him. His mates, seeing that the big loud mouth was getting a thorough hiding, moved forward to help him. Before they had taken a single step, they were stopped in their tracks and firmly warned to leave it *'one on one'*. Glancing around at the faces in the bar, they immediately realised they were way out of their depth. The big Maori quickly indicated that he had enough and was carried out by his shocked mates. By the time Johnno climbed out of the base drum, it was all over and he mumbled to no one in particular, *"What the fuck was that all about"*.

The team was in fine form and we hadn't even started work.

Finally, we sailed for the west coast of Malaya to begin the first exercise. The whole team transferred across to HMS Monkton, a British minesweeper which was to be our support vessel for our phase of the operation. A large field of ground mines had been laid to make the exercise realistic. The Aussie minehunters had to find everything in to a depth of 180 feet and we had to locate, identify, render safe everything between them and the beach. Monkton would then recover our mines as we found them. As these were genuine mines (minus explosives), we had to use our Drager mixture sets *(being both magnetically and acoustically safe)*. This meant a lot of hard work as our mixture cylinders had to be filled from larger storage cylinders via a hand booster pump - memories of CD training. The storage cylinders when full were only around 1800 psi and we needed to pump our sets to 3000 psi. Once again we lived on the upper deck and slept on canvas stretchers. There wasn't a lot of fresh water available for showers but that wasn't unusual on British warships. As a consequence, we only used our ration of *'freshers'* to wash down our diving equipment at the end of each day.

On completion of the exercise we sailed for Penang which was home to RAAF base Butterworth. The team was invited to a number of parties on the base and the *'Bubblies'* were a major social hit with all except the male half of the airbase. Several events occurred there which I feel should not be put in writing as I don't wish to incriminate or embarrass any of my old teammates.

From there it was on to Manila Bay to exercise with the US Navy. Same sort of thing but a little less organised. Once again we transferred to a minesweeper for the operation. This time to an old WWII US minesweeper, the USS Force. Lots of flavoured milk, doughnuts, hamburgers and the American way, which brought back many memories for the ex Team 3 members. When we made our final departure from the *'Force'* at 0730 one morning, we souvenired their Ensign (flag) and the ship's bell. So at 0800 that morning when the Officer of the Deck ordered the bell to be rung and the flag hoisted, there was no bell & no flag. We had a good laugh about it because we could imagine the absolute pandemonium on board. A week or so later we were told that after sailing from the Philippines, the Force had caught fire and sank. Nothing was saved and so nothing remains of this ship other than the CDT1 souvenirs, and these sadly were in turn souvenired by some thieving low-life after we returned to Waterhen. In later years we tried to track them down so we could return the flag and the bell to the USS Force Association - sadly without success.

With the Aussie ships taking several days for R&R in Manila, the Team jumped at the opportunity to visit the huge Subic Bay Naval Base 54 kms to the north of Manila and catch up with the resident US Navy SEAL and EOD teams based there. SBNB with the city of Olongapo situated right outside the base, was one of the most famous and popular ports of call in the world for both US & Australian sailors.

During the Vietnam War, Subic Bay became the US Seventh Fleet's forward operating base. The average number of ships visiting the base per month rose from 98 in 1964 to 215 by 1967. The base, with 6 wharves, 2 piers, and 160 mooring points and anchorages, had about 30 ships in port on any given day. About one-third of these were Military Sea Transportation Service ships bringing in 45,000 tons of food, ammunition, and supplies and 2 million barrels of fuel oil, aviation gasoline, and JP-4 jet fuel each month. During 1967 alone, visiting sailors purchased more than $25 million in duty-free goods from the Navy Exchange. The base also provided employment to fifteen thousand Filipino civilians.

The wild nightclubs along Ramon Magsaysay Drive outside the naval base main gate were notorious amongst sailors the world over. Talented Filipino musicians and singers, inexpensive San Miguel beer, attractive teen-age bar-girls, (said to number over 30,000), floor shows, Jeepney rides back to the naval base and children diving for coins tossed from the bridge by sailors over the drainage canal in front of the naval base main gate.

Soon after our arrival the US teams dragged us out to the high spots of downtown Olongapo with Johnno once again making a name for himself in the *'New Jollo Bar'*. Subic Bay had a well-deserved reputation for providing a good time and we weren't disappointed. The town's main street, Ramon Magsaysay Drive, was called *'Shit Street'* by sailors and consisted of wall to wall bars which spread down every side street as well. As you left the Naval Base gates you had to cross the *'Shit River'*, aptly named because of what it contained. Every night there would be young boys swimming under the bridge waiting for sailors to throw one peso coins into the river. They would then duck dive in the filthy water to recover them. They never missed a coin....

The town of Olongapo and its bars existed solely to service visiting warships, the US Naval Base and the nearby Cubi Point Naval Air Station.

About halfway along Shit street there was a bar which kept a young crocodile out the front in a fenced enclosure. Every so often the owners would feed a duckling to the crocodile for the amusement of the American sailors. One night a slightly inebriated Aussie sailor, thoroughly disgusted and feeling empathy toward the defenceless little duckling, jumped the fence, wrestled with the croc for a few minutes and finally heaved it out onto the road, straight under the wheels of a passing Jeepney (US

Jeeps copies converted into very colourful Philippino taxis), much to the delight of his fellow Aussies.

Sadly, the time soon came for us to return to Stalwart and re-enter the real Navy. We weren't the most popular sailors with the Stalwart's wardroom and Mac also found it difficult to relate to the officers from the regular navy. One evening just after the beer issue, there was a knock on the door of our mess deck. The Stalwart sailor who answered the door was taken aback to see a Lieutenant standing there with a half a dozen or so cans of beer in his arms asking *"Are any of my boys here?"*. Mac came in and joined us, sitting on the floor of the Mess sharing our beer issue. The other sailors couldn't believe it – a naval officer sitting in their Messdeck drinking with his sailors. Mac told us he was sick of talking to *'those wankers'* in the wardroom and would rather have a beer with us. Not surprisingly, Mac was one of the most highly respected and well liked officers in the diving branch.

From Manila we headed for home and back to the more mundane diving jobs and ongoing training. As the year came to a close, I was advised that I had been posted back to the Diving school as a student on the next Advanced Diving course.

11
ADVANCED CD COURSE – 1973

On the 30th January 1973, along with *'Cowby'* Garrett and *'Occa'* Howarth from my AB's course, I posted into HMAS Penguin to begin advanced CD training which would provide me with the qualifications for promotion to Petty Officer Clearance Diver – a *'Senior Sailor'*. This course was something of a repeat of the AB's course in terms of PT and run jumps but we were treated with a touch more respect than we had received on our AB's course. The difference in the level of training was that we were to come out at the other end fully qualified to supervise all forms of Navy diving, EOD and demolitions.

Throughout the Advanced course, the students pretty much ran the everyday evolutions under the watchful eyes of our instructors, each of us taking turns planning and supervising the day to day diving, demolition and EOD activities. An ABCD course under training, which was running concurrently with our own, allowed us to practice and develop our supervision and planning skills. The learning curve was quite steep as there was no room for error. If we were to be trusted to supervise all forms of Naval diving and the handling and use of explosives, we were expected to *'have our shit in one bag'*.

One vivid memory of the EOD and Demolitions phase at Marangaroo in the Blue Mountains was a forced march prior to commencing night demolition training. In addition to our packs we each had to carry two 4.5-inch naval shells. Weighing 25kgs (55lbs) each, it was an extremely awkward and uncomfortable evolution.

General Purpose 500lb bombs were regularly dropped into the deepest creeks with the steepest banks that our instructors could find and the class would have to firstly find them, render them safe and then recover them from the creek-bed using nothing other than initiative and lots of muscle.

It was quite obvious by then that the Vietnam experience had had a major influence on the direction in which the Branch was evolving. There was an increased focus on infantry tactics and playing soldiers. We used commando type *'Klepper'* canoes for night insertions, patrolled and set all night ambushes in the scrub. We searched mock-up Vietnamese villages and practised contact drills. We had learnt that it was necessary for the Branch to be proficient in multi-role warfare. In my opinion there was a definite need for some of the SEAL type skills. The Branch had learnt from its Vietnam exposure.

I particularly enjoyed the Advanced Demolition phase of the course. My interest in explosives was continuing to grow. I also discovered that I was gaining a great deal of satisfaction from being given increased responsibilities for planning and supervision of diving and EOD operations.

In those days the RAN also trained Malaysian Navy Clearance Divers and we had two of them attached to our advanced course. They were good blokes but a bit of a handicap. They pretty much had to pass no matter what. The Malaysian government was paying for their instruction and expected them to qualify whether they were good or bad.

The mind games never let up. Often, after completing a full days diving, we'd wrap up around midnight, have a quick shower and head for our bunks on the diving tender Porpoise. The Chief instructor would regularly allow us just enough time to doze off and then it would be lights on and *"Let's go boys, we've got work to do."*

Finally, on the 30th November the long course came to an end and we were all qualified for the next step in our promotion to Petty Officer. Once again, much to my delight, I had topped the course. It was then a matter of us each working our way to the top of the Promotions list over time and waiting for the next vacancy for Petty Officer Clearance Diver.

12
CDT1 – 1974/75

On the 7th January 1974, I posted back into CDT1 at HMAS Waterhen for 2 years to fill one of the Leading Hand billets.

Team one was the plum posting in the CD Branch. It was the Branch's fully mobile team and was ready to respond immediately to anything the Navy threw at it. Many of the tasks involved trips to SE Asia. Being sailors first and foremost, these were the highlights of the posting to CDT1.

As usual, the year began with diving, EOD and demolition workups which brought all team members up to speed with the latest equipment and procedures.

The three high points of 1974 were our participation in SPECWAREX '74 in the Philippines, the Crown of Thorns starfish survey on the Great Barrier Reef and the joint exercise 'Kangaroo One'.

Much to our delight we had been invited by the US military to participate in their SPECWAREX (special warfare exercises) in Subic Bay, just north of Manila in the Philippines. Team 1, along with SAS troops from Swanbourne in Western Australia and a handful of New Zealand SAS troops boarded a RAAF C-130 Hercules out of Richmond Air Force base in Sydney bound for Subic with an overnight stop in Darwin. Also taking part in the exercises were US Navy SEALs, Green Berets, Marine Recon and Philippino special forces.

I was the only ex CDT3 Vietnam vet in our contingent but I was very pleased to see that many of the SEALs and EOD unit had served in Vietnam. I felt very comfortable socialising and working with these blokes. It was a bit like a family reunion.

The main purpose of this multi-national get-together was to cross train and in the process pick the eyes out of the skill sets each unit excelled in. We operated with the SEALs from the US Navy Special Warfare submarine USS Grayback, conducting day and night submerged launch and recoveries, wet deck launch and recoveries and periscope tows, ops with Swimmer Delivery Vehicles (SDVs), conducted covert ship attacks and covert beach reconnaissance. We fired thousands of rounds of ammunition with every weapon the SEALs held in their inventory and spent a lot of time practising the art of instinctive shooting - and we drank lots of beer whenever the opportunity presented itself.

In one of the EOD evolutions, we disposed of forty-eight 1,000 pound bombs and 2 large ground mines in about 30 feet of water. A particularly spectacular shot for the younger members of the team.

We averaged about one night off in three and not wanting to waste a minute, we hit the high spots of Olongapo. The EOD team was permanently stationed in Subic Bay and so they had their favourite bars downtown. One in particular I recall with very fond memories was the *'Bamboo Grove'*. There was a Navy imposed curfew every night from midnight so most of the regular Navy would be back on base as the clock struck 12. Naturally we would all be tucked up in one of our favourite bars where Mamasan would lock the doors and we would party on into the small hours. When we'd had enough, the girls would bring out mattresses and we would sleep on the floor or the tables, whichever looked the most comfortable at the time. As 0600 rolled around and the curfew was lifted, it was back onboard for a quick shower and breakfast and into the day's exercises. Thankfully we were young and fit enough to be able to keep up this pace for the duration of the exercise. Sadly, after 2 weeks it all came to an end and it was back onto the noisy C130 for the flight home. We were all very disappointed to be leaving one of the best sailor's runs in the world.

Kangaroo One was Australia's largest multi-national defence exercise and included armed forces from Australia, New Zealand, the UK and the USA. Some 15,000 servicemen (3,500 RAN), 38 ships (22 RAN) and 200 aircraft participated. Our main role was to survey and clear the approaches to the beach-head prior to landing craft assaulting the beach and disgorging several hundred Marines into the exercise area. Ours was a joint operation with the US Navy's SEAL Team One and UDT (U/W Demolition Team) 11. Once we had cleared the approaches to the beach and the immediate hinterland, we demonstrated fast drop and pick-ups for the fleet sailors before transferring to a heavy landing craft to continue *'cross training'* - supposedly more diving and demolition training. Instead we found some nice sandy beaches well clear of the war games, ran the LCH up onto the beach and proceeded to catch fish, swim, sunbake, barbecue and drink beer. What the Navy calls a *'banyan'*. One morning at low tide we discovered a very large sea turtle stranded by the outgoing tide. We dragged him up onto the beach and kept him damp with wet bags until the tide came back in. Before we released him, we painted in large red letters across his back, *'CDT1, SEAL Team One, UDT 11'*. I have often wondered if this old fella is still swimming around the Pacific Ocean. It is quite possible as their lifespan is about 80 years. They are an amazing animal - green sea turtles can stay under water for as long as five hours. Their heart rate slows to conserve oxygen and nine minutes can elapse between heartbeats.

One of the SEALs operating with us was a Vietnam Veteran by the name of Darryl Wilson. *'Willy'* and I hit it off from day one and we spent many an hour just bullshitting about life in general and nothing in particular. When we returned to Sydney, Willy came to my home for dinner and Antoinette cooked him roast lamb. Being a farm boy from Missouri it was the first time he had ever tasted lamb. Unfortunately, Willy and I lost contact after he returned home to the States and left the Navy. It was to be more than 30 years before we caught up again.

In 2004 my brother Mike and I were travelling by train from Los Angeles to New Orleans to meet up with an old friend of his from his Vietnam days before driving north with him to a reunion of the *'Inshore Undersea Warfare Group'* being held in Indianapolis. One evening while sitting in the train's dining car, Mike noticed a lady wearing a jacket with a *'Navy'* patch and proceeded to strike up a conversation. One thing led to another and we discovered she was returning home to Texas from a Navy SEAL reunion in San Diego. We mentioned to her that we had known a few SEALs from our Vietnam days so next morning when she joined us for breakfast, she handed me a book called *'The Men behind the Trident'* (the Trident being the badge worn by qualified SEALs). I casually flicked to the photo section in the middle of the book and the first photo I saw was of three SEALs cammed up, armed to the teeth and ready to go out on a night Op in Vietnam. I chuckled and said *'That's Willy!!!!'* Her jaw dropped and she said, *'You know Willy?'* I told her he had been a good mate of mine but I had lost touch with him more than 30 years earlier. She picked up her cell phone and dialled a number, then said *'Willy I'm with someone on the train who knows you'* and passed me the phone. I just said *'How the hell are you Willy?'*. I guess my deep voice and Aussie accent was not hard to pick but it had been over 30 years. There was about a 2 or 3 second pause and Willy exclaimed, *'Goddamn Tony!!!!'*

It's a very small world....

Willy and I have again become the best of mates and since catching up with him, I now travel to the US once a year to spend 2 months with Willy riding our Harleys all over the Rocky Mountains and riding to the annual reunion of SEAL Team 1 in Coronado, California. Following the SEAL reunion, we also make the pilgrimage on our *'Hogs'* to Oregon for the annual *'Inshore Undersea Warfare Group 1'* reunion. These blokes crewed the River Patrol Boats (PBRs) in Vietnam from which SEALs and CD's often operated. While in the US, Willy and I usually average about 4,000 miles on our bike trips. I have every intention of continuing to attend these annual reunions until I'm too old to get on an airplane or throw my leg over a Harley.

On the subject of it being a small world, several years ago I was standing at a boarding gate at Bangkok International airport when I heard a voice call out *"Hey Tony"*. I turned to see Gary Parrott - Willy's SEAL platoon officer from Vietnam and also a good friend of mine. He was travelling on the same flight as me....

In 1974 the Australian Institute of Marine Science (AIMS), located at James Cook University in Townsville, requested the assistance of CDT1 as part of their ongoing research into the *'Crown of Thorns'* starfish. This extremely ugly and unpleasant character is an unusually large starfish and can grow to more than 30 inches (80 cms) in diameter. It has up to 21 arms with the entire upper surface of its body covered in long venomous spines. A crown of thorns starfish begins to breed when it is 2 to 3 years old and breeds for 5 to 7 years. Each female can produce up to 60 million eggs during a single spawning season and while population blooms of these animals are considered a naturally occurring event, their frequency has increased from once in 80 years or so, to approximately once in every 15 years. When the starfish find living coral, they extrude their stomach out through their mouth to cover the living coral tissue which is then liquefied by digestive enzymes that are secreted from the stomach. The starfish can move up to 20 metres in an hour and they have an incredibly ability to regenerate from just one severed arm and part of the central disc.

At that time - 1974, not a lot was known about their feeding and migration habits and the overall effect they were having on live reefs. AIMS intention was to conduct a survey of a number of outlying reefs to determine population density and the damage inflicted by the apparent surge in their numbers.

We, along with several Marine biologists, deployed with all our gear aboard a Navy Landing Craft (Heavy) to the outer reef. With accommodation being a little tight aboard the LCH, several of us were billeted on a civilian charter boat which accompanied the survey. As luck would have it, the Skipper was not only a mad keen fisherman, he was a qualified Chef and did all the cooking. For the next 6 weeks those few of us who were lucky enough to be living on his boat dined on freshly caught and superbly cooked reef fish. While we were out conducting our starfish surveys during the day, he was reeling in Sweetlip, Coral Trout, Red Emperor and numerous other reef delicacies for breakfast, lunch and dinner. It was a tough life but somehow we managed to survive.

The AIMS objective was to survey a selected number of reefs to obtain a reasonably accurate estimate of the number of live starfish, overall percentage of live coral remaining, percentage of dead coral and the number of feeding scars on a reef.

Interestingly, the Crown of Thorns often destroyed a patch of reef about the same diameter as its body and then for some unknown reason would move up to several metres looking for greener pastures. This left a patchwork of bleached feeding 'scars' all over a reef. We found reefs virtually untouched and others totally destroyed.

Due to the difficulty in swimming over the top of a reef at anything but high tide, we confined our survey to the reef's very outer edges which coincidentally were where the large Tiger sharks liked to prowl. It certainly gets your attention when you spot a 12-foot Tiger approaching you on a reciprocal course.

At the end of the survey the LCH pulled into the town of Bowen for a well-earned break. On the first day ashore, all dozen or so of the team walked into the main bar of the local hotel intent on enjoying a few cold beers. We immediately attracted the attention of the barmaids – not every day I suppose that 12 well-tanned and very fit looking young men walk through their front door. After being asked who we were, our Chief, John Kershler explained to the girls that we were Navy divers and had been working out on the reef for the past 6 weeks. One of the girls beamed and told us that one of the Hotel's barmen was an ex-Navy Clearance Diver who had served in Vietnam. When she told us his name we knew we had discovered another *'wannabe'* bullshit artist. He was due to begin his shift within the hour so we thought we would hang around for a bit. John asked the girls not to say anything about us to this clown when he arrived to start work. When he eventually got to serve at our end of the bar, John mentioned we were from the Navy Landing Craft down at the wharf and said we heard he had been a Clearance Diver. Assuming our group to be just regular sailors, he, with a little encouragement from John, eagerly began spinning us war stories about his time as a Clearance Diver. The same stories he had been telling the regular customers for years. In fact, the entire bar had gone quiet so as to listen to his incredible long winded war stories. After 20 or so minutes of listening to his bullshit, John said in a voice that everyone could hear, *"Well that's very interesting, but see all these blokes here at the bar with me, they're all Clearance Divers and half of them are Vietnam vets, and none of us know you. You're full of shit."* You could have heard a pin drop in the bar – he just stared at John for a few seconds with his mouth open and then bolted for the door, never to be seen again.

One Friday afternoon – 19 July '74 – as we were changing into civvies to head home for the weekend, the Boss came out of his office to tell us that the landing craft, HMAS Buna, had just lost her bow door while returning to Sydney from Norfolk Island in heavy seas, forcing her to stop and turn stern-to into the sea. All team leave was immediately cancelled and we were to get ourselves across to Garden Island where HMAS Parramatta was standing by to go to the rescue. As soon as we were aboard, Parramatta slipped her lines and we raced through the Heads at 26 knots, ploughing into a head sea. At that point we were under the impression that Buna's bow door was hanging vertically in the water and we would have to cut it away with our underwater cutting gear. For the next several hours we ploughed on into a huge easterly swell. Sleep was impossible. The Captain asked to see us all on the bridge to discuss what our options were once we arrived at Buna's location. To my great surprise, it was JD Foster, my ex divisional officer from Yarra days. The very same officer who had saved my backside so many times. He recognised me at once and began grinning like a Cheshire cat, obviously very pleased to see me again. The rest of the team stood around while JD and I briefly reminisced about old times. I think the Bridge watch was a little taken aback to see their Captain chatting to a Leading Seaman like they were the best of mates. Then it was down to business. We told JD we were ready to go but until we saw the state of Buna's bow and the sea state, any firm plans would have to wait until we arrived.

The further east we travelled, the larger the swells became. As we finally approached Buna we were advised that the bow door had actually broken off at the hinges a little earlier and was now at the bottom of the ocean. We were quite relieved as the only task remaining now was to take her in tow back to Sydney. The sea state was horrendous so if we had had to cut away the door, it would have been very close to suicide. Buna had her stern facing into the oncoming swells and had her engines going astern just enough to maintain steerage way. Had she been bow on to the sea, she would have gone down like a rock.

With great difficulty, as it was still the middle of the night, a towing hawser was eventually passed to her. During this evolution, while needing to stay close to Buna, the hawser unfortunately became wrapped around Parramatta's port screw. That meant she immediately lost the use of that propeller which left Parramatta at the mercy of the sea and we were soon broadside on to the huge swells. What followed were a couple of extremely uncomfortable hours. There was nothing we could do until daylight. As the much awaited dawn approached we realised that there would be no alternative other than to put a diver in the water with a hacksaw to cut through the nylon hawser. Parramatta was still abeam the swell and was steadily rolling through about 90 degrees. To make matters worse the stern was constantly rising up out of the water and thumping back down with a tremendous crash into the sea. The task looked near impossible and extremely dangerous but there was no other option – we had to have a go. The boss of the team, LCDR Dave Ramsden, flatly refused to risk any of his team in the water under such conditions. He said he would do it himself. We argued that it was our job but he wouldn't budge. The team's nickname for Dave was *'chicken man'* because if he turned sideways he barely cast a shadow. But it became obvious to us all that day that he had the heart of a lion. I still don't know how he managed to hang onto the propeller shaft while it was pounded by the relentless swells but he finally cut through the hawser. It was one of the gutsiest and most dangerous things I have ever seen. We had a new respect for the *'chicken man'* from that day forward. He should have been given a medal for bravery but in those days the Navy wasn't particularly generous with awards.

Finally, Parramatta took Buna under what proved to be a very difficult tow – she had to be towed stern first. We eventually returned to Sydney on 24 July, 5 days after our mad dash to the east.

The remainder of the year passed relatively quietly as did the early months 1975. On the 13th June 1975 I received the exciting news that I had been promoted to Petty Officer Clearance Diver.

The last few months of that year were taken up with several routine trips to the Great Barrier Reef to dispose of WW2 sea mines which had been discovered embedded in the reef. The Defence Film unit had gotten wind of our ongoing role in removing these old WW2 hazards and decided to produce a movie documenting the discovery through to the subsequent disposal of real live sea mines - to be called *'Mine on Channel Reef'*. This involved several trips to Cairns with the unit filming the Team doing our *'thing'*. Unfortunately, the unit didn't have an underwater cameraman so I was seconded to do the U/W filming as well as supervising the operation.

As '75 drew to a close, I was advised of my next posting. I was returning to HMAS Penguin as the Demolitions instructor at the EOD school, a posting which appealed to me greatly as I loved anything to do with explosives.

13

DEMOLITION INSTRUCTOR - 1976

To be posted as the CD Branch's Demolition instructor was one of the many highlights of my career. To my mind, diving instruction was relatively boring when compared with the opportunity to *'play'* with and instruct in the use of high explosives.

The EOD school was situated within the grounds of HMAS Penguin but quite separate to the Diving school so the three senior instructors were pretty much left to run their own routines.

Mick Cook was the Chief Petty Officer and in charge of the school. His responsibility was instructing surface EOD while POCD Russ Steer instructed underwater EOD and my baby was surface and underwater Demolitions. I taught the students how to blow things up - safely. Can't get much more fun than that. I was ably assisted by Leading Seaman Geoff Bascombe, a very competent and conscientious sailor. We were all responsible for training the basic CD courses, the advanced CD courses and the Officers courses in every aspect of surface ordnance recognition and disposal, underwater ordnance recognition and disposal, improvised explosive devices, sabotage and the use of high explosives as an effective tool.

The handling and use of explosives is a very precise occupation and there is no room for error. Not too many second chances – in fact none. I took my responsibilities very seriously and expected my students to do the same. I had zero tolerance for anything less than the greatest respect for explosives. My goal was to graduate Clearance Divers who could say of their demolition skills with justifiable pride – *'Tony Ey trained me'*.

As there were only several classes a year, Geoff and I had enough spare time to experiment with explosive techniques and produce training aids for the school's EOD museum.

We conducted all of our *'Demo'* training on the Army ranges at Marangaroo in the Blue Mountains to the west of Sydney. The Army depot (223 Supply Company) was the storage area for many of the Army's larger munitions and its warehouses were set back deep in the mountain valleys. We had the full use of what were referred to as the *'internal'* and *'external'* ranges.

The internal range had a lower explosive weight limit than the external so there we conducted the initial training where students were introduced to the basics – safety, testing firing circuits and firing small charges. Later in the course we would move out to the external range where much larger quantities of explosives were handled and students were introduced to the awesome power of the high explosives at our disposal.

I had a natural inquisitiveness about explosives and their properties and regularly had my head buried in every text book I could lay my hands on. I was particularly interested in the fact that in the right hands, explosives could be used with extreme precision to perform useful work. To my mind there was no reason why explosives could not be used as skilfully as a carpenter uses his wood working tools.

High explosives *'detonate'*, they do not *'explode'*. The amount of work and the type of work they perform is very much determined by their velocity of detonation (VOD), or the speed at which the shock wave front proceeds through the explosive compound – for example in PETN (the core of detonating cord), the VOD progresses at 8,400m/second or 27,000ft/second. Low explosives are generally compounds which do not detonate but *'deflagrate'* or burn very quickly (e.g. black powder and gunpowder) whereas in high explosives, an instantaneous chemical decomposition takes place and as a result, huge amounts of energy are released.

Explosives with low VODs are used where a pushing or shoving effect is required whereas high VOD explosives produce an extremely violent shattering effect. Both very useful tools if used correctly....

Between classes I took the opportunity to advance my own skills and knowledge. I completed the Army's IED (Improvised Explosive Device) course at Bandiana in Victoria. An extremely professionally run course conducted by the Army's Ammunition Technicians. To keep our minds on the job 24 hours a day, we could never simply walk into a classroom or even our accommodation without assuming that everything had been booby trapped. It would take our class the best part of 30 minutes to an hour just to get into the classroom to begin the day's theory. When we left for lunch, we had to assume that the instructors had booby trapped everything all over again. It never stopped... For our practical training they would seed a large number of buildings with IEDs, including all lines of approach. We had to assume nothing was safe and everything was a potential IED. An excellent course.

Towards the end of my 12-month stint instructing at the EOD school, I was *'kidnapped'* and underwent Code of Conduct training – probably the most unpleasant experience of my life, all the more so because it was so totally unexpected. Several of us were nearing the final phase of *'escape and evasion'* training conducted by No 1 Commando and as we entered a storeroom to be issued with our kit, we were pounced on, handcuffed and a bag tied over our heads. Thrown into the back of a truck we were then driven around for several hours until we were completely disoriented.

The course, designed to simulate being a prisoner of war of a Communist Asian country was conducted by Army SAS and Commando NCOs. After our release several days later, we discovered that the course had been conducted in old underground WW2 bunkers on Middle head in Sydney, only a short distance from the Diving school.

We never saw the light of day, only candlelight, so had no idea where we were or if it were midday or midnight. We were kept in solitary confinement in dark damp cells and sleep was out of the question. I spent a few nights – I think they were nights –

with my wrists handcuffed over an old overhanging water pipe, high enough that I either had to stand on tiptoe to relieve the weight on my wrists or accept the cutting pain from the handcuffs to relieve my aching ankles. All the time with an old smelly wheat bag over my head and repetitive communist music and propaganda blasting away from somewhere near my dungeon. At irregular intervals we were taken away to a larger cell for interrogation where we received the *'good guy/bad guy'* treatment. Our interrogators were of Asian appearance and wore North Vietnamese uniforms. The unpleasantries continued non-stop until we had completely lost track of time with no idea when it would end.

Our only occasional meal was overcooked sloppy rice, covered in greasy fat. When the course finally came to an end, I was beginning to believe that I had somehow actually been taken captive by the North Vietnamese.

Along with a number of NCOs from No 1 Commando I also participated in a *'Small Scale Raid Commanders'* course. This training culminated in an exercise where the class parachuted at night into an exercise area with *'Klepper'* canoes and proceeded to paddle for 2 long nights and hide up during the day. Our target was a civilian power station. We carried dummy demolition charges which we were to place at critical locations around the power station after infiltrating the civilian perimeter security. The regular army were out searching for us and the local Police had been asked to arrest us on sight. It was on the 2nd morning after we had just hidden our canoes and gone into hiding for the daylight hours when I was advised via a routine radio check that I had been selected for the Personal Exchange Program (PEP) with the US Navy's EOD Group One, based in Hawaii. After receiving that piece of outstanding news, I sailed through the rest of the exercise with a very large grin on my face. Two and a half years in Hawaii, all expenses paid. Not a bad life being a Navy Frogman.......

I had one last demo course to put through and on my second to last night at Marangaroo, the Sergeants mess bought me a bottle of Jack Daniels and of course I felt obliged to drink it all. When the rest of the Sergeants Mess went to bed they said I was unconscious but still sitting bolt upright on my bar stool. When I woke up in the early hours I was still on the barstool.... I spent the rest of the night in the company of a toilet bowl. The next day I was so ill that Russ Steer, who was up there for the Surface EOD phase, had to take my class and I spent the forenoon asleep in the explosives trailer.

For the best part of 12 months after that I could not even look at a bottle of Jack Daniels let alone drink any.

Nevertheless, it was a great send off and one I'll always remember.

14

USA – 1977/80

As the time approached for us to depart for the US, Antoinette and I decided to arrange a stopover in New Zealand for a few days to catch up with her sister and brother in law who lived on the North Island. After several days of visiting her family, we came close to missing our onward flight to Hawaii from Auckland airport as the New Zealand Immigration officials refused to allow us to board the flight without return tickets. Only after arguing with the most senior official that we had diplomatic visas and would not be returning to Australia for 2½ years did he reluctantly agree to let us board the aircraft. He was concerned that US Immigration may not allow us to enter the USA with one-way tickets and as our last point of departure was NZ, the Kiwis would then be responsible for returning us to Auckland. Dumb and dumber!!!!

So early on the morning of the 24th January 1977, Antoinette and I landed at Honolulu's International airport, as excited as two kids on Christmas morning, knowing that this exotic Pacific island paradise was to be our home for the next few years. Emerging from Immigration and Customs, we found two US Navy Chiefs from my new unit waiting to welcome us with the traditional Hawaiian greeting, *'Leis'* made from the beautifully scented flowers of the Frangipani - or Plumeria tree. The Master Chief of the Command, Master Chief Petty Officer John Hazeltine, CPO Larry Aanarud (known as *'Double A'*) and his wife Peggy delivered us to the Hotel Ilikai on Waikiki Beach with the very sound advice that we should get some sleep.

Over the next few days we touched base with the Australian Consulate and took the opportunity to take in the wonderful climate and lifestyle that was Honolulu. It was love at first sight. We hired a car and began exploring our new island home of Oahu.

I was the third RAN Clearance Diver to be posted for exchange duty with the US Navy. The first was POCD John Thompson who had spent his entire tour with the Navy's Salvage Divers based in Pearl Harbour. The second, CPOCD Harry Brankstone, began the long running exchange (which continues to this day) with the USN's Explosive Ordnance Disposal Group One (EODGRUONE), then based at West Loch situated on the western side of Pearl Harbour. For some obscure reason the Navy had posted Harry back to Australia 2 weeks prior to our arrival, leaving me without a handover or the benefit of his valuable experience gained from 2½ years working with the US Navy. We were not overly concerned, however it would have made life a little easier with respect to settling in, finding accommodation, shopping etc. After several days of playing tourist around Oahu and downtown Honolulu at the Navy's expense, we moved to a motel at Ewa Beach to be closer to West Loch so that I could begin my assimilation into the United States Navy.

Our first priority was to find a house and buy a car. Harry and his family had lived in an area known as Makakilo so we thought it was as good a place as any to start looking. The Americans had offered us a married quarter at the nearby Barber's Point Naval Air Station, but that had all the drawbacks associated with on-base living, so we settled for a house situated on the rising slopes of Makakilo overlooking the ocean on the south west corner of Oahu.

After drooling over the latest Ford V8 Mustangs which cost around US$5,000, we finally decided on a brand new 1977 fuel injected Volkswagen Rabbit (Golf). At the end of the day we were swayed by German engineering, reliability and resale value over American chrome and horsepower. Due to the Rabbit's popularity in the US at that time, large numbers were being flown in from Germany aboard B747 freighters in an effort to keep up with the demand. We paid US$4,200 for our new acquisition and it was one hell of a buy considering the Australian dollar bought US$1.15 at that time.

EODGRUONE was under the command of a Navy Captain (he was given the courtesy title of Commodore) who was also a qualified EOD technician as were all the officers and men of the Group with the exception of the administration and support staff. They were a completely self-sufficient Command and comprised an operational mobile unit, a training unit, vehicle and machine repair shops, a boat section, dive locker, parachute locker, and a sick bay complete with Doctor and medical corpsman. To my surprise, the Group headquarters were housed in old WW2 Quonset huts.

EOD Group Two was its east coast equivalent; responsible for supporting the Atlantic Fleet.

During the Vietnam War, EODGRUONE had been the command group for teams deployed to Vietnam, including our own RAN Clearance Diving Team 3, designated by the Americans as EODMUPAC Team 35.

To become an EOD technician in the US Navy, selected personnel underwent initial training at the EOD Chemical School at Redstone, Alabama. Students received classroom and practical instruction in the methods of identification, render safe, and disposal procedures for a wide variety of chemical and biological munitions. Daily physical conditioning readied students for diver training which occurred later in the course. Upon completion of this 5-week phase, students reported to Navy EOD School, Indian Head, Maryland, for 34 weeks of intensive study. The course was taught in five phases: the core phase, which was the foundation for the rest of the course included instruction in the use of EOD publications, special tools, explosive charges, and principles of applied physics; the ground phase dealt with land mines, booby traps, and fusing of launched or thrown ordnance. The air ordnance phase examined ordnance launched from aircraft; the underwater ordnance and diving phase studied torpedoes, contact/influence mines, and depth charges. In this phase the students were taught basic diving skills using open circuit SCUBA, semi-closed circuit SCUBA, MK 5 (hard hat surface supplied air) and MK 1 Bandmask (light weight surface supplied air). The final phase of training focused on nuclear ordnance and associated equipment. All phases utilised both classroom and practical instruction. Upon graduation, the Basic EOD Technicians were assigned to either EOD Group One, Pearl Harbour, Hawaii, or EOD Group Two, Fort Story, Virginia. At both Groups, EOD techs then received further on-the-job training and made at least one 6-month deployment aboard an Aircraft Carrier or Ammunition ship as a member of a 4-man EOD Team. On completion of their training they qualified for $110 per month incentive pay and at a later date were sent for parachute training.

It came as quite a surprise to me to discover that a diving supervisor remained current only in his present command. When arriving at a new posting, he was required to satisfy his command that he was up to date before being allowed to supervise diving. A diving supervisor could hold a qualification for any individual or combination of rigs and could be of virtually any rank whereas in the Australian system only Petty Officers and above could supervise diving, EOD and demolitions, however our supervisors remained current until they left the branch.

My previous experience had shown that CD's were more thoroughly trained in the areas of diving, demolitions and general seamanship and the US EOD sailors were more technically qualified in the field of EOD. Aussie CD's being *'jack of all trades'* are also more comfortable and capable around explosives. I believe this is a result of there being so few CDs when compared to the vast numbers churned out by the US system. The Mobile Unit alone was as large as the entire Clearance Diving branch of the RAN. Fewer numbers meant Aussie CDs had a much greater exposure to a broader range of tasks and as a result our sailors after 5 years' service can have as much practical experience if not more than a US sailor with 20+ years' service.

My predecessor, Harry Brankstone, had spent the initial part of his tour with the EOD Training Unit and his last 12 months as Training Officer of the widely travelled Mobile Unit which enabled him to participate in several operational deployments.

The Americans were keen to take advantage of our *'jack of all trades'* training and diving skills to enhance their training programs however I was determined not to waste my tour stuck in Honolulu conducting refresher training for EOD technicians. I felt the only way to maximise the benefits of the exchange program would be for me to serve my entire tour with their operational Mobile unit. After a long and candid talk with the Commodore about the aims of the exchange program and what I hoped to gain from the experience, we agreed that I should be attached full time to the Mobile unit. The first thing I had to do was undergo a familiarisation course with their diving equipment and safety regulations. Fortunately, I had already used most of their equipment during special warfare exercises in the Philippines and of course we had used US scuba equipment exclusively during my tour in Vietnam.

In addition to rank titles, the American Military classify their rank structure by a numerical system to allow cross recognition between the services. For enlisted ranks there are 9 levels with E1 being the lowest, through to the dizzy heights of E9 Master Chief. As they have three different levels of Chief Petty Officer, it has always been difficult to clarify the exact equivalents in the Australian system which had only five levels including one level of CPO (the senior NCO level in the RAN at that time). As an Australian Petty Officer, I was recognised as the equivalent of the USN E7 Chief Petty Officer. When I was promoted to CPOCD in Nov '78, I was accorded the equivalent rank of their E8, or Senior Chief Petty Officer. In the whole of Group One there was only one E9 and he was the *'Master Chief of the Command'*. The American Navy accords its Chiefs enormous respect and its officers are taught from day one in the Navy to *'listen to the Chief'*. Trained along the lines of the British class system, many Australian officers assume through ignorance and arrogance that only they have the intelligence and ability to make decisions, whereas the American officers are very aware that their Chiefs keep the wheels from falling off. It is an area where the Yanks leave some of our lot looking like pompous little *'Lord Fauntleroys'*. I regularly witnessed very senior American Naval officers displaying this deep-seated respect for their Chiefs and it stimulated enormous pride and loyalty within the US Navy.

While waiting for my first EOD task with the Mobile Unit, I was asked if I would like to attend a 3-week Outboard Motor technician's course at the *'Johnson OMC'* (Outboard Marine Corporation) factory in San Francisco. As this would allow me my first trip to the US mainland, I didn't need to be asked twice. We flew into SF on a commercial flight and I can clearly remember my excitement as we crossed over the California coast.

We were taken to our accommodation at the Oakland Naval Base and provided with a Navy station wagon to allow us to commute daily to the OMC factory. I was billeted in the CPO quarters along with Petty Officer 1st class John Conway who was also billeted in with the Chief's due to a lack of space in his own mess. He was one crazy dude. He had some Irish blood in his lineage and was I believe, the oldest 1st Class PO in the US Navy. Apparently he had been denied promotion permanently due his inclination towards giving the odd officer a belt in the mouth when he disagreed with them. John showed me around San Francisco and we had a ball. One night is cemented in my memory. A mate of his from the San Francisco EOD detachment took us on a Yankee version of a pub crawl. Cruising through the downtown area, I was sitting in the back of a brand new white Pontiac Firebird drinking Budweiser and John and his mate were in the front drinking beer and puffing on a joint. The windows were down and *'Seals and Croft'* were cranked up on the stereo. I thought to myself, *'Only in America'*. At that point in time marijuana smoking was quite widespread in the US military although I never felt the slightest inclination to try it.

I thoroughly enjoyed the Outboard technicians course as I have always had an interest in all things mechanical. During the 3 weeks we learnt the fundamentals of marine outboard engines while we each stripped and reassembled a 4 cylinder 85 HP Johnson. The same factory also produced the identical Evinrude outboard motor. Outside of working hours we enjoyed the hell out of the social life available in a major US city. I loved San Francisco. To me it epitomised everything American. Fisherman's Wharf, Alcatraz, the famous cable cars and sour-dough bread.

A sad ending to the course occurred during the final days. One of our fellow EOD mates became quite anxious and was desperate to go home earlier than our scheduled flight. We couldn't understand this as the rest of us were having a ball. Only after we returned to Hawaii did we discover the reason for his sense of urgency. He had been tipped off by a mate that another sailor was having an affair with his wife. By arriving home early, the poor bugger had actually caught them in the act.

We completed the course and went away qualified as OMC Outboard Service Technicians. While everyone else flew back to Honolulu, I stayed on, taking 2 weeks leave. I hired a huge 2 door Ford LTD and Antoinette flew in to SF International. She was very impressed with my choice of car. We spent a couple of days at a Military motel at Oakland while exploring Fisherman's Wharf and riding the cable cars before heading north along the Californian coast. It was a beautiful drive taking in everything from old whaling villages to the massive Californian Redwood forests. Some of the trees were so large that the road passed through cut out sections of the trunk. We moved on into Oregon, a very clean and pristine State. Every 20 or 30 miles there were rest stops with toilet facilities, picnic tables and lots of green grass. We never saw a scrap of rubbish anywhere, not even a cigarette butt.

We continued north to Portland and crossed into Washington State. I still have a great photo of Mount St. Helens taken on that trip. This supposedly dormant volcano was to suffer a catastrophic eruption 3 years later on May 18, 1980, the deadliest and most economically destructive volcanic event in the history of the United States - 57 people were killed; 250 homes, 47 bridges, 15 miles (24 km) of railways, and 185 miles (298 km) of highway were destroyed and half the mountain was blown away.

From there we headed east up the Columbia Gorge to Lost Lake at the foot of Mount Hood and then turned south. Wonderful places like Klamath Falls, Crater Lake National Park, Reno and Virginia City spring to mind and stir great memories.

One hot afternoon in the middle of nowhere while passing through a little one-horse town, I decided to stop and pick up a couple of cold beers to keep me going. I was very surprised to find they sold 26-ounce cans of *'Tooths KB'* (a Sydney beer) and what's more, it was cheaper than buying it in Sydney. We went to Reno Nevada where even the barber shops had poker machines and a full breakfast at most casinos cost only 49 cents, then onto Las Vegas where the casinos didn't have locks on the doors because they never closed. We drove through Yosemite National Park and up into the Sierra Nevadas to an old mining ghost town called Bodie. The town's *'Boot Hill'* had numerous graves of babies who had died before the age of one because of raging diseases and sub-zero winters. A land of incredible contrasts.

EOD like all other Special Forces types are very fitness conscious. Every morning PT was led by one of the Chiefs or senior Petty Officers. This was followed by a typical US Military run of about 1.5 miles. Everyone was fallen in and ran in 3 columns singing a cadence as we went. At the halfway point most turned back and a few of the keen runners kept going to complete the 5-mile circuit around the West Loch Base. I was one of those and I usually ran stride for stride with PO 1st Class Harmon Slappy who became a very good friend of mine. After I returned home, Harmon was promoted to Chief and posted to Australia under the PEP program, so we spent another couple of years together. Harmon was one of the strongest runners in the Group and by pairing up with him I improved my distance and pace considerably. He also ran every lunchtime so I thought, bugger him, if he can do it so can I. So on most days we ran 10 miles with the odd day when we were feeling energetic we completed 2 circuits of the base at lunchtime, bringing our daily total to 15 miles, or 24 kms.

One lunchtime, Rich Mahone, a young Seaman not long out of EOD school, asked if he could join me for a run around the base circuit. I knew what he had in mind – he wanted to kick the old Chief's ass. We went out at a nice comfortable pace but at around the 3-mile mark, Rich (*6feet 1inch tall and couldn't cast a decent shadow*) started to steadily pick up the pace. Much to his surprise, I stayed with him, stride for stride. I could see that he had bitten off more than he could chew and was starting to hurt so around the 4-mile mark, I started to crank on the pace and Rich learnt a valuable lesson – never underestimate a Chief...

At the completion of the run he just grinned at me and said, *"Goddamn it Chief, you kicked my ass."* Many years later, Rich became the US exchange Chief with our Clearance Divers.

Occasionally I ran the 8 miles to work. A very pleasant run with the road winding through fields of sugarcane. Sometimes when I was feeling particularly sprightly and after running in from home, I would keep on going and run the base circuit as well. Feeling on top of the world, I would often continue on and complete a second circuit. That made 18 miles before I started work. Long distance running provides a *'high'* that cannot be explained to anyone who hasn't been there. I loved it and running became an obsession.

I went into training for the Honolulu marathon, running 14 to 18 miles on Sundays with the Aussie Vice Consul, Mike Williams (also a Vietnam Vet). At about that time the Honolulu *'Hash House Harriers'* were just getting started so I joined them and we would run quite hard every Tuesday night and like every other Hasher worldwide, partake of a drink or two after the run.

Apart from the marathon, I ran in two other major races and both I felt were much tougher. The first was the *'Oahu perimeter run'*. This was a 140-mile relay race beginning at 8pm and going through the night. Each team consisted of 7 runners and it was personal choice whether your team ran it in 20 mile sections with each runner running only once, or split the race so that each member ran several legs of 4 or 5 miles through the night. My team opted to do the latter. We had 2 support vans following us so that we could rest between legs. We could drink fluid but eating was out of the question. When it came time to run your next leg, your muscles had cooled and tightened so that it was sheer agony for the first mile until you began to warm up again. No-one slept as we were all so hyped up. It was a very long night. Being the team captain I felt obliged to run the first and last legs with a few in between to make up my 20-mile share. As the night wore on, each leg became more difficult. By the time I ran the final leg through downtown Honolulu and across the finish in Kapiolani Park it was 9 am, the sun was up, it was hot, and I was totally buggered. The cheering crowd however spurred me on for the final sprint to the line. I remember this event as being far more demanding than a 26-mile marathon. The second race was a 58-mile relay run through the hills around the Schofield Army base. From memory there were 7 man teams, so each runner had to run a single 8-mile leg at close to sprint pace. It was a very hard run.

Much to my delight I discovered that the US Military sponsored Flying Clubs at most of their Air bases. These clubs were only open to military personnel and flying lessons were considerably cheaper than civilian clubs. I had always wanted to learn to fly and was determined to take advantage of such a great opportunity. After checking around, I discovered a few EOD sailors were already taking lessons at nearby Barber's Point Naval Air Station. I actually drove through the base twice a day on my way to and from work. After confirming that I was eligible to be a member of the club I got stuck into it. I attended theory classes two nights a week and after about 3 weeks was ready to begin practical lessons. I loved it from day one and took to it like a duck to water. Most of the flight instructors were military aviators themselves with the CFI (chief flying instructor) being a civilian employed to ensure the training curriculum met with FAA (Federal Aviation Administration) standards. My instructor was aircrew on Navy P3 Orion aircraft.

From memory the theory phase of the course cost $35 in total and my flight time was $18 an hour wet (fuel included). $13 for the aircraft (a Cessna 150 Aerobat) and $5 for the instructor. I managed to fly at least 2 afternoons per week and once on the weekends. It was important to fly often enough so that each new lesson was not wasted going back over old ground.

I breezed through the course, going solo in 10 hours. My first solo flight was something I will never ever forget. We were doing touch and go's on Ford Island airstrip (next to the USS Arizona Memorial) when my instructor told me to turn off the runway and stop. He opened the door, got out and casually said to me *"You're on your own. Do three touch & go's and then come back and pick me up"*. I thought I wasn't hearing correctly but he had already closed the door and walked away.

As I accelerated down the runway and pointed the nose skyward, there was a brief moment when I wondered if I was ready for this. About 50 feet above the ground I glanced to the right to make sure I was really on my own and couldn't stop myself from breaking out in a huge grin. I was airborne, I was flying, and I was in command. It was just me and this little plane. It was about 15 minutes of sheer albeit very focused bliss. I was quite disappointed when I had to pull off the active runway and pick up my instructor. He climbed back into '*my aircraft*' and we returned to Barbers Point to review my first solo.

From that point on, we began cross-country flying, across to Maui, Molokai, Lanai and Hawaii - the *'Big Island'*. The day arrived when I was to do a solo flight from Barbers Point through Honolulu controlled airspace, across to Molokai, over Maui and on to land at Kona on the west coast of Hawaii. What a feeling; 5 hours of flying on my own with the spectacular scenery of the Hawaiian Islands unfolding beneath my wings. To land at Kona, taxi in and refuel *'my'* aircraft, just like a fair dinkum pilot. Heady stuff.

Every time I went down to the club I would look at the bigger and more powerful aircraft parked at the ramp and look forward to the day when I would be able to fly them.

I sat the FAA theory examination and my instructor said I was ready in all respects to take my final flight test. He advised the CFI who then took me up for a final check ride. We went out to the training area and flew turns around pylons and conducted a variety of stalls and spins before heading off to Honolulu International for a few touch and go's. I was cleared for runway 4R but on short final was told by the tower to immediately move over and land on 4L. As I rolled out on 4L it became immediately obvious why I was directed to change runways. Out of the blue we heard an ear shattering roar as a Boeing 747 screamed past us on 4R in full reverse thrust. The CFI said no big deal - when the controllers realised we weren't going to land and clear 4R in time, they just moved us over to the parallel runway. All in a normal day's flying.

Back on the ground the CFI gave me an *'above average'* assessment and said I had passed the FAA flight test with flying colours. What a buzz to be told you are a qualified pilot. My new licence allowed me to fly with passengers both locally and cross country. I could also fly locally at night providing I maintained three night take-offs and landings every 3 months.

My next priority was to get checked out in a 4 seater. I began with a Cessna 172 and progressively became qualified with taildraggers, retractable undercarriage and constant speed propeller aircraft such as the Piper Arrow, Beechcraft Sierra, Cessna T41 and my all-time favourite aircraft, a Beechcraft T-34B *'Mentor'*. This fantastic airplane had been the standard trainer for US Navy and Air Force pilots for many years and had been replaced by the 'C' model which was basically the same aircraft but was fitted with a gas turbine engine. The then effectively obsolete T-34B's were given to military flying clubs. It was a retractable constant speed tandem seater with sliding Perspex canopies. The cockpit was set out like a real jet fighter with its instrument layout, joystick, throttle quadrant and huge rudder pedals. It certainly felt like what I imagined flying a jet would be and I loved it. The aircraft was fully aerobatic and handled like a dream. At the controls, flying over the Hawaiian Islands in perfect weather at 160 knots with the canopy wide open, there was no place on Earth I would rather have been. When I first read the poem *'High Flight'*, I understood exactly what the author was talking about: -

"Oh! I have slipped the surly bonds of Earth
and danced the skies on laughter-silvered wings;
Sunward I've climbed, and joined the tumbling mirth
of sun split clouds - and done a hundred things
you have not dreamed of - wheeled and soared and swung
high in the sunlit silence. Hov'ring there
I've chased the shouting wind along
and flung my eager craft through footless halls of air.
Up, up the delirious burning blue.

> *I've topped the windswept heights with easy grace*
> *where never lark, or even eagle flew -*
> *and, while with silent lifting mind I've trod*
> *the high unsurpassed sanctity of space,*
> *put out my hand and touched the face of God."*
>
> Pilot Officer Gillespie Magee –
> RCAF, KIA 11th Dec. 1941.

For the next 2 years I flew at every opportunity. Once I had obtained my taildragger rating on a fully aerobatic Citabria Bellanca, I set my sights on a multi-engine rating. I'll never forget the sense of achievement, sitting in the left hand seat of a Cessna 310 and hearing the growl of the two engines as they responded smoothly to my inputs and we *"slipped the surly bonds of Earth."*

Whenever we had visitors from Australia I flew them around the islands. We watched migrating Humpback whales frolicking off Maui, flew along the edge of Molokai's towering 2000 foot cliffs, flew into the crater of Mount Haleakala, flew over Kilauea, the active volcano and roared along the crests of Oahu's famous surf beaches. We saw more of Hawaii in 3 years than 99% of the local residents could hope to see in a lifetime.

Often on the weekends I would wake and say to Antoinette *"Where would you like to go for lunch? Maui or Kauai, or perhaps Molokai."* Then we would call a few friends to see if they wanted to join us - what a life. When Aussie ships came in during RIMPAC exercises, I would take the CDs up for a scenic flight over Oahu and Pearl Harbour.

Once I flew the Australian Consul and his wife over to Hana on the island of Maui, dropped them off for the weekend and returned to pick them up a few days later. I took my parents to every island, staying a few days on each. They always remembered it as the best holiday of their lives.

I was to discover that one of the regular tasks for the Mobile Unit was to visit the island of Kahoolawe, situated off the south western tip of Maui, about 160 kilometres (100 miles) south east of Honolulu. This uninhabited island has been used by the US

Military for gunnery and bombing practice since 1941. Native Hawaiians had been lobbying the US Government to have at least part of the island returned to them as part of their cultural and religious heritage claims. EODMUONE was tasked with clearing part of the island of unexploded ordnance to allow limited access by the native Hawaiians. It was estimated that the project would require 10 EOD techs 10 days per month for at least 18 months.

I once took part in a cull of the island's large population of goats, an introduced animal which deserved most of the blame for the desert-like conditions on the island. These goat hunting expeditions were only conducted by Navy EOD personnel due to the dangers of the aging unexploded ordnance littering the island. We spent several days at a time hunting with the US issue 5.56mm M-16s. Not a particularly good hunting weapon as the sights are not well suited to small targets. We camped under the stars and lived on C-rations.

One evening I decided against all advice to cook a meal of curried goat. It turned out as tough as old boot leather. I was advised by the old Master Chief to place a large stone in the pot at the same time as I cooked the goat meat. He said that I should stew the goat for about 24 hours and then throw away the meat and eat the stone. It would be the more tender of the two. He was right....

By the time our chopper arrived to pick us up for the return trip to Honolulu, we were a dirty rough looking lot, unshaven and covered from head to foot in the red dust of the island. How the goats survived there, and why the Hawaiians wanted the island back, I'll never know.

Kahoolawe is situated in the rain shadow of Maui so it was argued whether the goats or lack of rainfall were most responsible for its bleak landscape. We were also regularly tasked with escorting government and archaeological personnel on their regular visits as parts of the island were supposedly rich in Hawaiian artefacts.

My broad range of diving and EOD experience often paid off as the CO of the Mobile Unit always called me to his office whenever a task was assigned and asked if I wished to go. Of course I jumped at every offer. This allowed me to have numerous trips to the mainland where I always took some leave on completion of the job. Antoinette would then fly over and we would continue our travels. In all we managed to visit some 32 states.

One of my most interesting deployments was to Florida. The US Navy was developing decompression tables for a new piece of diving equipment known commercially as the *'Electro lung'*. The Navy called it the SLSS (Swimmer Life Support System) and it was state of the art. Its greatest advantage was its ability to automatically provide the optimum oxygen percentage at any depth thus conserving the breathing medium to provide 'unheard of' endurance. However, this constantly changing percentage of both O2 and the inert *'diluent'* meant a completely new set of decompression tables had to be developed – and that could only be arrived at by trial and error.

Divers were selected from across the US military spectrum to take part in the decompression trials. They came from all branches of the Navy diving community including SEALs, EOD, Salvage divers and Army Green Beret dive troops.

Three EOD sailors were selected from Hawaii and I was extremely pleased to be one of them. We departed Honolulu on a commercial flight on New Year's Eve 1977. CPO Norm Case, Seaman Rich Mahone and I saw in the New Year sitting in an airport bar at LA International awaiting our onward flight to New Orleans. There were just the three of us in the bar with the Negro barman when the clock struck 12.

Once aboard our flight, the hostesses told us they intended to take a nap as all the other passengers were now asleep and we were welcome to help ourselves to the bar service. Being sailors, we jumped at the offer and moved back closer to the galley. For the next 5 hours we celebrated the New Year and drank them out of beer. We arrived in New Orleans in pretty bad shape having had no sleep. A *'Dixie'* beer in one of the airport bars finished us and for the next two legs onto Mobile Alabama and finally into Panama City Florida, we slept like babies.

Thirty divers had been assembled for the trial and to our delight we were told that we would be deploying to Puerto Rico for a 3-week familiarisation with the SLSS before returning to the Experimental Diving Unit (EDU) at Panama City to begin the actual decompression trials. A US Navy DC9 flew us across the Gulf and the Florida Keys to our final destination in the Caribbean.

The diving familiarisation entailed gradually increasing the duration of each dive until we were comfortable with dives of 6 hours' duration. During these long dives I searched for sea shells and managed to acquire a great collection, none of which I had ever seen in the southern hemisphere.

We had quite an interesting flight back to the mainland as we flew into a very intense tropical depression as we neared Panama City. On our final approach there was torrential rain with continuous lightning flashes in every direction. The pilot was crabbing the aircraft on approach to compensate for the very strong gusting cross-winds and as I looked out of my window, I was looking directly up the length of the runway. Using rudder and aileron to align the DC9 with the runway just prior to touchdown resulted in an extreme bank angle. There was a flash of sparks from the port wingtip and the engines immediately went to full thrust. It was a very close call. We were diverted to Eglin Air Force base and landed safely. After the engines were shut down, the pilot came out of the cockpit and apologised to his passengers, saying that it had been a very close thing indeed. We all chuckled and said how much we had enjoyed it....

Back in Florida we conducted all our dives under strictly controlled conditions in a huge wet recompression chamber.

The Ocean Simulation Facility (OSF) simulated ocean conditions to a maximum water depth equivalent of 2,250 feet of seawater (686m) at any salinity level. The chamber complex consisted of a 55,000-gallon (208,000 litre) wet chamber and five interconnected dry living/working chambers totalling 3,300 cubic feet of space. Wet and dry chamber temperatures could be set to anywhere from 28 to 104 °F. The dry chambers were also capable of altitude simulation studies to altitudes of 150,000 feet (over 28 miles).

We dived in groups of 10 so one day's diving was followed by 2 days' stand-down. During these dives we spent up to 6 hours underwater at depths of 150 feet (46m). This routine continued for 3 months.

We were living in brand new condominiums right on the beach, 3 divers to a unit and for each unit we had our own rental car. I can remember some great nights kicking up our heels in the numerous *'shit-kicking bars'* around Panama City. What a life. I shared my condo with Norm Case and a Green Beret Top Sergeant. One of the EDU's resident diving chiefs, Dusty Rhodes, owned a bar called *'Down the Hatch'* just outside the main gate so it became our regular stop for a game of darts and a beer or two. Dusty kept a selection of about 8 or 10 beers on tap.

On my days off and in between games of tennis, I would jump into our car and head off to see as much of northern Florida, Alabama and Georgia as I could.

During the course of the trial, several of the team were *'bent'* (suffered from decompression sickness). Fortunately, I was not one of them.

On completion of the trials, I submitted a full report including my recommendations on the SLSS to OIC Diving and Navy Office back in Australia and never heard it mentioned again. I find it interesting that 25 years later, this same set became the mainstay diving set of the RAN Clearance Diving Branch.

The EOD Group had its own parachute locker staffed by a Senior Chief Master Parachutist and a PO 3rd class parachute rigger. An operational requirement for US Navy EOD is the ability to be inserted by parachute into both the land and water environment, day or night. At that time, it was not a requirement of the RAN.

Soon after my arrival I was asked to supervise the recovery operations for their water jump training. Once EOD sailors obtained their jump wings it became the Group's responsibility to conduct their water jump qualifications on their return to Hawaii. It didn't take too long for me to decide that I wanted to be part of this jumping business. Jumping out of an aircraft over the Hawaiian Islands into clear blue water was too good to miss.

After a quiet word to the CO of the Mobile unit, I sent off a request to the Australian Embassy in Washington seeking approval to attend US Jump School. This put a *'cat amongst the pigeons'* as it would be a first for the RAN. Fortunately, and quite surprisingly, approval was given by the Canberra paper shufflers.

In short order I was packing my bags and on a civilian flight to Washington. The Navy parachute school was situated at Lakehurst Naval Air Station in New Jersey. A very famous location as it was at Lakehurst in 1937 that the German Dirigible airship *'Hindenburg'* had caught fire and crashed.

The Navy had its own parachute school to train their Special Forces and pilots and differed from the Army training in that at Lakehurst they taught you to pack chutes first and when actual jump training began, trainees jumped with the chutes they had personally packed. Makes you pay attention knowing your first jump is with a main and reserve parachute that you have packed.

My class was made up of Navy SEALs, a bunch of young trainee Navy pilots and a couple of EOD types. The first event on the program was a 1.5-mile sprint to confirm our fitness levels. It turned into a race and I was pretty pleased with myself when I sprinted across the line a clear winner. There were a lot of very surprised young pilots and Navy SEALs when the 31-year-old Aussie Chief kicked their ass.

Training got under way with a combination of PT, packing lessons, and practising parachute landing falls (PLFs). Each morning the class fell in neatly, three abreast, and ran the circumference of the airfield singing typical American military *'hoo-ya'* songs. Our PLFs were practised from a wooden stage about 10 - 12 feet high to simulate the impact of landing. I was quite surprised how hard you can hit the ground from only 12 feet.

Military chutes at that time were steerable but unlike modern chutes they could not be flared - flaring reduces the speed of descent just prior landing. From memory it was about day 6 before we were due to have our first jump. Unfortunately, at the last minute we were told our aircraft had been made unserviceable so we had to wait a couple of extra days before it was all go.

Our first jumps were from Navy Trackers which surprised me as they are a very small aircraft (conventional design with twin engines, a high wing and tricycle undercarriage). We had to exit from a side door which was barely big enough to fit through with a parachute strapped to your back. Kneeling in the open door, all you could see was the port engine nacelle about 4 feet away. The Jumpmaster assured us that we would not hit it as we flung ourselves out the door because the 100 knot slipstream would almost knock us unconscious anyway as it slammed us sideways. My final thought in the door was '*I hope I packed these damn chutes properly*'.

That first jump was something you could never forget. What a buzz - the roaring din of the engine in your face and the wind blasting by, followed by the adrenaline rush from launching into empty space. Then the shock of the opening chute as the harness almost cuts you in half, followed by the total tranquillity of being under a canopy, gently drifting earthward. And finally, absolute relief as you mumble to yourself - '*thank Christ, my chute opened*'.

During the second week we were shuffling in line out to the aircraft dressed in full kit when I turned my ankle on an aircraft tie down point. It hurt like hell but I thought '*I'm not telling the instructors or they'll stand me down*'. The next few jumps were OK but on the final jump for the day, it caught up with me. The drop zone was a dirt paddock with a heavily compacted dirt road running through the centre. On my approach to the target I was flying downwind before turning into wind for my final approach. I had slightly misjudged the wind strength and as I turned over the road to fly into wind to the target, I discovered my forward speed matched the wind speed which meant my ground speed was zero and I was in a straight drop to the hard compacted road. I suspect that I was subconsciously concerned about my still sore ankle so landed with most of the impact being taken by my good ankle. It snapped like a twig. An ambulance took me to Fort Dix Army hospital where they had to operate and pin my ankle. Prior to going under the anaesthetic, I overheard the surgeon, an Army Major, say he wanted a quick operation as he might be late for his golf game. If I ever ran into this incompetent shit for brains again, I would wrap a golf club around his neck. He made such a mess of the operation that I was to spend a total of 3 months in a cast and on crutches. When the cast was removed back in Hawaii 6 weeks later, I discovered that my ankle was locked solid. The orthopaedic surgeon at Tripler Army hospital was quite shocked at the complete botch-job made by the golfing Major. Another operation followed; re-breaking two bones, more screws and another 6 weeks in a cast. I was really pissed off as it brought my running, parachuting and flying to a complete halt.

The one very positive outcome of my being a patient at home was Antoinette became pregnant.

Eventually I recovered sufficiently to complete the water insertion phase of EOD Jump qualifications. The night jumps were the best. We would load up a CH-46 Sea Knight (multi rotor) helicopter with chutes and jump out over Kaneohe Bay to the north of Honolulu. We would exit the aircraft at sufficient altitude to see the lights of Honolulu across the mountain range as we stepped off the ramp. A magnificent sight. On hitting the water, we were recovered by a support boat and then our chopper would hover above us to winch us back aboard before climbing back to altitude for the next jump. What a life!! Doesn't get any better.

One of the truly great characters I met during my 3 years with the US Navy was Senior Chief EOD Technician Stanley Milward Ryley Jr.

Stan was a Vietnam Vet and a Navy legend, known and respected far and wide by Seamen and Admirals alike. He was definitely a man's man who *'had his shit together'*. As strong as an ox and built like a brick shithouse, nobody messed with the *'Senior Chief'*. We became firm friends and I never tired of his sense of humour and his company.

One night I will never forget - several of us were drinking at *'Buddy's Lounge'* in Waipahu when one of our 2nd Class Petty Officers had sufficient to drink to think that he could beat *'Stan the Man'*. There was no animosity involved, just one alpha male thinking he could kick the ass of the top dog. Jim Reed told Stan he reckoned he could beat him and asked him outside. Jim was no small man but no one had any doubt as to the outcome. Stan replied, *"OK Jim, you go outside and practice falling down and I'll be out there after I finish my beer."* No one even bothered to go outside to watch. Within seconds of Stan leaving the bar, he was back as if nothing had happened. A few minutes later Jim staggered back in looking a bit starry-eyed. After a few sips of his beer, Jim said, *"I still think I can beat you Stan"*, placed his beer back on the bar and walked outside again. Stan sighed, put his beer down and said to us, *"This won't take long."* Ten minutes later Jim staggered back in and resumed drinking with us as if nothing had happened. No anger, no bad feelings. They were the best of mates again.

Men amongst men……

Towards the end of my exchange posting, I wrote the following summary of my tour.

"I am posted to EODGRUONE but have in fact been detached to EOD Mobile Unit One (a subordinate unit).

The Group is mainly the administrative area for all EOD units in the Pacific and these detachments range from the west coast USA to Japan and from Alaska to the Philippines. At the moment there are 16 - 18 four man teams detached throughout this area. Most of these teams are located on Naval Air Stations or on Naval Magazines and are tasked with providing EOD/diving services to the local command.

There are two subordinate commands of GRUONE, EOD Mobile Unit One and the EOD Training Unit One, both of which are run by Lieutenant Commanders.

The Training Unit consists mainly of the more experienced EOD technicians with the majority of the Unit being Chiefs.

Their major task is to provide refresher training for the detachments, which come back to Hawaii every 18 months for 3-week refresher courses. They also provide training to the Mobile Unit's teams before they deploy onboard ships to the Western Pacific as well as carrying out a certain amount of testing and evaluation of new equipment before service approval and use in the Fleet.

The area of the Training Unit which is of special interest to us is the Dive Locker. It is staffed by EOD technicians as well as Fleet divers. On request, they will supply instruction and refresher training in ordnance locators, hand held sonars (passive & active mode), small boat navigation, chamber operator/supervisor and diving supervisor - air through mixed gas to MK. 1.

An interesting point here is that a diving supervisor is only current in his present command. When he arrives at a new command, he must satisfy them that he is up to par for his particular supervisory category and he will then be able to supervise diving only within his new command. A diving supervisor can hold a qualification for any individual or combination of rigs and he can be of virtually any rank - e.g. a young sailor just out of SCUBA school could theoretically become a SCUBA supervisor shortly thereafter.

All EOD divers are qualified to 130 feet on air on graduation from EOD school and have completed familiarisation dives using MK-6 (semi-closed circuit), MK-1 (surface supply rigs using Kirby Morgan type facemask) and MK-12 (the replacement for the MK-5 hard-hat rig). With the MK-6 re-breather they use 60/40 (80 ft.) and 32/68 (180 ft.).

Part of the Group's equipment includes a 74 ft. LCM 8 aluminium landing craft which contains a complete fly-away MK-1 diving system. This consists of a 10 man 100psi aluminium RCC housed in a Mil-van (a large Conex type box), 2 x 150cu.ft/min. air compressors, one 230psi volume tank, 4 x 3000psi flasks and 2 x 4Kw 110/220VDC generators. This entire system will fit into a 17½ ft. x 46 ft. area and is designed for a fly-away capability in a C-141 or C-5 aircraft. The Diving Locker maintains a large inventory of diving gear which includes 250 sets of 90cu.ft. aluminium cylinders and 2 x 15 cu.ft./min. 3000psi compressors.

The Mobile Unit at full strength is assigned 25 officers and 75 sailors but at the moment is below full strength due to recruiting problems. A core of approximately 3 officers and 10 enlisted men remain at all times in the unit and the remainder are split into 4 man teams which deploy to ships and carry out EOD/diving tasks as required.

Due to the present shortage of EOD personnel, they are sending 3 EOD techs to sea with the 4th man being a SCUBA diver just to make numbers for their 4-man minimum for diving operations. This is an interim measure until they get back to full strength.

They usually have 5 - 7 teams deployed at sea at any one time with the remainder being in the Hawaii area carrying out local tasks and maintaining training between deployments. Their normal sea deployment is 7 months, with a year back at the unit before deploying again but at the moment this time at home is down to 6 months.

The teams normally comprise one officer, one CPO and two sailors. They work as a team providing EOD/diving services to the ship and do not work as ship's company or keep regular watches. They are onboard only for EOD and diving jobs.

One of the most regular tasks for the Mobile Unit is on the island of Kahoolawe situated about 100 miles SE of Honolulu. It is an uninhabited military target island which is causing a few headaches due to the fact that it has been bombed and shelled consistently since 1941 and now the native Hawaiians want it back for ancestral and religious reasons. EODMUONE has been tasked with clearing part of the island for limited access by the Hawaiian population. This is an enormous task and will probably require 10 EOD personnel 10 days a month for at least 18 months. Since I have been here, we have taken part in tree planting operations to control erosion which has required explosives to make the holes for planting. Also due to a large population of wild goats contributing to the erosion, we have taken part in the culling of these goats using M-16 rifles.

I have visited Midway Island twice on reports of WWII ordnance being discovered, one being a 750lb. GP bomb and the other a reported mine which turned out to be a mooring buoy. The buoy received the same fate as the 750 pounder.

In the local area I have participated in a Minex, disposal of retrograde ordnance and general demolition work.

As my main job while in the local area has been supervising maintenance of boats, outboards and Cornelius diving compressors, I was lucky to get the opportunity to attend Johnson's Outboard Motor School in San Francisco and completed the factory technicians course on Cornelius/Stewart-Warner air compressors.

Late last year I had the opportunity to visit and work with the detachment in Guam. I spent 3 months diving in Truk Lagoon in the East Caroline Islands and Kwajalein Atoll in the Marshall Islands. I had the opportunity to dive on seven of the more than 50 Japanese shipwrecks including a submarine (*the I-169. 1400 tons & 331 ft. in length*) which in 1944 was the largest class of submarine in the world.

During World War II, Truk Lagoon was Japan's main base in the South Pacific theatre. Truk was a heavily fortified base for Japanese operations against Allied forces in New Guinea and the Solomon Islands, serving as the forward anchorage for the Japanese Imperial Fleet. Truk Lagoon was considered the most formidable of all Japanese strongholds in the Pacific.

On the various islands, the Japanese Civil Engineering Department and Naval Construction Department had built roads, trenches, bunkers and caves. Five airstrips, seaplane bases, a torpedo boat station, submarine repair shops, a communications centre and a radar station were constructed during the war. Protecting these various facilities were coastal defense guns and mortar emplacements. The Japanese garrison consisted of 27,856 Navy men, and 16,737 soldiers. Due to its heavy fortifications, both natural and manmade, the base at Truk was known to Allied forces as "the Gibraltar of the Pacific".

A significant portion of the Japanese fleet was based at Truk. At anchor in the lagoon, were the Imperial Japanese Navy's battleships, aircraft carriers, cruisers, destroyers, tankers, cargo ships, tugboats, gunboats, minesweepers, landing craft, and submarines. Some have described Truk as Japan's equivalent of the Americans' Pearl Harbor.

About 1,800km north-east of New Guinea, it is located mid-ocean at 7 degrees North latitude, and is part of 'Chuuk' State within the Federated States of Micronesia. The atoll consists of a protective reef, 225 kilometres (140mi) around, enclosing a natural harbour 79 by 50 kilometres (49 by 30mi).

In 1944, Truk was devastated in one of the important naval attacks of the war. Forewarned by intelligence a week before the US raid, the Japanese had withdrawn their larger warships (heavy cruisers and larger vessels) to Palau. Once the American forces captured the Marshall Islands, they used them as a base from which to launch an early morning attack on February 17, 1944 against Truk Lagoon. Operation Hailstone lasted for three days as American carrier-based planes sank twelve smaller Japanese warships (light cruisers, destroyers, and auxiliaries) and thirty-two merchant ships, while destroying 275 aircraft, mainly on the ground. The consequences of the attack made *"Truk lagoon the biggest graveyard of ships in the world"*.

The Atoll is protected by law and nothing can be removed from the wrecks so everything is pretty much the same as when the ships went down.

In the massive ships' holds are the remnants of fighter aircraft, tanks, bulldozers, railroad cars, motorcycles, torpedoes, mines, bombs, boxes of munitions, radios, plus thousands of other weapons, spare parts, and other artefacts. Most of the wrecks are accessible to divers in 60 to 140 feet of water.

Of special interest to us was the wreck of the submarine I-169 *'Shinohara'* which was lost when diving to avoid the bombing. The submarine had participated in the attack on Pearl Harbor in December 1941.

Our prime objective was to clear the airfield of any WW 2 ordnance prior to it being enlarged, as the area had been heavily bombed during the war.

In Kwajalein, where there are also large numbers of Japanese wrecks, we were tasked with removing and disposing of a large number of depth charges still on board the ships. Much to the dismay of the local diving fraternity we also removed a dud-fired US 500-pound bomb which was wedged between the bathtub and the deck in the Captain's cabin of a Japanese freighter. This was obviously the favourite photographic subject of the local diving community. We safely removed the bomb and the bathtub remained completely undamaged.

One of the highlights of Kwajalein was a dive on the German heavy cruiser, the *'Prinz Eugen'* (she was escort to the battleship Bismarck when they encountered and sunk the British battle cruiser HMS Hood – 47,000 tons). I was also lucky enough to have several chopper flights over the numerous reefs of the Atoll which still hold the remains of many Japanese wrecks, including a mini submarine.

My most recent trip was to the EOD school at Indian Head, Maryland where I had a close look at all their different phases of EOD training as well as their Research and Development Facility which was quite an eye-opener.

From Indian Head, I went to the Naval Parachute School at Lakehurst, New Jersey which is quite well known in the US as it was here that the German airship *'Hindenburg'* burned and crashed in 1937.

The parachute course is 3 weeks long and consists of a lot of running, PT, practising landing falls, learning to pack your own main and reserve chutes and completing 5 land jumps.

Apart from Kahoolawe, the Mobile Unit's tasks in the immediate future are a WWII small arms ammunition dump in 60 to 100 feet of water about one mile off this island (Oahu) and the clearance of a WWII ammunition dump off Guam which was used originally by the Japanese and later by the US. It contains everything from small arms through to artillery and Naval projectiles and is estimated at 64 tons of ordnance. This will be a major task for the Mobile Unit and every spare man will be utilised for the 5 months it is estimated to take.

I feel the exchange program has been a very valuable experience for me and I hope it will benefit the Branch as a whole."

My posting was for only 2½ years but as I neared the end of my tour, the Mobile Unit was tasked with the major EOD job in Guam – mentioned in my report. The CO advised me that he wanted to utilise my underwater EOD experience on this job and as a result he requested Washington to extend my tour by 6 months, providing I had no objection. Being of reasonably sound mind I had no objections.

Sadly, this posting of a lifetime came to an end, but nothing lasts forever. CPOCD Blue Furner and his family arrived in January 1980 and after a 2-week handover, which included my flying them all around the Hawaiian Islands on a sight-seeing tour, Antoinette and I headed for home.

For me, a brief leave before taking up my new posting as the Operations Chief of CDT1.

15
CDT1 – 1980/83

On arrival back in Australia our major priority was to buy a home as Antoinette was due to give birth to our first child (*Jason*) in early '80. We found a place we liked in the northern Sydney suburb of Wahroonga in time for the arrival of our son. He was to be a much loved boy as we had waited for over 8 years to have our first child.

CDT1 was the Navy's operational team based at HMAS Waterhen in Ball's Head Bay. It was by this time made up of 24 Clearance Divers - two Officers, two CPOs, a number of Petty Officers with the balance being Leading and Able Seamen.

The first month or so of every new year was dedicated to refresher training for the team in every aspect of the CD role. This included my favourite demolitions work-up at Marangaroo. As the operational Chief, I was responsible for the conduct and supervision of these workups and I always enjoyed the explosives/demolitions phase immensely.

The team was at the beck and call of the Fleet Commander. We had a unit which responded to diving requests from Fleet units for everyday diving/maintenance tasks at Garden Island and the remainder of the team were regularly deployed up and down the East coast of Australia as well as overseas.

The OIC pretty much stayed in his office carrying on the mundane official paper war required of a Naval unit. The executive officer was normally a young recently graduated MCDO who was there to support the Boss and tag along on jobs consolidating his training and gaining hands-on experience by working with the more experienced Chiefs and POs.

My responsibilities rotated between day to day running of the team as the Team Coxswain and being the Ops Chief in charge of ongoing training, planning, preparation and conduct of operational tasks both on and off the Australia station.

Things had changed a little since my earlier days in Team 1. It had obviously grown in size to cope with its increased responsibilities but also jobs like the annual 3-month deployment to New Guinea were a thing of the past. Since gaining independence and becoming Papua New Guinea, Australia no longer had any responsibilities towards clearing the enormous amounts of WW2 ordnance scattered about the country. I assume we would have continued to perform this much needed role if requested to do so by the PNG government but as with most recently independent countries, they wanted to cut the ties with their previous colonial benefactors.

Fortunately trips to our northern neighbours had not come to a complete standstill. An agreement called the Defence Co-operation Program (DCP) had been hatched between the governments of Australia and the Solomon Islands. Under this program CDT1 was to make an annual trip to the Solomons using obsolete anti-submarine mortars to blast channels through the outlying reefs of the more remote islands allowing them improved access for their boats in bad weather. This allowed them to both bring in needed stores and ship out the local produce thus much improving the lives of these otherwise forgotten villages.

Several months prior to each deployment, the CO and the Ops Chief would visit all the sites which had been selected for channel blasting to ascertain both their suitability for blasting and the explosives and time frame required to complete the job. Not all sites were suitable and occasionally we had to tell a very disappointed village Chief that it was not feasible at his location. It gave him enormous *'face'* if he could *'arrange'* for the white fellas to blast a channel just for his village. It was pretty obvious they made a lot of mileage by bragging to the rest of the villagers how they had organised for the big Navy ship and white fella divers from Australia to come and blow a channel for them. The surveys were usually conducted on a government boat with a guide from the Solomon's Marine Department. Chugging along on an old timber boat which stank of stale fish, stale body odour and mouldy bedding was not exactly luxury cruising however it was more than made up for by the beautiful islands we visited. The reefs and beaches were magnificent and we couldn't wait to return with our diving gear. We dined on freshly caught reef fish with the occasional lobster thrown in.

For the operation, most of the team would fly into Honiara to meet the Heavy Landing Craft which had sailed up from Australia loaded to the gunwales with explosives, diving equipment, boats and Atco style huts for our accommodation. It was quite a simple operation to blow the channels. Once the location and direction had been decided, it was a simple matter of bringing in the armed mortars by assault craft, positioning the correct number with the correct spacings at high tide, connecting them at low tide with detonating cord and shooting the lot on the next high tide, taking advantage of the maximum water cover over the charges. Shooting at high tide served a dual purpose – it gave maximum tamping to the detonation thus increasing the effect of the explosives and also minimised the throw-out distance of shrapnel and reef material. The villagers thought it was *'white man's magic'*. Only the older men of the village who were young boys during the war had ever seen an explosion. When this perfectly straight sided and deep channel magically appeared in front of their village they were ecstatic. They also had no objection to the fresh fish they were going to have for dinner that night, courtesy of CDT1.

During my 3 and a half years as a Chief of the Team, I managed several trips to the Solomons both on surveys and running the actual blasting operations. They were great trips and I never tired of going back.

For these visits we usually carried a medic and engineer, so while we were doing our thing, they would be ashore in the village. The medic fixing minor medical ailments and the engineer usually repairing and improving their fresh water distribution. Of an evening we would usually go diving on the splendid reefs catching crayfish while the crew of the LCH would show a movie for the village. For most of the villagers, it was their first glimpse of the silver screen and they were like kids at Xmas. We would arrive back about 10 or 11 pm in time to cook up a big feed of crays for the crew.

On one trip, my old mate CPO Harmon Slappy USN from my days with the US Navy in Hawaii came along. He was on the same exchange program I had been part of and was attached to CDT1 for 12 months. Harmon had a diving light which I think must have been a stolen landing light from a Boeing 747. When night diving, we just tagged along behind him as he lit up the reef like broad daylight. Night diving in the Solomons was some of the most enjoyable diving I have ever experienced. The spectacular corals and sea life were breathtakingly beautiful.

On one occasion the LCH had to anchor several miles from the blast site and there was a reasonable swell running with passing rain squalls. My boat had left with the first load of mortars and Jake Linton, the OIC and my old boss from Vietnam days was to follow later with the next load. We arrived at the site, placed our mortars and looked around expecting Jake to appear at any moment. No Jake. I got on the radio to check on his ETA but no reply. The LCH advised that he had departed 20 minutes or so before so should have arrived. Keeping a sharp lookout as we backtracked towards the LCH, it wasn't long before we noticed what appeared to be a small mast in the distance. Our civilian guest on this particular trip was Dave Burchell, a renowned civilian diver known for his exploits in locating the wreck of the Australian Cruiser HMAS Perth, which was sunk by the Japanese during the battle of Sundra Strait in Indonesia in 1942. Dave was known for his sense of humour and as we closed the gap, the small mast became a paddle being held horizontally aloft by Able Seaman Husband on the upturned hull of the half submerged assault craft. Dave remarked, *"Bloody hell - it's JC, and he's walking on water"*. Jake and the rest of the crew were looking wet and embarrassed but still managed shit grins all over their faces. They had hit a particularly nasty wave which had capsized the boat sending its load of mortars, radio, personal gear including cameras, to the bottom of the Solomon Sea. We were able to laugh at their misfortune as nobody was hurt, just a bit of wounded pride. I knew Jake would have a bit of explaining to do to Navy Office in Canberra as about 1700 pounds of high explosive had been *'deep sixed'*. As the saying goes, shit happens....

Back in Honiara the young and fit Navy divers were a big hit with the local male starved expatriate female population. Being Clearance Divers, they took every advantage of the situation. The Chiefs as usual, led by example.

One frequent task for the team was dealing with World War II mines which were regularly found up and down the length of the Great Barrier Reef. Thousands of buoyant mines had been laid to the north of Australia during the war and hundreds had broken adrift from their moorings, finally coming to rest somewhere along the broad expanse of the reef. These mines were usually found and reported to the local police by civilian skin divers. Although the actuating mechanisms were long rusted away and useless, the explosive content of the mines was often intact and made more dangerous by age. Certain explosives become increasingly unstable with time so can never be written off as harmless. The only choice available albeit a simple one, is to counter-mine the explosive charge where it sits with plastic explosive. Not very reef friendly but the only option. On one such job Harmon Slappy came with me. The mine had been picked up in a fisherman's nets and he had dragged it to Magnetic Island and cut his nets free in shallow water. I went into the water to examine the condition of the mine. It was half full of mud and by feeling around inside the mine casing I soon discovered that the explosive charge had completely eroded away. With the assistance of a friendly local resident and his tractor, we dragged the mine up onto the beach. Upon emptying the mine case of water and mud, we discovered to my shock and horror that the casing contained two deadly Stonefish. How I never managed to touch their spines I will never know. To this day I thank my lucky stars as the poison from their 13 needle sharp spines is fatal.

After this particular mine incident, Harmon and I were sitting in the Sergeant's mess in Townsville having a quiet beer before we were to return to Sydney the following day aboard a RAAF Caribou. We struck up a conversation with the crew of a P3 Orion fisheries patrol (a four-engine turboprop anti-submarine and maritime surveillance aircraft). They were overnighting in Townsville before continuing on their patrol around Australia searching for foreign fishermen trespassing in Australia's territorial waters. Over a few beers they suggested that we should come with them through to their next stop in Darwin so Harmon could see the Great Barrier Reef from an altitude of 500 feet. They assured us they could get approval from their skipper providing we could clear it at our end. I said no worries. Just a quick call to the Boss in the morning to let him know what we were doing. The RAAF advised us that a scheduled C-130 transiting Darwin from Butterworth in Malaysia to Sydney would give us a ride home. So that was that – all organised.

Next morning, we departed Townsville with both of us on the flight deck heading east until we picked up the reef and then turned north, following the outer edge of the Great Barrier Reef all the way to the Cape. The view was spectacular. For Harmon, all his dreams had come true at once. He was an avid diver and this was a piece of Australia most Australians would never get to see, let alone an American. All from 500 feet.

Over our beers the previous evening I had mentioned to the Sergeant flight engineer that I was a pilot and he must have told the Captain. Once we were established on our northerly course at 500 feet the skipper said, *"Do a bit of flying do you Chief?"* I replied *"Sure do. Love it."* He turned to his co-pilot and said *"Why don't you go for a brew. Jump in Chief"*. After a quick rundown on the handling characteristics of the big four engined Orion he said, *"You've got it Chief"*. He then shut down one engine to conserve fuel and for the next two and a half hours I flew the aircraft whilst being given vectors to steer by the radar operators in the rear as we investigated every surface contact on our way north. What a buzz. It was the most fantastic flight I have ever experienced. About six and a half hours later we landed in Darwin. Another few beers with the crew and then the following morning they continued on their way westward while Harmon and I headed back to Sydney across the dead heart of Australia. Harmon remained glued to the window for the entire trip home. He was mesmerised by the immensity and isolation of the Australian *'outback'*.

Life continued at a hectic pace in Team 1. In early '81, the 3-week Special Warfare Exercise known as Specwarex was fast approaching. I had last participated in one of these exercises back in '74 as a Leading Seaman. The Boss decided our young XO, Lt *'Little Squiz'* Taylor should lead the deployment to gain some experience working with foreign forces. Squiz, and I as the ops Chief, were responsible for selecting and preparing those who were to go. I suggested that Harmon, being the US exchange Chief, would be an asset as it was a USN run exercise. Australian and New Zealand SAS troops and NZ Navy Clearance Divers were also taking part. The RAAF provided a C-130 for the trip to Subic Bay in the Philippines with an overnight stop in Darwin.

When we departed Richmond Air base in Sydney, it was a full load, with us, the Kiwis, the Australian SAS and all our gear aboard.

On arrival in Subic Bay we were billeted at the large US Naval base at Olongapo where Harmon and I shared a cabin in the Chief's quarters. Our hosts for the joint exercise were the US Navy SEAL and EOD teams based in Subic Bay. Along with US Army Green Berets, US Air force and Philippino Special forces, we were to conduct joint operations allowing us to familiarise ourselves with each other's equipment and methods of operation.

The first few days were taken up with PT, surface swims and lectures. We then progressed to learning about and using each other's equipment and demonstrating our various in-house speciality skills. There were several areas where the Aussie CDs stood out. These included overt and covert beach survey/clearance, advanced demolition techniques, dealing with IEDs and covert ship attack using Oxygen rebreathers. We all managed to learn something from each other prior to moving on to the practical phase of the exercise.

Naturally on the nights when we weren't working, the US Navy SEALs took it upon themselves to introduce us to their favourite bars and the ever friendly and gorgeous girls of Olongapo. The favourite EOD hangout was the *'Bamboo Grove'* which I remembered well from 1974. It was located off the main drag and on the 1st floor of a dingy little wooden building. The

Mamasan loved us as did the girls. Before the night was over, we were all attempting the traditional Philippino dance called the *'Tinikling'*. Two long bamboo poles were banged together about 6 inches above the floor. The object was to *'trip the light fantastic'* in and out of the clapping sticks without breaking your ankles – a lot of fun with a few beers under the belt and the girls all laughing as we regularly fell ass over head.

At that time there still remained a military imposed curfew and no US servicemen were allowed on the streets of Olongapo after midnight. So it was either hightail it back to the base, or camp in a bar. We always opted for the bar. We would continue to party into the early hours and when we had had enough, the girls would bring out mattresses to be placed on the tables or the floor. We would all then bunk down for the night, the girls included. Nothing had changed in the 7 years since I was last there.

Unfortunately, these nights on the town were not as often as we would have liked. There was work to be done and often the exercises continued throughout the night.

Sadly, the exercise was to end on a tragic note. One of the final exercises involved a covert night insertion/extraction onto an outlying island utilising the US Air Force's super stealth, super quiet C-130s known as *'Blackbirds'*. This evolution required the aircraft to land and take off from a non-lighted airstrip without the use of landing lights. We were to exit the ramp as the C-130 turned for take-off at the end of the runway, secure the area, conduct the programmed exercise and wait for our covert extraction. On take-off from the airstrip the aircraft would depart out over the water and remain at wave top level to minimise the risk of detection. Due to our numbers, we were split into two groups spread over two nights. CDT1 was tasked in the first op and it was completed without incident. On the second op on the final night of the exercise, the C-130 took off from the darkened airstrip, banked over the water just after departure, clipped the surface of the water with a wing tip and cartwheeled in, completely disintegrating. All onboard with the exception of the Electronic Warfare Specialist crewman were killed, including two Australian SAS Sergeants. It was a very sad finale to a very successful SPECWAREX. A hastily arranged memorial service was conducted that very morning prior to us loading our RAAF C-130 for the long trip home with the bodies of our two mates in metal coffins at the rear of the aircraft.

I had been back in CDT1 as the Ops Chief for perhaps 12 months when during a casual conversation with the Boss, – my old boss from Vietnam, Jake Linton - I mentioned that I had been quite disappointed that after 3 years on exchange with the US Navy as one of the more senior enlisted NCO's, I had never had a debrief of any sort on my return. He was also very surprised.

After a few phone calls from him to Canberra I was on my way south to Navy Office for a debrief, or so I thought. My reception and treatment in Canberra made me realise that nothing had changed in the Navy since I had returned from Vietnam 10 years earlier.

My first stop was to see the resident MCDO (Mine Clearance Diving Officer) in Navy Office. I fully expected him to be most interested in what I had seen and done after 3 years' hands on experience with the US Navy's operational Mobile EOD Unit. Especially the 3-month trial of the SLSS I had completed at the Navy Experimental Diving Unit in Florida.

As stated earlier, I had sent home a very detailed report on the A5800 or Mk 16 dive set which was being introduced into the US Navy. This particular MCDO had either not read that report or just didn't give a damn. It is a damning indictment on that officer's level of competency that the Navy first had a closer look at the set some time in the '90s and it was still the RAN's mainstay Clearance Diving set until only a few years ago.

For the hour or so I spent with this officer I never got a word in. He spent the whole of our appointed time telling me about his personal problems. I left that meeting shaking my head.

In stunned disbelief I moved onto my next *'debrief'*, this time with the 'Director of Sailor's Postings', a 4 striped Navy Captain. Normally a senior officer shows quite a bit of respect to a Chief but the second I walked into his office he was on the attack. It was clear that he had every intention of closing down the exchange program at a Senior Sailor level as a waste of taxpayer's money and he was going to try to use me to justify his resolve to bring it to an end. Obviously if he were seen to be saving a considerable amount of money by terminating the overseas posting it would make him appear to be very efficient to his superiors.

After listening to this pompous officer give me his one-sided views and opinions for several minutes, I thought, *'I've had a gutful of this shit'*. So I interrupted him and for the next 15 minutes I told him exactly what I thought and tried to get through his thick skull how valuable the program was to the Diving Branch in particular and the Navy in general. He could see I was pissed off so he sat back and let me have my say. When I had finished, he at least had the decency to concede that I had persuaded him that the program should continue for the moment but be reviewed on an ongoing basis.

34 years later the program is still running. Hopefully I played a part in that happening.

After that shitfight, I thought, *'Right, what's next? It can't get any worse'*.

My next stop was the Navy's *'Intelligence'* section. After ID checks I was taken through several locked doors to their inner sanctum. Here I was met by an arrogant LCDR who had a particularly strong European accent.

Prior to my return to Australia I had submitted a very detailed report on my time in the US. I think this bloke must have been the only one to read it because he immediately began interrogating me about something I had mentioned in that report. I had been exposed to a top-secret project in the US, and without any niceties, or *'would you like a brew Chief?'*, he immediately began asking me direct questions about my involvement and knowledge of the program. I was not in a particularly receptive or friendly mood after my last two encounters and here was this arrogant LCDR with a foreign accent giving me the 3rd degree.

The Americans had treated me with the utmost respect and placed a great deal of trust in me and here was my own Navy grilling me like I was an undercover agent. My immediate conclusion was that Canberra wasn't much better than McHale's

Navy. I was not about to betray the trust the Americans had shown in me, even to my own Navy, although by that stage I was wondering what sort of Navy I belonged to. I had never in 16 years of service been exposed to the pen pushing bureaucrats who were wasting Australia's oxygen in Navy Office. I immediately made a decision, *'I'm not telling you shit. You want to know anything about that project, you go through the appropriate channels.'* So in a less than polite tone, I told him that I knew bugger all because the Americans had kept me, as a foreign national, isolated from the nitty gritty of the program. In fact, I had a very high US Security clearance. As far as I know I was the only foreign serviceman to ever attend the EOD *'Presidential Security'* course conducted by their Secret Service.

So that was my debrief... By the time I returned to the Team the next day, I had resolved to finish my 20 years and move on. I had decided that I had had enough of egotistical, arrogant and incompetent naval officers.

Fortunately, back at Team One I was again amongst my own. I was the Chief and in the main I only dealt with other CDs. We knew our job and we got on with it, without too much interference from the rest of the Navy. It was in my opinion the best job in the Navy. I was surrounded by competent young sailors who were reliable and professional. It was a pleasure to lead such men.

A major event in the developing history of the CD branch took place while I was at CDT1. The Prime Minister, after discovering that our Counter Terrorist forces (SAS) did not possess the capability to covertly retake an offshore oil rig if seized by terrorists, decreed that the Military had better find a solution - and quickly. After a lot of shoe shuffling at senior levels it was put forward that CDs had the perfect training to adapt to this role. The Army however was not prepared to just simply hand over its jealously guarded control of any aspect of counter terrorism to a bunch of sailors. Under extreme political pressure to do something and not having the skills to fulfil the role, they finally relented under the condition that CDs would have to first show they were up to their standards by completing the full SAS cadre course. They were quietly thinking that the SAS course would be too tough for a bunch of sailors and they would all fail, so that idea would be shelved once and for all and they could keep the role in-house.

Much to the Army's surprise, CDs proved they had the stamina, mental toughness and intestinal fortitude to handle everything the SAS could throw at them – they failed to realise that CD training was every bit as tough as SAS training - so eventually CDs became part of the Maritime Counter Terrorism force. How this all came about is another book in itself.

The first team to be sent to the SAS was being formed and my Team boss, CMDR Jake Linton asked me if I was interested in throwing my hat into the ring to be the Team Chief. It was just the sort of thing which most CDs, myself included, would jump at. But it wasn't that simple anymore for me. After thinking it through, I decided not to volunteer. For most of my 12 years of married life, I had been away from home and I now had a 2-year-old son and my wife was pregnant with our daughter. It was time to think about them. Later when I discovered the demeaning way in which our blokes were treated by the Army, I had no regrets about staying in Team One. To this day there is still some very bad blood between the senior ranks of both outfits.

Another offer was to come my way. The Navy had introduced a *'something nothing'* Warrant Officer rank in the late '70s, mainly to console the Army and Air Force. Those two services didn't much like the fact that a CPO (the senior enlisted rank in the RAN) was equivalent to their Warrant Officers – it was nothing short of snobbery. The introduction of the WO rank to the Navy had the effect of diminishing the position of Chief Petty Officers even though the Navy had no idea what to do with their newly promoted Warrants, as Chiefs still filled their same roles and billets. Senior Chiefs were being promoted to become Warrant Officer *'various'*. In other words, they effectively lost their Branch category and a job within their own Branch. They were given the demeaning jobs of very junior officers. Many, as I did, thought it to be a retrograde promotion. While in Team One I was quietly asked if I were interested in the promotion. It would mean immediately leaving the Team and probably posting into a job totally divorced from Clearance Diving. So my choice was to go from the most senior and satisfying operational position in the Branch to one of total insignificance and boredom. The thought of being posted to Navy Office was enough for me to flatly refuse to even think about it. A good friend of mine, another CD, on promotion to Warrant officer was made the *'Blocks'* officer at HMAS Penguin. He organised and supervised the cleaning of the accommodation blocks and admin buildings. It broke his heart and he resigned.

When the time came to move on from CDT1 after almost 3½ years alternating between Operations Chief and Team Coxswain, I had only a little over 2 years remaining before my retirement from the Navy. As it was to be my final posting in the RAN, I had a call from Navy Office asking me if I had a preference as to where I would like to spend it. I felt I had pretty well done everything the Diving School and Teams had to offer so after taking into consideration where we wished to live after I retired, I opted for HMAS Moreton in Brisbane. My parents and brothers were all living in Queensland so it seemed as good as a place as any, and we had no desire to remain in Sydney any longer than necessary.

16
HMAS MORETON – 1983/85

And so on the 18th April 1983, I took up my final posting in the RAN.

I realised it would be very mundane and perhaps a little boring after 3 years with the US Navy followed by 3½ years of running the operational side of CDT1 but I must admit I was looking forward to a quiet relaxed job for a change.

Moreton was the base for the Navy's Amphibious Squadron which included the heavy landing ship HMAS Tobruk and all the Landing Crafts - Heavy (LCHs). It also had a billet for a Chief Petty Officer Clearance Diver whose major responsibility was Command Diving and EOD supervisor for Queensland and keeping the Naval Reserve Diving Team (DT8) up to speed. In addition, I was given the roles of Boat's officer, OIC of the Amphibious Beach Team and I also kept Officer of the Day duties.

We bought a house in the northern suburbs of Brisbane and I bought my younger brother's 750cc motorcycle to commute to work and soon settled into the quiet routine that was Moreton. The Reserve diving team was pretty much self-sufficient so it was just a matter of being there to keep them on their toes. They were a good bunch of blokes who loved their part time military diving.

I was surprised to find that the Amphibious Beach Team and boats took up so much of my time. I was responsible for training and examining potential boat coxswains and issuing boat licenses. Whenever the Amphibious Landing ship HMAS Tobruk was tasked with a beach landing within Australia, it was the task of my team to guide her in to ensure she beached in precisely the right location. This was a little more complicated than may be first assumed and the team had to be regularly worked up with new personnel constantly being rotated through the training.

To maintain my fitness, I ran for up to an hour every lunchtime, usually accompanied by one or 2 other senior sailors who like me were also fitness nuts.

From time to time EOD jobs came in but usually turned out to be just expended Navy or RAAF flares which had washed up on a beach somewhere along the Queensland coast. An exception to this routine was the report that a fisherman had pulled up some unusual military type shells in his nets from the seaward side of Moreton Island. Along with two Army Ammunition Technicians, I was flown out to the island by chopper to check them out. None of us recognised the shells and we could find nothing similar in our publications. The Army Major in charge decided we would open one of the shells explosively – it would either open harmlessly or detonate, one of the two. We stayed far enough down the beach to be safe should it contain high explosive. After the plastic explosive did its job, it appeared that the shell was a dud - empty. As we approached the remains of the empty shell, we recognised a very distinct smell of freshly cut hay. It was then that we recognised it as Phosgene gas. Phosgene is a highly toxic chemical warfare agent used extensively during World War 1. The gas disrupts the blood-air barrier in the lungs causing suffocation. We had received a good whiff of it so when it was reported back to Army HQ, by radio, they hit the panic button and the 3 of us were immediately airlifted to the Army hospital at Enoggera Barracks. None of the Doctors had ever seen the effects of the gas so we were quarantined and put under intense observation while they took regular blood samples. I felt like a Guinea pig but thankfully all ended well and we were released after a few days with no ill effects.

A change of pace to the regular Navy routine was provided by the annual Birdsville Picnic races in western Queensland. Birdsville is in the middle of the Australian outback .... miles from nowhere with only rolling sand hills and desert to the west. The nearest town is Windorah, 400kms or 250 miles to the east along a rough dirt road. The town in those days consisted of the famous Birdsville Pub, a gas station, a store, a small airport and of course a dusty racecourse. Most years over 200 light aircraft flew in for the race weekend. Aircraft were neatly parked in rows all over the airfield and all the pilots and their passengers slept in tents next to their airplanes.

I hired a Cessna 210 *'Centurion'* and along with my brother and four of the reserve diving team, we packed our bags and we were on our way. Two fuel stops to stretch our legs made for a full day. Our second fuel stop was at the remote town of Windorah. As we taxied in to the fuelling point, two locals were standing in the shade alongside the tin shed which passed for a terminal. They were both casually waving their hands back and forth as they watched us approach. My brother Mike, who was sitting in the front seat alongside me remarked, *"They're a friendly couple of blokes"* and started to wave back at them. After I had shut down the engine and opened the doors, we realised why they appeared so friendly – the flies descended on us in droves and we were soon *'waving'* madly as well.

The final approach into the Birdsville strip took us to within about 200 metres of the pub and several hundred drinkers just prior to touchdown. With an audience of that size, it called for a *'greaser'* of a landing....

One of the reserve divers was an excellent trumpet player and we talked him into volunteering to play the bugle call for the start of the races – it was a first for Birdsville.

After 3 days of solid drinking - with the exception of the pilot, it was time to head home. One of the reserve divers had friends who owned a very large sheep property called *'Welford'*, to the north east of Windorah, so we agreed to stop in for the night on our way home to Brisbane. We all slept in the shearers' quarters well away from the homestead so the boys decided to have a big last night. As I had to fly the next day, I was the only sober one and tried my best to get an early night. There is an old Navy saying, *'Payback is a bitch'*. So at first light the following morning, I dragged our bugler out of bed and had him play *'Reveille'* as loud as possible on the veranda. I had five very tired and hungover passengers for the return flight to Brisbane.

During my last months at Moreton I was contacted by Ron Wood, an ex US Navy EOD officer whom I had met in Hawaii. He had started an explosives demolition business based in Clarksville, Florida and knowing I was about to leave the Navy, offered me a job with his company. At that time, he was demolishing a substantial sized bridge in San Francisco Bay so I immediately began looking at the various ways I might get to the US to catch up with Ron and discuss my options.

Fortunately, the RAN offered what was called *'Resettlement training'* prior to discharge. This allowed an individual to spend up to two weeks with a prospective employer at Navy expense – full pay, accommodation and, travel within reason. After studying the DI[N] (Defence Instruction - Navy) I discovered that nowhere did it say that the training must be conducted within Australia. The only real restriction was *'travel within reason'*. It occurred to me that if I could arrange my travel to the US there would be no justification for the Navy to say no. My past contacts with the RAAF now came in handy. I knew the Air Force often sent aircraft to the US, so after a few enquiries I discovered that a Boeing 707 was scheduled to depart on a training flight to the US west coast later in the week. It was to carry 2 complete crews and they were to conduct flight training under snow conditions in Canada. Fortunately for me they were going via McClellan Air Force base located just outside Sacramento, California. It was not scheduled to carry passengers however I was told by my contacts that if my travel was approved, they would get me a seat.

Initially a desk jockey in Canberra said it wasn't possible – only because it hadn't been done before. After sticking the DIN up his nose, he reluctantly approved my resettlement training in San Francisco. To my knowledge, it was a first and it was obvious that Canberra didn't like a precedent being set by a mere Chief Petty Officer. My message to them was *'never under estimate a Chief'*. One of my all-time favourite Navy sayings was: *As the Chief said to the Seaman –'Watch this shit!!'*.

So it was off to California for about 10 days. The only other passenger apart from crew was a Navy Warrant Officer who I knew from when we were both young sailors. Somehow he had wangled a ride for whatever reason I can't remember. We had a great trip as the cabin crew had no-one else to look after. We had an overnight stopover in Honolulu which enabled me to catch up with Jim Henry, the Aussie CPOCD on exchange at that time. We caught up with a lot of my old mates from my exchange days with a beer drinking session at one of the on-base bars before proceeding to Jim's place for an impromptu party with half of the USN EOD Group showing up. Following a day recovering and touring Oahu in a mate's Chevy Corvette, we departed Honolulu late in the evening, bound for San Francisco.

As the WO was just on some sort of *'jolly'*, we decided to team up and share expenses. It was his first trip to the States so I told him if he stuck with me, I would give him a Cook's tour.

On arrival at McClellan AFB, we hired a 2 door Ford Thunderbird convertible and headed for San Francisco – he was very impressed with my choice of car. I caught up with Ron and it took only 24 hours for us to sort out the details of my employment with his company. So Jeff and I had about 9 days to see the sights of California. Ron's daughter lived in the *'Bay'* area so she showed us the normal tourist sights before we decided to make a run to Las Vegas. We headed off late in the afternoon and drove straight through, making the odd fuel stop where we bought a 6 pack of Coors beer for the non-driver. Beer could be bought at any gas station. We arrived at the gambling capital of the world in the early hours and headed straight into the casinos. We wandered, gambled, had a few drinks and finally had breakfast before deciding we had seen more than enough of Vegas.

So next stop was the Hoover Dam. No sleep; too much ground to cover. After the Dam it was on to the Grand Canyon - one on the most spectacular sights in the world. The entire canyon was lightly dusted with snow when we arrived, a sight I will never forget.

From there we drove down to Los Angeles where a girlfriend of Ron's daughter had invited us to camp for several nights. After a much needed sleep-in, she showed us some of LA's nightlife. A day at Disneyland and it was then time to head back to

Sacramento to meet our flight home. Another short stopover in Honolulu, and then back to Aussie.

My last few days at Moreton were taken up with discharge procedures and plenty of farewells and beers in the Senior Sailors Mess. I had mixed feelings about leaving the Navy. Having been my life since I was 17 years of age, it felt very strange knowing I would never wear a uniform again. I knew I would miss the camaraderie, the job satisfaction and the blokes I had worked with. Sailors are unique people and my exposure to civvies had not given me much encouragement, however it was time to move on and start a new life for the sake of my family. My wife had not seen a lot of me in our 14 years of marriage and my son of 5 and daughter of 3 deserved to grow up with their father around. So finally, after 20 years' service in one of the best jobs in the world, I was discharged from the RAN on the 27th Aug. '85.

17

USA – 1985

Within 5 days of my discharge I was on my way back to the United States. Once again I had managed to organise a ride aboard a RAAF 707 which was carrying Aussie soldiers over for a joint Army exercise with the US military. So another overnight stop in Honolulu to catch up again with my EOD mates. They were beginning to think that all I did with my time was fly backwards and forwards across the Pacific.

Ron Wood lived just outside a little town called Clarksville on the Florida panhandle, just north of Panama City. My old stomping grounds from the late '70s where I had spent 3 months with the USN Experimental Diving Unit. Ron and his family had 30 or 40 acres set amongst tall pine trees with a lovely lake on their doorstep and he was in the process of building his own airstrip. Ron was also a mad flyer and had his own M20 Mooney, a particularly fast single engined 4 seater. He checked me out in the aircraft and we often flew to quote on various demolition jobs around the southern states of the US.

Over the years Ron had taught his son to dive and how to use explosives, along with the necessary associated skills of underwater welding and cutting.

When I arrived, they had just started to demolish a road bridge in southern Alabama. The new bridge had already been built only 100 yards parallel to the old one. Our task was to remove all traces of the old bridge without causing any damage whatsoever to the new one – not even a scratch…. Initially, with the use of linear shaped charges, we had to cut and collapse the steel girders into the river. While cranes with clamshell buckets removed the cut steel beams, we drilled the concrete piers and loaded them with Gelignite (*unlike dynamite, gelignite does not suffer from the dangerous problem of sweating - the leaking of unstable nitro-glycerine from the solid matrix. Its composition makes it easily mouldable and safe to handle without protection, as long as it is not near anything capable of detonating it*). Using heavy steel shot mats laid across the piers to contain the flying concrete debris resulting from the blast, we detonated the charges separately until very little remained above the surface of the riverbed. Once the clamshells had removed all the shattered material, it was over to us again. All traces of the bridge had to be completely removed to below riverbed level.

Coffer-dams are welded steel structures consisting of sheet piles and these contained the reinforced concrete which made up the footing of the vertical piers. Our final task was to use oxy/arc cutting equipment to cut the sheet steel piles to below the natural level of the river bottom.

After a few months I decided to bring Antoinette and the kids over to join me. They departed Sydney to fly via Cairns on their way to Los Angeles. As the aircraft was taxi-ing for take-off from Cairns, some lunatic reported a bomb had been placed on board. So after an overnight stop while the aircraft was thoroughly searched, they were finally on their way. I knew they had a connection with Delta Airlines from LAX via Dallas-Fort Worth and on into Tallahassee. Being an aircraft nut, I had checked all their flight details and knew they were flying on a Lockheed L-1011 from LAX to Dallas. During the 2 hours' drive to the airport to pick them up, a flash news announcement came over the radio. A Delta L-1011 out of LAX had just crashed on approach to Dallas airport and there were no survivors. It is impossible to explain how I felt but I pushed on to the airport, fearing the worst. When I arrived, the airline staff told me Antoinette's flight was OK and on time. The fatal crash had been the Delta flight from LAX following her flight. I cannot describe the joy and relief I felt seeing my family walk through that airport arrivals door.

Ron had a very large fully self-contained Mobile home set up on his property which was large enough for the 4 of us. Jason was at school age so we enrolled him in the Clarksville pre-school. He loved the fact that the *'big yellow'* school bus stopped outside the property every morning and afternoon just for him.

In between jobs, we toured around Florida and the neighbouring states. The highlight was seeing Disneyworld with the kids. The smiles on the faces of a 5 and 3-year-old when they met Mickey and Minnie Mouse for the first time was absolutely priceless.

Crunch time however was fast approaching for us. If we were to remain in the US, we would have to start thinking about buying our own home and about the future of our kids. Jason and Kimberley had both picked up quite a southern accent so it basically came down to the question of whether we wanted our kids to grow up as Australians or Americans. After a number of round table discussions, we finally decided that our kids should grow up in the land of their birth close to their grandparents and cousins.

So we up anchored again and headed back to Brisbane where we camped with my parents while we considered our future prospects. I bought a caravan to give us some independence and then decided to head down to South Australia for a long overdue holiday and explore the possibilities of settling down there.

My favourite uncle in South Australia was at that time thinking about retiring and selling the farm on which my mother had spent her childhood and I had spent so many happy times as a youngster. I had so many emotional ties to the house and property and I didn't particularly want to see it in the hands of a complete stranger. For the following several months I worked the property to get a feel for what I might be getting into. The kids absolutely loved it. Running around the paddocks in their gum boots, hand feeding poddy calves and riding on the tractor. It was exactly the environment that I wanted my kids to grow up in. Sadly, after numerous round tables with my uncle and his accountant, it became apparent that it would be a backward step for me. There would be a large initial outlay, many years of hard work ahead with very little return for the foreseeable future. My father was also advising me against it as he had struggled on the land for years after returning from the war.

Torn between both emotional and practical considerations, we finally came to the decision that it was for the best to head back to Brisbane and begin our new life a little closer to my parents and brothers.

18

DUPONT – 1986/96

On arrival back in Brisbane I applied for a position with the international explosives company, DuPont. They were hiring university graduate Mining engineers but I thought I could match it with anyone when it came to explosives - I had nothing to lose and I was keen to do something related to my favourite occupation – blowing things up!!! Surprise surprise, I got the job.

Luckily it was a travelling job and we had decided we wanted to settle in Brisbane, so next step was to buy land and build a home. Head Office for DuPont Australia was in Sydney and incredible as it may seem, I was giving technical marketing responsibility for NSW, Victoria and Tasmania. I initially spent a fair bit of time at Parkes in western NSW where the company had a Watergel explosives manufacturing plant. My responsibilities ranged from the big Broken Hill mines in far western NSW, the new mines in Cobar, through the gold mining districts of Victoria and the large mines at Mt Lyell and Roseberry on the west coast of Tasmania. In a very short time I learnt a lot about underground blasting and mining. It was at complete odds with most of my background because several hundred tonnes of explosive would be detonated underground using complex millisecond delay systems which effectively created numerous explosive ripples which shattered and moved the ore. I completed my circuit of the mines every two or three weeks and I soon discovered that DuPont was an excellent company to work for. For one, they never questioned our expense accounts. We stayed in the best accommodation, ate the best meals and I was free to decide on where I went and how often I flew backwards and forwards. Because of the constant travelling to remote locations, I proposed to senior management that it would be more time and cost effective for me to fly myself around the countryside. After a check-ride to confirm my flying skills, they approved my request. The really good news for me was that it was DuPont's worldwide policy that no employees were allowed to fly in single engined aircraft for safety reasons, and this included me flying myself around the country. So not only was I able to fly at company expense, it was to be all done in a Twin. For a mad keen pilot like myself, I had hit the jackpot.

Later in 1989 when the Pilot's dispute grounded all domestic aviation in Australia for several months I hit the jackpot again. Business had to go on and our people still had meetings to go to and mines to visit so I effectively became the company pilot for the duration of the national strike. Doing what I loved and being paid for it.

As time went on and I established a reputation for my underwater blasting expertise, the company managed to win some very large contracts based on my knowledge and experience. Two in particular come to mind. One offshore operation off the coast of Onslow in Western Australia which created a shortage of cartridged product at our primary Watergel plant in NSW because of the demand to manufacture product 24 hours a day for Onslow, at the expense of all other DuPont cartridged explosives, which was put on hold.

This task required a crucial combination of the right explosive for the job and the correct method of initiating the charges. Prior to DuPont being given the opportunity to trial my proposed methods, they were advancing their parallel anchor channels at 60 metres a week through a very hard Calcarenite (*type of limestone*) seabed. I flew to Perth to firstly convince their board members as to why my methods were superior to our '*opposition*'. After the first trial blast, their rate of advance increased to 170 metres a day. The contract was ours and the plant at Bogan Gate in country NSW swung into top gear to keep up with the demand.

The other huge contract was blasting the Kutubu pipeline trench through the highlands of Papua New Guinea. We won this job solely because of a hemispherical shaped charge I had developed and patented for DuPont. For two years running, these two contracts turned DuPont's business from the *'red'* to very handsome profits indeed.

An interesting sidelight to the PNG job occurred on the second shipment. We manufactured the cartridged explosive requirements in the Philippines and it was shipped across the South China Sea in specialised explosive carrying ships. I had just arrived in Manila and when I walked into the General Manager's office he informed me that the latest shipment had been caught in a major typhoon in the Philippine Sea, capsized and sank with the entire cargo. Fortunately, no lives were lost. This meant that the plant had to go back into full production to replace the lost explosives as quickly as possible. It also meant that as the cargo was fully insured, DuPont sold an additional shipload of product for a very healthy profit.

The GM and I then spent the remainder of the day in his office drinking Red Horse beer to celebrate the company's good fortune. As I had overall responsibility for the project, it made my bottom line look great and his plant produced hundreds of tons more product than had been budgeted. A good result for both of us.

By this stage I had been transferred to the International division and had pretty much a free hand. I visited the Hong Kong airport project where DuPont was contracted to supply US$48 million of explosive product to level the island of Chep Lap Kok and I attended a very interesting international conference on Advanced Explosive Techniques in Beijing, China.

My next adventure was back to Vietnam. The communist regime was beginning to open the door and to allow limited foreign investment as a way to improve their stagnant socialist economy. I was aware of the country's mining potential so when an Australian owned PNG drilling company approached me to accompany them on a fact finding trip to Vietnam with a view to providing drilling and explosive expertise, I had no trouble convincing my General Manager that it was worth a look.

This was 1993, and Hanoi in particular was still very much like it had been at the turn of the century. There was one set of traffic lights in the entire city and apart from the occasional Russian Jeep used by government departments, the streets were filled with bicycles and the occasional Honda Dream (100cc) motorcycle. There were no modern buildings anywhere in the city and there was only one international standard hotel.

I loved it from day one. Tree lined boulevards with numerous picturesque lakes spread throughout the city. Old French colonial architecture and lovely little coffee shops with foods stalls on every street. Delightful food – especially their soups and bread baguettes.

When it came to doing business in Vietnam however it was a completely different story. Most of the government officials we dealt with were of my generation and had avoided the war with America by studying in Russia. They were communist to the core and had acquired the Soviet mentality of smile and agree to everything, but make everything as difficult as possible until a bribe is forthcoming. Even then there was no guarantee that they would or could keep their promises. It was like trying to deal with a grinning snake. I often recall the old Vietnamese saying – *"Everything is difficult until it becomes easy."*

After a few weeks our friends from PNG decided it was all too difficult and resolved to make do with an enjoyable holiday instead. I persevered in an attempt to form a joint venture with the Department of Mines to manufacture modern explosives for their coal industry. I should have realised that the *'grinning snakes'* weren't the slightest bit interested in improving the country's mining output. It was a clear case of *'Ask not what I can do for my country, but what can you do for me'*. It was my first exposure to the communist mind set and I was yet to discover that it is near to impossible to do business with them. They can only visualise what is in it for them *'today'*.

Over the following few years I travelled back and forth knocking on doors and pursuing every avenue within government but alas, to no avail.

Back home, DuPont had become DuPont Wesfarmers and had opened an office in Brisbane. I continued chasing specialty blasting projects for the company until a new CEO, who incidentally knew absolutely nothing about explosives, decided to close the Brisbane office. I flatly refused to move my family to Sydney so after commuting on a weekly basis between Brisbane and Sydney for several months, I decided to take a redundancy package and leave them after 10 years. I knew the CEO and I would never see eye to eye after he noticed the sign hanging in my office –

'It is difficult to soar with Eagles when you work with Turkeys.'

I think he thought I was referring to him – and he was 100% correct. The company was now being run by accountants and not experienced operators. Time to move on....

An old neighbour of mine had been keenly following my experiences in Vietnam and we had often talked about the flood of interest in investment and manufacturing opportunities as Vietnam slowly opened up to the West. In particular, we discussed the huge shortage of accommodation available in Hanoi for visiting businessmen. After talking to a very wealthy business associate of his, we all visited Hanoi so they could see for themselves what was happening on the ground.

To cut a long story short, we formed an Australian company and I was to be the man on the ground to find a suitable Joint Venture partner in Vietnam to construct a 5-star hotel. The law required all JVs to be with government ministries or companies owned by ministries – very convenient.... As the Ministries owned all the best land, it was the only way we could proceed. After finding a most appropriate site for a hotel across the road from the International Convention Centre, we discovered the land was owned by the Ministry of Interior, the ministry responsible for national security – akin to the Russian KGB.

'In for a penny, in for a pound'. At least we knew they would have considerable pull at the highest levels of government.

The Joint Venture license was granted about 18 months later. We were now officially the *'Aus-Binh Minh JV Company'* and I was the General Director.

My friends at home had been busy and had employed a prominent Sydney architectural firm to design the 10 story 50 million US dollar hotel. I was negotiating with a major German construction company already established in Vietnam to build our pride and joy. Meanwhile I had obtained the exclusive rights to market and sell paint from a well known Australian manufacturer. During this time, we paid the bills from paint sales to large construction projects including Australia's brand new 18-million-dollar Embassy in Hanoi.

In the meantime, our primary financial partner decided he wanted to hedge his bets so he offered a substantial share to one of the largest casino operators in the world. They happily agreed to come onboard on the condition that we could obtain a casino license for the hotel. So back to the drawing board for me. I knew the government had an anti-gambling position but after speaking to our Vietnamese partners they assured us no problem.... the Minister himself had said it could be done.

So I spent another year or more in meetings negotiating a Casino licence. Fully aware of the grinning snake syndrome, I assumed nothing until we had the actual licence in our hands. After a lot of hard work and time wasting, we were finally given the firm decision by the Prime minister – no casino licence would be forthcoming. His argument was that gambling on a large scale was not in the best interest of the general population or in line with communist ideology. We had assured the authorities that we would only be encouraging serious international gamblers from neighbouring Asian countries, but all to no avail. With that door closed our new casino partners pulled out of the deal. They told us they were in the business of operating casinos, not hotels. The time and effort required to find a new partner for the project proved too much for my partners so they decided to cut their losses and walk away. I was left with no other choice but to do likewise.

I had thoroughly enjoyed my time in Vietnam. I had been a committed *'Hasher'* with the Hanoi Hash House Harriers for the whole time and I loved the magnificent tastes and variety of Vietnamese food available along with the everyday hustle and bustle of life in Hanoi. Small soup kitchens and fresh beer (Bia Hoi) stalls on the sidewalks, people forever streaming past on their bicycles and pretty young girls in their *'Ao Dais'* – the beautiful national dress of Vietnam.

It saddened me in lots of ways to be leaving that complex and beautiful country. The many contradictions of Vietnam troubled me and I felt compelled to put some of my thoughts and observations on paper while they were still fresh in my mind. In my final weeks in Hanoi I wrote the following words one evening whilst sitting in my Hanoi office reflecting on the intricacies of Vietnam. Many changes had taken place while I was there but very few that had actually improved the lot of the average Vietnamese.

I have included these thoughts in this book because Vietnam has had such a major impact on my life: -

WORDS from HANOI – 1996

"When I first returned to Viet Nam in January 1993 after a 22-year absence, my first impressions were of an intelligent, friendly, hardworking, extremely poor, but relatively honest race of people. Some of those impressions were to change dramatically as I came into more direct contact with the incredibly bureaucratic and corrupt communist state system. In many respects most of my opinions about the peasantry haven't changed a great deal, however as anywhere in Asia, nothing is as it first appears. Most are certainly happier with the apparent easing of iron fisted communist control, the literacy rate is approaching 90%, and they can be very hard working individuals. Unfortunately, honesty as we perceive it is not a strong point in the dingy corridors of power in the larger cities and the rabbit warrens of the central government in Hanoi.

In 1993 this was a country struggling to overcome the extreme poverty that it had endured for generations. Its constant struggle for nigh on a century to shrug off the oppressive and parasitic yoke of the French colonialists, followed soon thereafter by the war against America and her allies (Australia included), had left the country in ruins, both economically and physically. Not only had it lost millions of its young men and women to the ravages of war, its economy remained geared for battle and with little aid other than that provided by the socialist bloc countries, there was not much light on the horizon. There was insufficient to eat for most of the population in a country where totally corrupt hard-line Communist Party puppets controlled food distribution. Farmers were allocated only a meagre ration of the rice they produced and the remainder rotted in warehouses because of red tape and the total incompetence of these petty communist bureaucrats. In fact, many of the peasantry were starving and Viet Nam needed to import rice to feed her millions, and this in a country which has the potential to feed most of SE Asia. Children spent their days standing in queues waiting to buy bread while their parent/s struggled to earn sufficient money to pay for it.

The real crunch came for Viet Nam when the Soviet empire collapsed during the 80's. All of Viet Nam's socialist friends were also in dire straits and it was time for the Socialist Republic of Viet Nam to sink or swim. The older Party cadres still worshipped the Soviet model and religiously followed the dark and evil philosophies of Marx, Lenin and Stalin. By the mid 80's inflation was out of control *(437% in 1986)*. All industries were state owned, heavily subsidised, badly managed, controlled by corrupt officials, and completely run down with antiquated and obsolete Soviet made equipment. Fortunately for Viet Nam, a few wiser heads somewhere within the *'Party'* machine decided it was time to take a good hard look at where they were leading the country. If Communism was to survive, it was necessary to halt the downward economical spiral.

Doi Moi - *'the Policy of Renovation'*, was implemented in 1986. Sufficient numbers within the Party had wisely decided that the only way to improve the standard of living and climb out of the quagmire which had evolved, and more importantly, feed its growing population *(1996 - 75 million in total, 27 million under the age of 15).* was to follow the lead of its *'Tiger'* neighbours such as Taiwan, South Korea and Singapore. This was a very courageous move by some, as the deep thinkers of the Party must have realised that a major shift in direction from the existing command controlled economy to a Western style market economy would threaten the very existence of their entrenched Marxist/Leninist policies and consequently the very power base of the dictatorial Communist machine. To this day there are still many hard-liners who are trying to take Vietnam back to the dark old oppressive days of Leninism. Since 1945 North Viet Nam had been solidly communist after the founder of the Vietnamese communist party; Ho Chi Minh *('Uncle Ho's' real name was Nguyen Ai Quoc. He founded the Vietnamese communist party in 1930 and died in 1969)* declared Viet Nam to be an independent nation. Unfortunately for Viet Nam, the United Nations, steered by the United States, chose to ignore this legitimate declaration and handed the country back to the French on a silver platter with the US providing huge quantities of arms and money in support of France's barefaced aggression. It was to prove to be one of the most expensive mistakes the Americans have ever made *(the Viet Nam war ultimately cost the United States 58,000 dead and somewhere between US$146 and $165 billion).* After the French were finally defeated by the Vietnamese, the Americans once again made a fateful decision to support the despot Catholic President Diem in the south. This ultimately led to the Vietnam war as we know it.

Since the communist victory in 1975, the whole of Viet Nam has been under a very tightly controlled one party communist system and its foreign exposure was confined to the Soviets and their communist satellites. With the US embargo effectively cutting off all contact and aid from the West, Viet Nam remained in the *'dark ages'*. Their socialist allies had neither the capital to spare nor the technology to provide Viet Nam with anything other than antiquated equipment and technology. Everything was completely run down and all that remained was *'socialist ideology'*. Unfortunately, this could not feed the bulk of the population. Viet Nam was at the crossroads.

Enough of the politics, as my real intention is to convey a personal perspective of this country, observed over the past three and a half years as its people have struggled to come to grips with the massive and rapid changes that are occurring daily before their eyes as western culture steadily infiltrates their lives.

I liken the changes which I have seen in this short time to watching a racehorse which has been released from the starting barrier when the rest of the field is over half-way to the finish line. The Vietnamese people are in a race to catch up to the living standards that the bulk of their *'Tiger'* neighbours have taken for granted during the past 15 to 20 years and the West has enjoyed for at least 40 years.

The Vietnamese government is attempting to strictly control the rate of change to ensure that the socialist philosophies prevail, however they have opened a floodgate which cannot be closed, other than by heavy-handed Police or Military intervention.

I often make the observation to acquaintances in Hanoi that the worst thing to happen to the Vietnamese people during the past 25 years was winning the war against the Americans. The US has proven in the past that it is exceedingly generous in victory, but as the Vietnamese have discovered, it can be bitter in defeat.

Compounding the recovery process for the Vietnamese has been the long standing trade embargo placed on them by the US government (lifted only a few years ago). The US has never forgiven them their victory. Australian author Terry Burstall says in his book 'A Soldier Returns' – *"Even though your people refused to stand aside and won, you've still really lost. Those powerful interests will never forgive you and will keep you in poverty for the rest of your life to appease their own egos."*

Viet Nam has remained completely isolated from the real world with its bureaucrats and technocrats remaining totally ignorant of the workings of a market controlled economy. They have believed that the Communist Party in all its wisdom would see them through and that ideology was more important than rice on the table.

I still believe that the average rural Vietnamese remains an open, friendly, hardworking and honest individual. Unfortunately, it is rapidly becoming a different story in the major cities. Communist propaganda, lies, corruption and greedy self-serving bureaucrats have taken a heavy toll on this country. Everything I have read suggests Ho Chi Minh possessed a genuine nationalist vision for his country, but in the hands of many lesser individuals it has degenerated into a race for personal gain and self-serving indulgence. As Viet Nam has progressively opened its doors to foreign investment, the hard liners constantly espouse the social evils which are being introduced by the West whilst secretly lining their own pockets with US dollars. As with all politicians of any persuasion, the only real social evils as perceived by them are the ones which threaten their comfortable lifestyle and survival as members of the Party elite. The communist system has bred a particularly corrupt self-serving bureaucracy which takes full advantage of 'Uncle Ho's' god like stature in the hearts and minds of the people, constantly preaching socialist dogma to the masses, yet at the same time perpetuating the entrenched corrupt system to their own advantage. Without exception, government officials use whatever power and influence they possess to squeeze every cent from foreign investors and Vietnamese alike. To arrange a simple meeting with a senior government official entails heavy bribing of his underlings – US$20,000 to meet the Prime Minister. This also applies to the Ministry charged with encouraging and assisting foreign investment. I believe without exception; every level of the Vietnamese government is on the take. If palms aren't greased, applications or requests, big or small, seem to remain forever on the bottom of the pile, with many empty promises. Sadly, one of the very worst examples in the country is the Police force. From what I have witnessed, being a policeman is little more than a license to exploit the common people. Anyone with party connections seems to be above the law. No one dares question that the majority of policemen own US$2,500 Honda motorcycles while drawing an official salary of perhaps US$250 per annum. It is an accepted practice that if anything is stolen and the police happen to *'recover'* it, a significant payment is payable to the local police before it is returned to the owner. A very lucrative business. Every house, every business, foreign or Vietnamese which wishes to remain *'unmolested'* is subject to monthly payments of some form to the local police station. If anyone refuses to be on *'friendly'* terms with the local constabulary, it is incredible the number of laws which they will have violated almost overnight. All this while the *'Party'* publicly congratulates the police for their outstanding contribution to the welfare of the people and for upholding the true socialist ideals of the State.

I can only presume that the long and bitter struggle of resistance and survival against foreign invaders and colonialists over the centuries, has bred a race that lives entirely for today's gain. There seems to be an undercurrent of urgency to become as wealthy as possible, as quickly as possible, and to hell with anyone who gets in the way. This attitude is unfortunately rampant throughout every provincial and government authority. As an example, most of the large construction companies in Viet Nam operate under the protective umbrella of the Ministry of Construction, making it almost impossible for the emerging small private companies to obtain a licence. A little investigation reveals why the door is closed. All the successful companies happen to be owned by the relatives of the Ministry's very own senior bureaucrats up to and including Ministerial level.

Since my return to Viet Nam, I have met a number of NVA veterans of the 'American war' and it is interesting to note that none of them hold comfortable government jobs. Most were very poor and received neither medical care nor pensions for their years of sacrifice. Without exception, all the middle aged senior officials I have dealt with just happened to be in the Soviet Union or one of its satellites furthering their *'education'* while the war of liberation was raging. The Party faithful avoided the draft while the peasants gave their lives. The world never changes.

The Vietnamese mistrust of any foreigner, Western or Asian, is in their blood. Viet Nam prides itself on the independence of its culture and the importance of maintaining its purity. I believe this to be a fine philosophy. Unfortunately, this has bred a certain arrogance towards other cultures which makes it difficult for them to readily accept new or improved ways of doing anything. As they defeated the French and the Americans, they are convinced their way must be the right way. In complete contrast to Australia's pursuit of a multi-cultural society, Viet Nam is hell bent on rejecting every philosophy from outside. It obviously has a lot to do with survival of the communist system which pours out a steady stream of propaganda designed to fuel the national fervour regarding the dangers of democracy and the belief that only the *'Party'* can possibly know what is best for the Vietnamese people. All opposition to the party is totally banned. The media is state controlled and strictly adheres to official policy of propagating the *'Party's lines and policies'* and criticism is unacceptable. The 80 odd year old Secretary General of the communist party (without a doubt the most powerful and hard line individual in the country) is regularly quoted as saying that *"above all else Viet Nam must adhere to its Marxist/Leninist beliefs and beware of the constant threat and subversion from the outside world to undermine the party's ideals and position"*. They seem to be blissfully unaware that those same ideals have brought about the collapse of Soviet society and its satellite countries. Without exception, communist led countries throughout the world suffer from food shortages, inadequate medical care, rampant corruption and constant oppression, and all in the name of Marx and Lenin. Viet Nam is no exception to the rule however they are more fortunate in that they happen to live in the rice bowl of Asia.

People are dying in hospitals because they don't have sufficient money to bribe the doctors. Only those able to pay are treated well. The Vietnamese people are a total enigma to most Westerners. If you are a member of the family or a close friend, they will gladly share everything they have, their home, their food, their cash. But if you are outside of this network you are fair game. As an Australian I grew up with the attitude that you give the other fellow a *'fair go'* and you do the *'right thing'*. To most Vietnamese this concept is as unfathomable as the blackest depths of the Universe. Whether you are walking on the footpath, driving on the street, trying to run a business or dealing with the bureaucracy, Vietnamese males in particular appear intent on obstructing foreigners every step of the way. I think it is a case of being totally, and probably intentionally, oblivious to others. I'm not sure if it is genetic or it is considered to be the macho thing to do, however it is the one thing you can be certain of when dealing with the Vietnamese. Power seems to be everything to the Asian male mentality, and causing as many problems as possible for everyone else is their way of wielding it, and perhaps setting the scene for future *'favours'*. There is a very real law of the jungle in this country.

Within the government bureaucracy the prevailing attitude is to cause as many delays as possible and only help those who are willing to pay. There is an old Vietnamese proverb which says *'Everything is difficult until it becomes easy'*. No doubt the author was talking about greasing palms with silver and it certainly remains valid in Vietnam today. For the foreign investor, it is still a very difficult *'row to hoe'*. Projects float from one Ministry to another and backwards and forwards between People's committees and central government while the hapless investor struggles to find out how much it will cost and who has the power to make a real decision. Many an investor has parted with considerable sums of money only to find they have been misled as to who has the real influence. *'Everything is difficult'* etc. etc.

I think it will be at least 20 - 25 years before Viet Nam will be in a position to join the lower ranks of the so called Asian Tigers. Before that can happen, many changes need to be made and these may take a complete generation to come about. The most needed change is the demise of the corrupt and self-serving communist regime. The difficult task will be to find enough honest bureaucrats willing to allow a real change.

Like any society that has endured years of war, the older generation is determined to see that their children don't suffer or go without as they did. Unfortunately, this is resulting in relative pampering of the new baby boomer generation which is growing up taking for granted the suffering of their parents. There is a disturbing and growing number of young and vain *'yuppies'* appearing in the major cities. These are generally children of the nouveau riche who see money as easy to come by and are content to do nothing other than keep up with the latest fashion and be seen at the newest disco in town. Not much different from any other country, however it is seen to be a very disturbing trend in the eyes of the older generation who fought the wars of independence. Hopefully this new generation will grow and mature sufficiently to lead Viet Nam out of its difficult past and present and into the next century.

Unfortunately, our Western upbringing with its somewhat parochial mentality has not prepared us well for dealing with any of our Asian neighbours. The Anglo-Saxon and Asian mentalities and outlook on life are as different as chalk and cheese. The Western perception of common sense and logic is at odds with the Asian mindset.

The policy of *'Doi Moi'* has most certainly unleashed a huge number of dormant entrepreneurs. The Vietnamese, like the Chinese, seem to have a natural flair for making money, normally at someone else's expense. Next to Thailand it is the land of the fake copy. From Rolex watches to Zippo lighters to rubies, there is a conman waiting around every corner for the unsuspecting tourist and businessman.

Having dwelt on a number of their shortcomings as perceived through my Western eyes, I am cautiously optimistic about the country in the very long term. I believe that Westerners who have the not insignificant capital necessary to pay for every slow and difficult step forward, and display sufficient patience and perseverance in an attempt to come to grips with the difficult national characteristics, may eventually succeed in Viet Nam. Success comes only from extreme perseverance as the Vietnamese bureaucracy and most Vietnamese joint venture partners will do their best to create as many hurdles as possible.

Looking back, I believe we (the US included) were perhaps on the wrong side, going back as far as 1945. At the end of World War II the Allies decided to give Viet Nam back to the French against the will of the Vietnamese people, hence setting the scene for the Indochina war in which the French were humiliated in 1954, and the prolonged Viet Nam/American war which ended in 1975 when the US hastily withdrew from Saigon.

Any race of people who were prepared to take on the awesome fire-power of the United States for well over a decade in the pursuit of their national identity *(I believe, with the exception of the hard-core USSR and Chinese trained communist cadres, the majority of Vietnamese were nationalists first and last)* possess a depth of character and conviction which deserve immense admiration. The Vietnamese people had few options after the United Nations rejected their claims for autonomy at the close of WW II. The nationalists were unfortunately hijacked by the communists as there was no-one else prepared to help them in their struggle for national unity and independence. The Southern Catholic regime was extremely corrupt, did not represent the people, and their lack of will to fight showed they had little conviction other than a ravenous appetite for the rapid accumulation of wealth and power. For the senior Vietnamese Military and Government officials, this war was an extremely fortuitous opportunity to rake off an enormous share of the billions of dollars the U.S. poured into the war effort. Many of them are living comfortably in the US today, their fortunes provided courtesy of the American taxpayer. This includes the Chief of the Saigon 'White Mice', a notorious butcher who took pleasure in personally executing his enemies and VC suspects.

Viet Nam has a vast potential. It is rich in natural beauty and with a population racing towards 75 million, its potential agricultural and industrial output is staggering. It is rich in natural resources and with the inherent dogged determination ingrained in the Vietnamese character, it has the capacity to become a major player in the mushrooming growth taking place in South East Asia. All it needs is an attitude shift away from the constant interference of the Communist mind-set, and applying the brakes to corruption. Unfortunately, these changes will probably take at least a generation to come about. I hope for the sake of the decent and hardworking Vietnamese, of which there are many, that it will happen sooner rather than later, as there is no doubt that as individuals, and as a country, they have suffered enough."

19
RETIREMENT

After I returned to Australia, I decided that I had had enough of the commercial world – time to call it quits. Time to review the *'Bucket List'*.

Life had finally settled down. I got back into my running and started to go to Gym again. Most importantly I was spending time with my family.

In 2001 Antoinette and I decided to look for a place to retire to with some decent water views. We settled on Redland Bay, a quiet little suburb set amongst market gardens and small farms to the south east of Brisbane.

Unfortunately, during this period I was diagnosed with prostate cancer and Antoinette with breast cancer – we were advised of the news within a week of each other. We continued however with our plans and built our new home overlooking the tranquil waters of the southern reaches of Moreton Bay. Antoinette underwent a course of chemotherapy and after ignoring two doctors who wanted to immediately remove my prostate, I found a specialist who preferred a *'wait and see'* approach to my problem.

What followed was the most difficult experience of my life as I watched Antoinette slowly succumb to this horrible disease. Eight months after we had moved into our new home, my wife, my partner and my mate of 31 years passed away. It left a void in my heart and soul that felt as wide and as deep as the Pacific Ocean.

What hurt me equally as much as the loss of my mate was seeing the pain and loss endured by my children. Jason was 22 years old and Kimberley only 20. Far too young to lose the mother they adored.

Time heals they say and we have all tried to move on with our lives. It has brought the three of us much closer together so I guess some good always comes from the bad experiences of life.

Incredibly my prostate cancer gradually disappeared altogether and there has been no sign of it since.

In the 12 years which have since elapsed, Jason followed in my footsteps and became a Navy Clearance Diver and has since married and presented me with a beautiful granddaughter. Kimberley became an international flight attendant and is also married. Both of them continue to make me a very proud father.

I am now more than satisfied with my life. I spend two months of every year in the US with my great mate Willy, riding our Harleys to Navy SEAL reunions in San Diego and *'Inshore Undersea Warfare Group'* reunions in Oregon. The blokes we catch up with at these reunions are all Vietnam Vets and I love them like brothers.

"I now know why men who have served together in war
yearn to reunite.
Not to tell stories or look at old pictures. Not to laugh or weep. Comrades gather because they long to be with the men who together had performed at their level best, who suffered and sacrificed, who were stripped of their humanity. I did not pick these men. They were delivered by fate and the military. But I know them in a way I know no other men. I have never given any others such trust. They were willing to guard something more precious than my life. They carry my reputation, the memory of me. It was part of the bargain we all made, the reason we were, if need be, willing to die for one another and for our country. As long as I have memory, I will think of them all every day. I am sure that when I leave this world, my last thoughts will be of my family - and of my comrades in arms - Such great men."

author unknown

Motorcycles have always been one of my greatest passions so I keep a Custom Harley Davidson *'Fat Bob'* at Willy's place in Colorado for my annual visits and I also have a Fat Bob at home in Redland Bay.

One of my simplest pleasures in life now is spending time in the Australian *'Outback'*. I have no problems with my own company and can happily spend weeks on my own. Anyone who hasn't experienced the incredible peace and tranquillity of the Australian bush, sat in the shade of a gum tree alongside a muddy creek drinking Billy tea, watched the spectacularly colourful sunsets, sat in front of a log fire eating yabbies under the incredibly infinite canopy of stars visible only from the outback, has in my opinion missed the best parts of life on this planet.

At a little *'one horse'* town in western Queensland called Adavale, I have a share in a property where I love to go hunting feral pigs and catch and eat yabbies (an Australian freshwater crawfish) with *'Fox'*, my old Navy mate from Yarra days. To regularly escape from the cities, highways, cars, traffic and crowds of humans helps to keep me sane.

Having several investment interests in Thailand also takes me to the *'land of smiles'*, Cambodia and Laos, at least twice a year.

As the clock ticks relentlessly on, I remain determined not to let the grass grow under my feet....

All in all, *"life ain't too bad"*.

'UNITED and UNDAUNTED'

20

POSTSCRIPTS

I have often reflected on the differences between my generation's war in Vietnam and the 2nd World War in which my father's generation fought.

We arrived in our war zone by commercial airliner after a reasonably comfortable overnight flight. During World War 2, my father and thousands of others arrived by sea after a long voyage of several weeks. We knew when we were due to come home. Dad's generation had signed up for the *'duration'* of the war. We fought a cunning, mostly unseen, guerrilla night fighter who often went underground or blended in with the civilian population during the day. Dad fought the might of the German Military machine in open desert country. We (I use the word quite loosely) had relatively good food flown in direct from the United States and slept in air-conditioned quarters when on base. Dad survived on bully beef and lived in a tent in the middle of the sandy expanses of the Western Desert. We had the most modern weapons available and traversed the countryside in modern well-armed helicopters. Dad flew in old dilapidated aircraft which were already obsolete at the beginning of the war. My father spent three years in the Middle East never knowing when or if he would come home to his new wife. We flew back to Australia after 4 or 5 months for 7 days Rest and Recreation leave.

They were different times, different wars, different enemies; however, one common thread runs through every war from time immemorial - the human suffering and personal tragedy resulting from the loss of loved ones, and all because of politics and/or religion.

My Father's wartime experiences have captured my imagination since I was very young and thankfully before Dad passed away, I managed to document one of those experiences which came very close to costing him his life. I think it is worth recounting here.

Reginald Norman (*Mick*) Ey was a 28-year-old Flight Sergeant when he arrived in East Africa in October 1941 aboard the *'Queen Elizabeth'*. He was soon promoted to the rank of Warrant Officer and while part of 454 Squadron he received a Field Commission to Pilot Officer. Before returning home to Australia in September 1944, he was promoted to Flying Officer. One of three crewmen of a Blenheim bomber operating as part of a R.A.F. squadron in the Western Desert, Dad's aircraft crash landed in enemy territory *(he was in a total of 5 crash landings)* and he and his crew walked across 140 miles (225kms) of uncharted desert for 11 days with next to nothing to eat or drink. During their long walk home they dodged enemy tanks and patrols and lived on a little rice which they found in a derelict Bren Gun carrier and water drained from the intact radiator of another deserted vehicle. When this water supply was exhausted they moistened their parched mouths with morning dew from the occasional desert flower.

As Dad has been reluctant to record the details of this incredible trek across the Libyan desert, I decided that I would - with a little help from Australian newspaper clippings of the day.

This is that story as he told to me: -

"It was in the Middle East during March 1942 and as a crew we had just joined 14 Squadron after completing our time in the Operational Training Unit in Kenya. I was the Navigator/Bomb Aimer, Pommy Mills the Pilot, and Johnny Hunt was the Wireless Operator/Air Gunner. On March 16th we took off on a 'Squadron Do' in our old Mk. IV Bristol Blenheim. These were a twin engined bomber and our registration number was *V5446*. There were 9 Blenheims in the formation and we had to fly out across the Libyan desert and into Tripoli to have a crack at a Gerry target up there. As Pommy recalled *(taken from **Adelaide Newspaper clippings**)*.

'Coming back from a bombing raid west of Benghazi we were sailing along for home when our starboard engine began to pack up. We were only a thousand feet at the time. The port engine wasn't giving full power either, so we were done. I kept the aircraft going without any oil pressure at all, and gave the 'duff' engine an extra burst now and again to regain a bit of height.'

We had been flying over ground troops earlier so we could have copped a stray bullet, although of course we will never know. We knew we had to keep well down into the desert to the south, well away from the German garrisons along the coast. We decided to jettison as much as we could, as Blenheims were notorious for flying like a brick on one engine and we wanted to get as far as we could. We dumped our remaining bomb load and that helped a bit although we were losing height all the time. We discussed our options as we knew we were definitely going down. The choice was a wheels down landing, or wheels up and belly it in. We all agreed to try a wheels down as the old Blenheim was a pretty slow old bird. When the crook engine finally seized after about twenty minutes, Pommy feathered the prop.

Adelaide Newspaper - *'There was nothing to do except get down as quickly as possible. I turned back into wind on the one engine and decided to do a wheels down landing in case she went up in flames. The country was full of rock shelves and I hadn't had time to pick or choose a suitable spot to bring her down'.*

As we steadily lost altitude Pommy said, *'Alright, this is it'* and we all knew there was only going to be one bite of the cherry - either we made it or we didn't.

Adelaide Newspaper - *'I steered clear of the worst rocks and we came to a standstill with the tail wheel broken off and the prop tips bent as we went over a bit of an escarpment.'*

As it happened, we couldn't have struck a worse place to land. It was all rocky outcrops, rough as the devil, anyway Pommy did a great job, no doubt about that. He touched her down while trying to heave the aeroplane over the worst of the rocky areas. She banged and bounced and finally she was on the ground for good and as we skidded along, the tail wheel and one of the main wheels was torn off, so one wing was low and this caused her to eventually ground loop. When we came to a halt, the high wing came to rest alongside a large rock outcrop about 6 or 7 feet high so all we had to do was walk along the wing and step off onto the top of this rock. It was an absolute miracle how Pommy managed to land on such rocky ground without injury to any of us. Being in enemy territory it was useless to wait besides our aircraft, so we decided to walk. We immediately took stock of what we had. We had a water bottle each, a first aid kit, a tin of peaches and a packet of Army ration biscuits.

I removed the aircraft's P6 compass from the pilot's position, ripped a small canvas bag from the inside skin of the aircraft, stripped some shroud line from one of the parachutes and made a little bag to hold the compass. With the shrouds looped around my neck, I could then carry it on my chest. So away we went. We walked for about 4 hours and stopped for our first night at the base of a fairly steep sand hill. It rained that night and hell it got cold too. We shivered all night but it wasn't a normal shiver, our whole bodies quivered with the cold. It was the only night it did rain. Later on we came to pray for rain but nothing happened.

The next morning, we got started pretty early because we couldn't sleep much and headed off on a compass course of 045°. The idea was that we wanted to bypass Tobruk as *'Gerry'* still controlled it. We had estimated that we were about 180 - 200 miles inland. We walked all day with the occasional spell when we would have a nibble of a biscuit and a bit of water. We knew we had to ration it all out. Our water bottles had corks in them so we decided to ram the corks home in the necks of the bottles so that we couldn't get them out. Each bottle had a pin on a chain and with this we forced a small hole in the cork. To get any water we had to blow through this hole to slightly pressurise the bottle so that when we tipped the bottle up, the pressure forced a few drops of water out. We knew that those few drops were all we could afford to have. We had our peaches that night with some of our broken biscuits which we also strictly rationed. Over the first two days and nights we made good progress and reckoned we covered some 40 miles. It wasn't until the third day that we began to realise the seriousness of our position. We wondered what our people were thinking, as by now we would have been posted as missing.

The worst part up until then was our flying boots which were wool lined. Our feet just slopped around in them and they played merry hell with our feet. We still had some parachute cord so we tied this around our boots to try and keep the boots tight on our feet. We just seemed to walk and walk. Some nights we would walk until about 8 or 9 o'clock until we found somewhere to camp. There were no trees, just a little bit of bush called camel thorn and we'd try and find a little bit of a ridge to dig a bit of a hole and fill it with this camel thorn, and we'd lie on that but it used to get that bloody cold, your teeth would chatter because we only had a pair of trousers and a shirt each; nothing else. What we used to do was toss to see who would be in the middle first, and we'd all face the same way so that we could fit in, and we'd stay like that until we got stiff and then righto, over we'd go. The bloke in the middle would get on the outside so we each had a turn being reasonably warm, but some nights were so bloody cold that by about midnight or 1 o'clock in the morning we'd say, *"Come on let's get cracking"*. The compass was luminous so we'd walk a bit at night and towards daylight we'd have a bit of a camp again because we knew we'd be walking all day; and that's how it went on. During the day it was bloody hot but at night it was as cold as charity. The compass only weighed about 6 or 7 pounds but it seemed like a half a tonne after a while. I had a permanent kink in my neck. On the fourth day we hit a stony plain. You could glimpse the horizon but nothing else - and we kept on seeing mirages. By the fifth day we were out of water.

One night we came on a depression and there had been rain there recently. It was a natural catchment area and there was quite a crop of Lucerne growing. Maybe the Italians had planted it. We camped in this patch for the night and it gave us some shelter from the bitterly cold night wind. We were out of water but we found a tortoise. It was bad luck for him because he got knocked on the head. We had no means of cooking so we ate it raw and drank the blood. It was fluid. In the morning we pulled the Lucerne between our lips to get the dew. We buried our feet in some moist sand to relieve the pain from our blisters.

Another night we found a British Red Cross pickup that had been knocked out. It was like a utility with a canvas top and had a large red cross on either side. Anyway, that night we decided that we were going to camp in this vehicle. After scratching around inside I found a roll of cotton wool and a tube of *Gentian Violet*. Our feet were so bad that I said to my mates that I couldn't go any further unless I pricked my blisters and got rid of some of the fluid, even at the risk of them turning septic. So that's what we did and we smeared this Gentian Violet all over our feet, and that eased the pain. That was one of the good nights we had even though there was one hell of a dust storm. Of course next morning when we started to walk, our feet gave us *'what-o'*.

One day we spotted some knocked out vehicles, so we walked over to them and we were all scouting around to see what was what. The one I was looking at was an Indian Bren Gun carrier and unfortunately its battery was whacked, otherwise I reckon I could have got it started. Anyway there was nothing I could do about it. Pommy came over and he said, *'What have you found Mick?'* I said, *'Well firstly, there's a 4-gallon tin of Indian curry and it'll burn your insides out, but it's something to eat. I've tried it, and bloody hell it's hot. Another thing, this radiator's got a lot of water in it'*. We found some empty Gerry cans and drained the water into them. We ended up with two cans about three quarters full. It wasn't the best of water but it was water and it saved our bacon. We were determined that we wouldn't part with those Gerry cans for anything, so we carried them for about 4 days I think it was. One bloke in the middle would carry both cans with one either side holding the can as well. When the bloke in the middle was buggered, we would change over. But I was stuck with that ruddy compass around my neck all the time. It kept us on course and we were right on track when we got picked up. We were aiming for the coast road east of Tobruk and if we knew if we made it, we had a good chance of running into our own troops.

Once we saw a Gerry patrol of 3 or 4 vehicles and as we were in a pretty bad way at that stage, we didn't give a bugger who picked us up. We tried to attract their attention but they just sailed by. Probably thought we were bloody wogs *(Bedouins)*.

Adelaide Newspaper - *'The mental strain was worse than anything. You don't realise how vivid your imagination can be. In the evening we could see our bar in the mess and all the boys around it. Our eyes began to go to, after about 4 or 5 days, and everything became blurred as a result of the glare and sand.'*

One day we came across some canisters lying around on the ground. We were pretty fuzzed up by this time; not exactly thinking clearly. These things looked like big thermos flasks and I thought, *'What the hell's this'*, so I picked one up and had a look at it. It must have been intuition but I thought, *'Hell'*. I let it roll off my hand onto the ground as I realised that we had walked right into a bloody German minefield. We quickly backtracked until we were sure we were clear of it. We hadn't had anything to eat for several days and we had run out of water. Things were getting tough. We were now on our last legs and had given up all hope of getting back alive.

On the tenth day I spotted something in the distance but I couldn't make out what it was, so I said to Pommy and Johnny, *'Let's deviate and go over and see what that is. There might be something to eat'*. So we altered course and when we got over there, we found a truck which had been a tanker of some sort. It had been knocked out and was sitting in a deep depression, and down in this depression it looked as though troops had recently been camped there. We were looking for water and thought that there may be a well there, so down we went.

We found three holes in the ground which we thought might contain water. Pommy went to one and I went poking around one of the others. When I got to this particular hole, I found a length of telephone wire which was tied to an old kerosene bucket so I picked up the bucket and sang out to Pommy, *'Hey come here, look at this, there's water in the bucket'*. There was a rock hole which we couldn't see into, but we knew there must be water in it. I said *'Thank God, we've found some water'*. I dropped the bucket down the hole and pulled up about a half a bucket of the best water you've ever tasted in your life. It was crystal clear so we all had a real good slug, and that perked us up quite a bit. Johnny then said, *'Come over here'*, and he showed us an area where there had been a lot of troops. It looked like there had been a bit of a fight as there were a lot of empty cartridges and little trenches where someone had obviously dug in. We decided to stay the night there and it occurred to me that the bucket must have been used that morning, as the evaporation rate out there was quite high, and there had been water in the bucket. I said, *'Someone is not very far away, so we'd better keep an eye open'*. Anyway, Johnny walked over to have a good look at the tanker and wedged between the tank and the step which ran around the outside he found a round tin. The label had gone and Johnny was belting it with rocks trying to get it out. He reckoned there was probably something to eat in it. Johnny finally got it out and brought it over to us. In the meantime, Pommy and I had been scouting around and we rounded up all the little bits of camel thorn that we could find as we intended to have a fire that night. Pommy said there were a lot of cigarette butts there so I said, *'Round them up because I have a packet of papers and two matches'*. So we picked them all up, knocked the ash off, broke them up and we had enough for a smoke each. Then Johnny turned up with his tin and it was a tin of rice of all things. I thought *'Jesus, we'll eat this up tonight'* as we had plenty of water, providing we could get the fire going. So I got to work and finally we had a fire going. With only two matches I couldn't take any chances. We filled our bucket with water and were watching it heating up when all of a sudden we heard a noise. We looked up and at the top of the little escarpment there was an Armoured car with its bloody guns trained down on us. I said to Pommy, *'Who the hell are they?'* and then we realised they were ours. They were Pommies. We sang out and waved. Down the side of the escarpment there was something like a goat track and it led into the hollow. Anyway, down this track came this Armoured car, then a second, and then a third one appeared on top with its guns pointed at us. The first car stopped about 50 yards away but kept its gun turret pointed directly at us. I could see an officer standing in the turret so I called out *'Thank Christ, you're the best sight we've seen'* and we heard him say, *'They're bloody Australians'*. It turned out that they used to come in and water there every few days and they knew that Gerry also used it. *(these British Army Patrols regularly operated behind German lines).* I asked *'Were you here this morning?'* and they said *'No, not today'.* I replied *'Well Gerry was, there was still water in that tin, so we picked the right blokes'.* The bloke in charge said *'We'll get the hell out of here now. We don't want to get caught in here'.* So they filled up their water tanks and one of us went to each car, and then we took off. The name of the well was *'Bir-Tengeddar'.* I'll never forget it.

We got well away somewhere out in the desert and the Sergeant said, *'We'll camp here for the night'.* They split up and each car camped about a quarter of a mile apart as they would never group. It presented too large a target.

Anyway, these jokers said, *'Right, we're just about due to go back and we're short on rations but we've got some powdered eggs here'* and that sounded like a banquet to us, so they cooked up these powdered eggs and we had army ration biscuits and had a great feed. But gee we were crook after, it bloody near killed us. Our stomachs were obviously in shocking condition.

It was the evening of March 26th *(38 years later to the day, Dad's third grandson and namesake, my son Jason Reginald Ey was born).* We had been in the desert for 11 days and had walked for about 140 miles. They made us as comfortable as possible and I had a good night's sleep for the first time in 11 days. The following day we headed back towards their advance base, and that consisted of only a few vehicles in a bit of a waddy.

The next afternoon they told us that they had organised a ride for us back to their main base on three of their supply trucks the following afternoon. On that day, just after lunch, we heard an aircraft approaching and next thing an old three engined Italian *Savoia* came over the top of us. They must have been the biggest dopes in the world because they were flying at about 300 feet and the whole crew were looking down at us. One of the Sergeants in the Armoured cars had replaced his standard issue Browning .303 with a Breda, an Italian gun and a damned good one; about an 8mm calibre which packed a hell of a wallop. As this bloody old thing circled at about 300 feet, almost over the top of us, the Sergeant opened up with the Breda and I could see those slugs tearing into that aircraft, hitting at the wing root, and the next thing I could see fuel pouring out. The next minute she dived straight in. I often remember there were 4 blokes in that Savoia looking down on us, and three seconds later, they were all dead. Just as quick as that.

Our rescuers turned out to be a Long-Range Desert Patrol from the Royal Dragoons and luckily for us they were prowling around behind Gerry lines. Anyway, their re-supply vehicles picked us up and we finally got back to our squadron. On the way back we rode one to each truck. I was in the lead one and there were tracks going everywhere. My driver was scarping along and all of a sudden something sort of gelled so I said *'Hang on a minute, pull up quick'*. The driver said, *'What's up Sarge?'*, and I said *'You won't believe it but we're in the middle of a bloody minefield'*. I stood on the running board and directed him back slowly, exactly in our tracks until we got back about 100 yards and onto hard stony ground. Our luck was still holding. Gerry had laid thousands of mines throughout the Western Desert. Pommy and Johnny came up in their trucks and asked what was wrong. I said *'Don't go down there, it's a bloody minefield'*. It had made my hair stand on end.

When we got back to base all our gear had gone. We reckon the Pommie stores blokes had got hold of it and split it up between them. They were a mob of vultures. The Medical Officer gave us a check out and we had a bit of a blowout that night with our mob in the mess. We were told that we were going up to Cairo on a month's special sick leave and they had a vehicle which we could drive ourselves if we wanted to. The MO gave us a couple of letters to take to Cairo to make sure that we would be looked after. I was only in Cairo for about 4 days when I collapsed from Enteric Fever (Typhoid).

However, we all got over it and as we were eventually away from the squadron for over 6 weeks, we were taken off Squadron strength and posted out to new squadrons. We were posted to 55 Squadron which was another English squadron.

That prang was on our very first raid. I had been in 3 earlier prangs while back in OTU *(Operational Training Unit)* so I said to Johnny one day, *'Jesus Johnny, we're not long for this world. The first one we do, we get whacked'*. After I joined 55 squadron, I was on my sixth op when we got hit with Ack Ack and I was wounded in the right foot by shrapnel, so I was off strength again for about 2 months because the wound wouldn't heal.

While I was in Cairo again on sick leave I heard that Johnny and Pommy had got split up, and one day I bumped into some mates and they said *'We've got bad news for you Mick'*, so I said *'What's up?'*. They told me that Johnny had bought it. The CO of the squadron had wanted a gunner and he picked Johnny to go with him. They took a direct hit by an 88mm shell, right on the bloody nose. They never knew what hit them.

I was then posted to 454 Squadron, which was a new all Australian outfit forming up in Iraq. This squadron had *Blenheims* but was in the throes of changing over to *Martin Baltimores*. That was where I ran into Paddy Archer again, my old Pilot from OTU. He said *'Who are you flying with Mick?'*, and I said *'You'*, and he said, *'That'll do me'*, so we teamed up. I'd been there about 4 days when the adjutant approached us and *said 'I've got a job for you fellas; a holiday'*, so we were immediately very suspicious. He told us that Ferry Command wanted a loan of an experienced crew to ferry an aircraft out to India, so that job took us a month. When we came back, we picked up with the squadron and went back to the Western Desert where we became fully operational again. It was a damn good squadron; they were all Australians. So that was that. I did another 12 months operational flying with Paddy on 454. When I tallied it up, Paddy and I did 87 operations together, for me a grand total of 93. It was a hell of a lot."

Back in Australia, my mother had received the following two telegrams from the Air Board: -

Date 20th March 1942 - *"Regret to inform you that your husband Sergeant Reginald Norman Ey is reported missing as result air operations in Middle East on 16th March 1942. Any further information received will be immediately conveyed to you. 12.40pm. Air Board".*

Date 4th April 1942 - *"Pleased inform you that your husband Sgt. Reginald Norman Ey previously reported missing has been found safe and has returned to Unit. Your husband's aircraft made a forced landing in Libya on 16th March. He with other members of the crew travelled on foot until 26th March when they were picked up by a British patrol".*

Pommy, Dad and Johnny (posthumously) were later made members of the *'Late Arrivals Club'*. Membership of this club was restricted to air crews who had been forced down or crashed in the Western Desert and had taken longer than 48 hours to walk to the safety of their own lines.

By war's end, there were only 80 or so members of this exclusive Air Force group. The badge consists of a silver winged Flying Boot.

The award reads: -

"LATE ARRIVALS CLUB

This is to certify, that Sergeant Reginald Norman Ey of 14 Squadron, is hereby nominated as a member of the Late Arrivals Club. Inasmuch as he, on 16th March 1942 when obliged to abandon his aircraft (a Mk. IV Bristol Blenheim) on the ground as a result of unfriendly action by the enemy, succeeded in returning to his squadron, on foot long after his Estimated Time of Arrival."

This marathon trek across the Western Desert behind German lines is also described in the official RAAF publication on WWII - *'These Eagles'*. It is part of a chapter titled *'But the Pilot is Safe'*.

ABOUT THE AUTHOR

The author joined the Royal Australian Navy in 1965 and spent the following 20 years as a Clearance Diver, retiring as a senior Chief Petty Officer in 1985.

His brothers, Mike and David and his son Jason all joined the ranks of Navy Frogmen thus making 4 members of the Ey family to serve as Clearance Divers.

Career highlights included;
- being a member of the 8th and final Clearance Diving Team to serve in South Vietnam during 1970 & 1971.
- 12 months as senior Demolitions Instructor in the RAN and numerous postings to operational diving teams, including 3½ years as Chief of CDT1.
- Personnel Exchange Program with the USN based in Hawaii from 1977 to 1980.
- diving in such magnificent locations as the Great Barrier Reef, Papua New Guinea, the Solomon Islands, Truk lagoon, Kwajalein, Hawaii and the Caribbean.
- obtaining a US Pilot's Licence.
- qualifying for US Navy Parachute wings at Lakehurst, New Jersey.
- several SPECWAREXs with US Special forces.

After leaving the Navy he worked for a short time in the southern United States demolishing bridges using specialised explosive techniques and on returning to Australia, was employed by DuPont Explosives as their Specialty Blasting Manager (during this period he developed a commercial *'shaped charge'* for DuPont which was patented worldwide) and afterwards had a business in Hanoi, Vietnam, until his retirement in 1997.

The author holds both US and Australian Pilot licenses with a multi-engine endorsement, and a Glider rating.

His hobbies include writing, international travel, photography, spending time in the Queensland outback and riding his Harleys in both Queensland and the western United States.

He resides in Redland Bay, Queensland, Australia and has two children – a son Jason and a daughter Kimberley.

The author – between reunions - California. 2013.

ADDENDUM

In 2016, after 19 years of a very enjoyable and satisfying retirement, it was suggested to me by an old American friend, who is both ex USN EOD & a Vietnam veteran, if I was interested, that I should submit a CV to *'Golden West'*, who had created a position of *'Chief of U/W Operations'* to manage, train and mentor the Cambodian National Dive team with a view to progressively growing both their diving and EOD skill levels.

A US based non-profit Humanitarian Foundation, *'Golden West'*, in partnership with CMAC – the Cambodian Mine Action Centre, agreed to train a team of locals to dive, conduct EOD, and to locate and recover ordnance remaining in the rivers and waterways of the kingdom.

'Golden West,' who specialise in EOD training, were seeking an ex-serviceman who was the equivalent of both a USN Master Diver and a US Master EOD technician to take over the dive program and was prepared to reside full time in Cambodia. They also wanted someone with extensive experience operating in Asia. Fortunately, I ticked all the right boxes and was more than happy to accept the challenge and come out of retirement and relocate to one of my favourite parts of the world.

And so began 12 months of mentoring & training in the *'Kingdom of Kampuchea'*, responding to reports of air dropped ordnance discovered in the rivers and waterways of Cambodia.

With the assistance of foreign aid, primarily from the Japanese & the US governments, the current Cambodian government had created the *'Cambodian Mine Action Centre'* (CMAC) to address the task of locating and removing/destroying the unexploded ordnance littering the countryside.

A number of CMAC de-miners volunteered and began the selection process.

Selectees were put through a very rigorous training program under the guidance and supervision of Golden West & serving/retired US Military Diving/EOD personnel.

Eleven eventually qualified as USN 2nd class diver equivalent, certified to 30 metres on air utilising USN twin 80 cu.ft. dive sets. After graduation as divers, they underwent training in English, Maths, Science and basic EOD – in accordance with IMAS guidelines (*International Mine Action Standards*).

The entire project was funded by the US Department of State through their office of *'Weapons Removal & Abatement'*.

During the Vietnam war (1955–1975, called the American war by the Vietnamese), over 7.6 million tons of ordnance were dropped on Vietnam, Laos and Cambodia, with 2.7 million tons of that total (*over 230,000 sorties*) being dropped on Cambodia – a neutral country.

Indochina now holds the unenviable record of being the most heavily bombed region in history.

Of the Cambodian total, approximately 26 million sub-munitions (*Bomb Live Units*) were dropped. The failure rate of these Cluster munitions was estimated to be at the very least 30% - some sources state as high as 80%, leaving between 8 million and 20 million units unexploded in the Cambodian countryside, and it is generally accepted that between 10 to 30% of conventional air dropped ordnance also failed to detonate. These statistics do not include the millions of anti-personnel mines laid indiscriminately by Lon Nol government forces and the Khmer Rouge during the 70's.

To put that into clearer perspective, the Allies dropped a total of 2 million tons of ordnance during the 6 years of WW2.

Since the Khmer Rouge were routed by the Vietnamese Army in 1979, Cambodian civilian casualties from UXOs and anti-personnel mines have totalled more than 64,000 (*with over 21,000 fatalities & 40,000 amputees*). Sadly, for Cambodia this has been in addition to the 3 million civilians (*37% of the population – UNICEF estimate*) massacred by the Khmer Rouge during their genocidal reign 1975-1979. (*Incidentally, while the merciless Khmer Rouge systematically slaughtered their own countrymen, they were recognised as the legitimate government by the UN & the West*).

Based at the CMAC training centre on the Tonle Sap river, 90 kms north of the capital Phnom Penh, the 11-man Team consists of one Team leader with 2 additional supervisors so the team can theoretically operate as 2 separate dive teams. My task was to mentor the team and train them to the point where I was satisfied to sign them off as competent Salvage divers able to operate in all environments without the supervision of an expat Technical Advisor.

Operating out of *'Wing'* inflatable boats and equipped with towed electro-magnetic metal detection arrays, hand held metal detectors, hand held sonars, dredging equipment and 1,000 lb mine lifting bags, the Dive team began to recover ordnance from the fast flowing and zero visibility rivers. Sunken barges loaded with a variety of ordnance and ammunition were a priority closely followed by the safe recovery of air-dropped ordnance from rivers and large ponds. Bombs ranging from 250 lbs to 1,000 lbs were dropped by the US with the majority being 500 lb US Mk 82s. These are frequently discovered by local villagers and fishermen who often only reveal their whereabouts after methodical questioning by CMAC personnel. Unfortunately, villagers are most reluctant to contact the police.

As an example of the team's work, a major task which had been on hold until the new 'Chief' arrived was a timber ammunition barge which had been sunk by Khmer Rouge troops using rocket propelled grenades (RPGs) in the mid-70s. It had been transporting a variety of US ordnance destined for the Lon Nol Government which, with US support, was fighting a losing battle with the Khmer Rouge forces. The manifest included 105mm howitzer rounds, 2.75-inch rockets, 60mm and 81mm mortars. It had been sitting on the river bottom for over 45 years, less than 20 metres from the edge of a large village. Clearing this ordnance was a major priority of the Cambodian authorities and with their new national diving team now fully operational, the task could begin. There were however a few obstacles to be overcome. Firstly, the Tonle Sap river flows at a considerable pace for most of the year – the only river in the world which flows in both directions over the course of a year, the visibility in the river is zero, the riverbed is mud to a depth of several metres, the bottom is covered with dead branches and tree trunks intertangled with old fishing nets, the surface of the river for the part of the year when the flow is at its slowest is covered by floating drifting broad leaf plants and lastly, the barge was below the actual level of the river bottom – buried in the mud.

After pinpointing the largest concentrations of magnetic anomalies, a search area was cordoned off. Firstly, the search area had to cleared of all tree branches and fishing nets. This was followed by searching with hand held Ebinger UWEX metal detectors to pinpoint ordnance down to a metre or so in the mud. With the use of a suction dredge, mud was then removed until ordnance was located and lifted to the surface – and all in zero visibility.

This detector/suction/detector/suction cycle continued for several weeks down to 3 metres below the riverbed until no further magnetic returns were detected.

The success of this operation demonstrated the ever-increasing value of the dive team.

During my tenure, the team refined their skills with hand held sonars utilising a variety of search schemes, completed training in Surface & U/W demolitions, small boat operations, emergency medical first aid and U/W medicine.

It was my intent during the second year to qualify the team to 40 metres, equip and train them in the use of Surface Supplied equipment and to become proficient in the use of towed side scan sonar. A necessity as parts of the Mekong river are in excess of 30 metres in depth.

It is with some pride that I make the claim this team of EOD divers to be second to none in South East Asia and perhaps unique in the world because of their constant operations in zero visibility and working continually under the very worst of conditions with unsafe ordnance.

I assume, in part to my positive monthly reports on the Team's progress, the US State Department decided, much to my disappointment, to cease funding for my role from December 2017 as they felt the Team was now capable of stand-alone operations.

It was my plan before leaving to make this Team, beyond any shadow of a doubt, the premier diving team in Asia.

Unfortunately, the bureaucrats in Washington control the purse strings.

The Team has however, cemented its position as an acknowledged and extremely valuable National asset, not only in diving and EOD but also with the Prime Minister's office now utilising the team on every occasion of the PM's appearances in or around the maritime environment to secure those areas from the threat of UXO and IEDs.

After a brief stint training the Solomon Island Police EOD Team in early 2018, I was offered a part-time role as a Program Advisor for Golden West in Vietnam.

Being back in semi-retirement allows me time to refocus on my bucket list and spend time in the Australian Bush, along with riding my Harley around the US catching up with old mates.

It has done wonders for me to work once again in the profession I have always loved. The old adrenalin rushes have returned and I continue to get an immense amount of personal satisfaction from the thought that perhaps my work may be just helping save a few innocent lives along the way.

An old retired Clearance Diver can't ask for much more out of life.......

GLOSSARY OF TERMS

ARVN – Army of the Republic of South Vietnam.

A/S - Anti Submarine.

A/Stroke - Acting Leading rank as in A/LS or A/PO.

Bells - signals were called "bells". They were given very lightly, and as if ringing a ship's bell - in pairs. 3 bells consisted of two short taps followed by a single short tap on the buddy line.

Billy Tea – Leaf tea brewed in a tin can (Billy) over a log fire.

Birdcage Mine – ingenious actuating mechanism used on VC water mines. Triggered by low pressure behind the bow wave of the target vessel.

B&MD - Bomb & Mine Disposal.

CDT - Clearance Diving Team.

CDT3 - CDT3 was formed for *'Special Operations'* in Vietnam. It was disbanded when the 8th and final team was withdrawn from Vietnam in May 1971 and was reformed again for the Gulf War.

CO - Commanding Officer.

Colours - The Navy White Ensign is hoisted with great ceremony every morning precisely at 0800.

Crushers – Naval patrolmen – hated by all and sundry.

Diving/Swimming - In Clearance Diving terminology, wearing fins is *'swimming'* and wearing boots is *'diving'*.

Drafted – posted/transferred to another ship/shore establishment.

Emergency Surface signal - This consisted of a small black powder explosive charge *(thunderflash)* being thrown into the water.

EOD – Explosive Ordnance Disposal.

Far East – Navy term for South East Asia.

Freedom Bird – the aircraft which flew troops home from Vietnam.

HMAS – Her Majesty's Australian Ship.

HMS - Her Majesty's Ship.

Hooch – Accommodation.

Horoscopes - This was a detailed no holds barred analysis of how we had stuffed up during the week.

Huey – UH-1 Iroquois helicopter.

IED – Improvised Explosive Device.

Liberty boat – the term refers to going ashore from both a warship and Naval establishment.

Matelot – pronounced *'mat-ell-low'*. Old term for a sailor.

NBCD - Nuclear, Biological and Chemical Defence.

NCO – Non-Commissioned Officer.

Knot – speed. A knot is approximately 1.15mph or 1.85kms/hr.

PETN – high velocity explosive Penta Erythritol Tetra Nitrate.

Pusser – the Naval supply system.

Quarterdeck – the aftermost exposed deck on a warship (Fantail).

Rack – Bed.

RCC - Re-Compression Chamber.

RDX – Research Department Explosive.

RMS – Render Mine Safe.

RPG – rocket propelled grenade.

Run Jumps - Running, swimming, pushups, PT etc. etc.

Saigon – renamed by the communists to Ho Chi Minh City in 1974.

SEAL – SEa Air Land (USN special warfare frogmen).

Shaped charge – an explosive charge shaped in a way to focus its explosive energy. Also known as the Munroe Effect.

SEATO – South East Asia Treaty Organisation.

SPECWAREX – Special Warfare Exercise with US Military.

TAS - Torpedo and Anti-Submarine.

USN – United States Navy.

USO – United Services Organisation – provided shows of touring entertainers.

U/W – Underwater.

UXO – Unexploded Ordnance.

Made in the USA
Lexington, KY
07 September 2019